MW00614087

A SHIFT IN BEING

THE ART AND PRACTICES OF
DEEP TRANSFORMATIONAL COACHING

LEON VANDERPOL

To all those who opened their lives to me
and to Hui-Ya, for your love and trust

Contents

PART I

The Journey of Awakening and Transformation

CHAPTER ONE

The Deep Coaching Potential

Evocation

Around the world, across cultures and religions, people are awakening to the potentials and realities of higher consciousness. More and more people are sensing and desiring a connection with their deeper essence, and feel compelled by an inexplicable life force to understand the greater nature and meaning of existence.

What does it mean to awaken?

Awakening is a rich and complex experience that defies a narrow definition, but the essence of awakening is the new-found awareness and experience of one's spiritual reality. It's not an event, it's a process—a process in which spiritual consciousness flows into the mind, reorienting the mind to a reality that lies beyond the 'veil' of superficial definitions and material boundaries. The veil then begins to lift and the awakened mind becomes aware of living in a distorted perceptual reality, a dream of self-imposed limitations, where what was thought to be true is in fact a shadow dance masking an expansive and encompassing Truth.

While awakening is not by any means the end of our evolutionary adventure, it is a significant transition point from one state of consciousness to another. When we awaken, we find ourselves at the beginning of an extraordinary *journey of transformation*, one that invites us to explore the depths and edges of our existence, to know more of *who we are*—the 'true Self,' the 'I' at the core of our being—and of our relationship to the divine life essence, the one consciousness or presence alive in every life form.

One of the benefits of awakening is a slow disassociation from the world of form combined with a deeper knowledge and appreciation of our spiritual nature. Discovering *who we are* at this level drives the experiences that shape our life and gives meaning, value, and purpose to our existence. Once we discover this reality within, we begin to view life very differently, and can make great progress in all areas—not so that we feel 'successful,' 'accepted,' or 'worthy' in the eyes of the world, but because we recognize that our life exists for a much higher purpose.

Another benefit is that we become increasingly adept at determining where we must grow in order to experience more of our true Self, our eternal spiritual nature. The courageous among us decide to *heal* by facing the darker aspects of our personalities, replacing them with spiritual attributes that nurture our evolving soul. Genuine healing requires complete honesty with oneself, and it is hard to acknowledge our deepest fears, our weaknesses, our vulnerabilities, and to abandon what we have long held to be necessary or true, even when it holds out the promise of a better life.

Awakening invites us to spend more time at the level of *being* and in the company of our true Self, and to observe how our life changes when we do. Those who progress along the transformational path become more intuitive and creative when facing the problems of daily living; they seem to find solutions with greater ease than do others, and they feel the impulses of inspiration more frequently. There is more energy available, as well as greater joy, peace, vitality, and connection with others and the natural world. This is the result of having a mind that now pays attention to those vital aspects of the inner realm that were always there but remained unnoticed due to the veil of egoic thought.

The journey of transformation takes us to a rich and rewarding discovery of the vast potential contained within ourselves and others, yet the discovery requires each of us to *undertake* that grand transformation. And many people who have awakened hesitate at this point; they hold themselves back from committing fully to their own transformation, from diving deep and getting to essence, from exploring the edges of their existence. Why do they hesitate? Because the unknowns of the journey trip their alarm bells. Deep down they question:

> Am I ready to take this journey?
>
> What will I gain? What will I lose?
>
> What will people think of me?
>
> What will become of me?
>
> Will I be safe?

They fear they don't have what it takes; they fear what they will find if they do; they fear because they do not understand what is happening and why they experience what they are experiencing; they fear the unknown, the uncertainty of what it all means; and most of all they fear they will lose themselves (which they will).

This is where transformational coaching steps in.

It's an exciting time to be a coach (or a facilitator of transformation, in any form), as we are participating in the beginning of a sweeping shift in personal and collective consciousness. And although this shift naturally engenders fear and trepidation, it can not only be supported, it can be accelerated.

If you desire to deepen your participation in this process, this book is for you. It's time to reveal and understand the dynamics, beauty, and potentials of the 'way of transformation,' the path of our personal and collective evolution that we all are invited to travel, and to learn how we can support this process for ourselves and all those with whom we work.

The Purpose of This Book

Every day I have the privilege of working with people from all corners and cultures of the world who feel a powerful inner call to participate in the flowering of human consciousness. They seek to know more about who they are, to bring meaning and value to their lives, to heal and to grow into more complete, radiant expressions of selfhood, and they desire to support others to do the same. These people label their work differently—they may call themselves anything from coaches, healers, facilitators, to teachers, leaders, storytellers—but what they all share is that they are becoming exceptional *facilitators of transformation* and guides to a greater reality.

Although this book is about Deep Transformational Coaching (or Deep Coaching, for short), it is written to address some pertinent questions: questions that, when answered, equip people, regardless of their work, to become facilitators of awakening and transformation:

> What does transformation actually mean?
>
> What does the human transformational journey look like?
>
> What are the optimal conditions in which transformation unfolds?
>
> How do we accelerate shifts in being and consciousness?
>
> What is the role of Spirit and spirituality?

These and many other such questions will be answered in this book. And as much as this knowledge and information will enable you to support the growth of others, this book is first and foremost for *your* growth. Its primary intention is to bring about a shift in your own consciousness, to help you experience more of the truth of Who You Are: your essential Self and nature. When accessed in the right way, this material and the practices will act as a catalyst for your own transformation.

What this book is not is a collection of tools and techniques to pick through and apply in your coaching sessions (or into your chosen field of service). You can read it in that way, but you would be missing out because it offers you so much more. This is a book about awakening and transformation—the most profound, sacred, and mysterious of human experiences—and how we optimally position ourselves to support it. *This work begins and ends with your own consciousness.* And your capacity to support others in their transformation is proportionate to the degree that you bring your own consciousness to the recognition of your own Reality. My request is that you allow yourself plenty of time to reflect on and assimilate what you will learn here, applying it to your own life before applying it to the lives of others.

Most importantly, the ideas and concepts presented in this book are intended to give rise to an experience, as they themselves are the product of the new consciousness. Concepts are wonderful, and tickle the intellect's desire for knowledge and understanding; however when it comes to deep transformation, *experience* is the best teacher. A question you can ask yourself at any time is:

What is the inner experience that is desiring to happen
in me?

As you assimilate the lessons, a shift will take place within you, and you will experience yourself as more complete, more real, more whole, more awake, and more alive. If your readiness is high, you may even experience a profound sense of who you are at your most essential level, as 'I Am.' A glimpse of this state of being is enough to act as a mighty accelerator of transformation, for any visceral experience of your essential nature fuels your ongoing efforts to expand your awakening mind.

Your unawakened mind will also be stirred as you read this book; it is a necessary part of the transformation of consciousness to recognize those aspects of the mind which are in need of attention and healing—how the unawakened mind thinks, speaks, and acts. We cannot grow into the fullness of our enlightened Self if we do not shine a light onto the shadowy aspects of our unawakened self. For most people, this part of the transformational process causes discomfort and dis-ease. I encourage you to stay with it and recognize it for what it is: your egoic consciousness fighting for its survival in the face of the emerging light of a new consciousness. And if you desire to support others in their transformation, it is important that you have experienced for yourself the process of facing and healing the shadows of the unawakened you.

As you work with the nine transformative practices that form the foundation of Deep Coaching, as you apply them to all the situations and circumstances of your life, you will become a transformational presence. One of life's great truths is that *your transformation enables transformation*. The more you allow the light of your awakened self to become your 'way of being' in this world, the more your presence will enable others to awaken and grow into their highest potential. What you call yourself or the kind of work you do is far less important to supporting transformation than the quality of your being. The light of your consciousness weaves the space in which transformation unfolds. Be that light and bear witness to what becomes possible.

The Rise of Coaching

You do not need to have any coaching background or experience in order to gain tremendously from reading this book, nor have plans to become a Deep Coaching practitioner in the future. At its essence, this book is about learning to *hold space for transformation*, a space in which ways of being and consciousness shift naturally and organically. And it is written for all

8

those who desire to understand and support the journey of awakening and transformation, for themselves or for others.

If you are not a coach it may be helpful to let go of the 'coach' moniker used throughout the book and replace it with a label of your choosing. I am, however, a professional coach, and this book is written from a coaching perspective. From years of experience, I have come to trust that, as an approach to human development, coaching has enormous potential. I recognize how clichéd the notion of 'changing the world' can sound, yet when coaching is done well it does a world of good. No matter your profession, you will benefit from an understanding of the transformative coaching principles and practices presented here.

In comparison with other professions which explore the human experience, such as psychiatry, psychology, or therapy, coaching is a newbie, having come into existence as a profession as recently as the 1980s. Yet within this short timeframe there has been a remarkable global surge of interest. Coach training schools are flourishing, more and more universities are offering coaching as a course of study, and progressive organizations are increasingly making it part of leadership training. Professional coaches abound.

Why is there such an extraordinary level of interest in coaching?

It may have something to do with the fact that in an awakening world many people are hearing an inner call to live purposefully: to set and achieve goals and aspirations, to realize more of their innate potential, to create meaningful, fulfilling lives, and to take ownership and responsibility when doing so. Coaching, through the process of inquiry and dialog, invites us to explore our beliefs and perceptions, often revealing those to be distorted ideas and images we have somehow bought into. Coaching simply enables people to move beyond such limitations into a space of clarity and expanded possibility.

My extensive experience mentoring student and professional coaches has shown me that people who study coaching share a desire to change lives for the better, including their own. I'm not speaking about just any kind of change, or change for change's sake (there is plenty of that happening, and it is not necessarily for our betterment), but rather the kind of change that we so badly need, change that invites in a higher order of life experience: vibrant, optimistic, intentional, and possibility-oriented.

In the Deep Coaching program, I like to ask participants the question: "What attracted you to coaching?" Invariably the response is something like, "Coaching is my calling. I don't know why it is exactly, but I know that I want to help people reach their goals and potential, and to support their personal growth. Coaching speaks to me as a way to do that." When I inquire further into the nature of the calling the response is usually along the lines of: "I've been going through a period of significant growth myself for a while now, and I've decided to make some changes in my life. I can no longer do the work I was doing or living as I was living, as it is not aligned to who I am. I see coaching as an avenue to realizing my own goals, dreams, and potential as well."

Perhaps you recognize some of this in yourself.

Is it a coincidence that the coaching profession has risen to global prominence at the same time that our world is moving through a period of collective awakening? Perhaps. But my interpretation is that we have somehow birthed a process that perfectly serves the needs of an awakening mind. At its core, coaching is about self-awareness and what happens when self-awareness expands beyond its current boundaries.

With its eye on the future yet tuned into the present, coaching is a force for good, seeking to bring out the best in each of us. When adopted by legions of practitioners, it becomes a collective force for global change because coaching embodies a mindset that chooses to see and enable the very best within each person, despite the limitations of our human condition. Coaching recognizes there is always some aspect of ourselves that is unseen, unexplored, untapped, and unrealized and which, when revealed, helps us to grow into more of our innate potential.

This is why I became a coach.

A New Paradigm of Coaching for a New Paradigm of Living

Coaching offered me the opportunity to sit with another person and draw from the well of life. These were soul-nourishing experiences through which I learned what it takes to support others to recognize and move beyond identity masks and layers of perceived limitation, and to connect with what was really going on. The deeper the conversation went, the more real we became: authentic, vulnerable, open, revealed, and truthful. Not only my clients, but myself as well. In the most powerful coaching conversations the experience is like an upward spiraling dance: both parties are elevated into higher levels of awareness, with a shared sense of profound connection to each other and the whole.

Deep Coaching can be, as this book aims to show, an exceptional means for fostering enlightened levels of being, thought, and action, enabling people to rise far above their daily thought processes and connect with a higher flow of consciousness where more truth, peace, understanding, and wisdom is available. As far as I'm aware, there are few approaches like it, and it is what makes this work a powerful facilitator for the ongoing awakening of our world. Yet what I have noticed from my years working in the coaching industry is that this potential has yet to be realized by the majority of coaching approaches and coaches.

Conventional coach training programs do not teach how to create the conditions in which a person can connect with the deepest part of themselves. So much coaching is issue-based, solution-focused, often process-driven, and with a strong emphasis on taking action to 'get there' as quickly as possible. Such coaching approaches generally access information that is readily available at the surface, and create little space for accessing a level of mind that is more than a slight deviation from one's predominant way of thinking and perceiving. Change and growth can and do happen, but the potentials of coaching to engender enlightened thought, action and ultimately *transformation* are the result of a *set of conditions* which enable connection with a higher flow of consciousness.

Deep Coaching, with its nine transformative practices, is about that set of conditions: an *optimal* set of conditions designed to create a coaching space where people can dive below the surface and connect with their most essential source of self-understanding and wisdom. Many people today are sensing that a new paradigm of living is possible, one which unfolds from the awakened mind and is grounded in spirituality, yet what that means and how to live into it with all the busyness and responsibilities of daily life remains a mystery.

Conventional coaching, with its emphasis on 'doing' over 'being,' simply cannot support a depth of personal exploration that takes people into that new paradigm. But Deep Coaching can and does. Here we are swimming at the deep end, bathing in the essence of life, and connecting with that which supports us into the embodiment of our vast, transcendental potential. It is possible, through Deep Coaching, to come into the fullness of your Self: to know Who You Are, your purpose and place in this world, and to recognize your relationship with All That Is. It is possible to live joyfully, peacefully, lovingly, and to express those enlightened aspects of being into all that you do and create.

Awakening is the starting point. Beyond awakening lies a journey of transformation that takes us into the heart of the new paradigm where we can experience what it means to become the *living embodiment* of our greatest human possibility. It is a journey each of us must consciously choose to take, and it is not for the faint of heart. The work of Deep Coaching is to foster connection, inquiry, reflection, dialogue, and ultimately healing so that the transformation that is a possibility for each of us can become a reality for those who have chosen to embark on the heroic journey of self-actualization.

CHAPTER TWO
The Coaching Continuum

In coaching, we can define two general approaches: transactional and transformational, and there are fundamental differences between them. Let me clarify that these are coaching *approaches*, not styles, methodologies, or niches (which are multiform), and can be placed on opposite ends of a 'coaching continuum,' with transactional coaching on one end and transformational coaching on the other. Understanding this distinction is helpful as one of the challenges of the coaching world has been the confusion over terminology.

Coaching Continuum

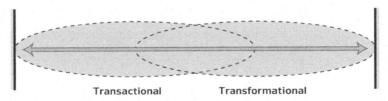

Transactional   Transformational

Generally speaking, during any given coaching engagement or session there is the potential to move along the continuum, from one approach to another. The degree of that movement depends on two factors. First, what the client wants. A good coach will determine what kind of coaching approach to use depending on what outcomes the client hopes to achieve and how they wish to get there—do they require or desire the approach to be more transactional or a more transformational? The second factor is the coach's capacity to coach transactionally and transformationally. The reality is that most coach training programs teach transactional coaching methods, and many coaches have not yet gained the ability to drop below the surface-level issue or situation. With an understanding of this distinction, you will have a clearer sense of the type of coach you are or wish to become.

What Is Transactional Coaching?

Transactional coaching can be described as an exchange (or transaction) between a coach and a coachee to achieve clearly defined goals. The coach's role in the exchange becomes one of listening and asking questions to help the coachee gain clarity on those goals, and then to explore ideas, perceptions, options, strategies, and actions which further their attainment. It is often conducted in a more systemized or process-driven way, with change happening primarily through cognitive thinking and action—by 'thinking and doing differently.' Because of this it can be perceived as a relatively impersonal approach.

In transactional coaching, goals are clearly defined and then pursued to success. The goal itself is often described in 'external' terms, such as: lose weight, grow my business, make more money, fix my relationship, or 'get better' at something (perform better, communicate better, feel better, live better, lead better). While all of these goals have the *potential* to lead to transformational work, they remain in the transactional realm when the primary interest is in clarifying techniques, strategies, and solutions to move from point A to point B in the most expedient way possible. The mindset of both the coach and coachee in a transactional relationship tends to be that the sooner the breakthrough (the 'aha moment') or goal is achieved, the better.

One of the key differentiators of transactional coaching is that there is less need or desire to delve into our 'internal operating system,' the level of mind which gives rise to *why* we do what we do, and *why* we experience what we experience. Our internal operating system is a complex system that includes our conscious and unconscious values, mental models, beliefs, assumptions, self-identity, and meaning-making processes. To use a computer analogy, transactional coaching is focused on upgrades to our operating system that enable us to be more effective at what we are trying to achieve; it is not concerned with understanding the nature of the operating system itself nor with any redesign of it.

Self-awareness, which lies at the heart of all coaching, is still essential to transactional coaching, and personal growth does occur despite the issue or goal-driven focus. But transactional coaching is what coaching ends up looking like when the coach or coachee doesn't want to get too 'touchy feely,' go into painful experiences or emotions, explore past events that shape present experience and influence future potentials, or look at deeply held beliefs and values, no matter how limiting they may be. Transactional coaching remains on the surface of our human existence.

A past client of mine is a good example. When she contacted me for coaching, she was completely overwhelmed. She was a work-at-home entrepreneur, aspiring author, and mother to a young family, and for some time had been pouring herself into her work. She had taken on numerous business projects while also contracting with a publishing company to complete a book. When I asked her what she was looking to get out of coaching, her answer was simply, "I want you to help me get stuff done." It doesn't get more transactional than that. With all that she had on her plate, and the enormous stress it was causing, she wanted to figure out a way to manage the workload in such a way that it would all get done in a timely fashion, albeit with far less stress. A transactional coach would take that objective at face value and run with it.

Through our conversations, and because I'm always listening with a transformational ear, it didn't take long for me to see that something deeply personal was driving her to take on this level of work. It also became clear that she was either not ready to admit that to herself or wasn't prepared to explore it (at least with me). Each time our conversation was about to turn in a deeper direction, she would slam the door shut and steer the discussion back towards getting stuff done. It went on like this for a number of sessions until one day, in a moment of exhaustion and despair, she said, "If I don't get all this stuff done and this book written, I guess I won't be rich." And there it was, the hidden driver of her behavior. Yet the moment she said it, she was aware it had slipped out. She artfully tucked that thought away and turned the conversation back to figuring out how to get stuff done efficiently. There would be no examination of that thought, nor the underlying beliefs and self-images that gave rise to it. To do so would require an examination of the choices she was making, which in turn would jeopardize her internal image of 'self as rich' becoming a reality. She was not yet ready for that level of disruption.

What I have just described is one of the reasons that coaching, which always has the potential to dive into our inner operating system, tends to remain at a transactional level. People generally see 'going deep' as risky—after all, who knows what will be revealed when they take a good look at what is there? ("Why is writing this book so important to me?" "Why do I really care about making a million dollars a year?" "Why do I really go to church every Sunday?" "Why do I really spend so much time online?" "Why is having a flash car so vital?") When we shine a light on the beliefs and self-images that give rise to our choices and behaviors, it will reveal hidden drivers. And if we have pursued a particular path based on a particular belief system for a long time, to seriously question the validity or efficacy of that system will feel like we're putting everything at risk. And in a sense we are, because a kind of 'insanity of thought' can be revealed. Yet the disruption to our life that stepping out of that insanity would cause is seen as a far greater risk than remaining within the insanity itself (especially if life is good; why rock the boat?). The underlying belief structure therefore remains safely unchanged, allowing us to make surface level change which maintains the status quo of the deeper realm.

Transactional Coaching in a Nutshell

Focus: Think and Do Differently

- Issue-focused

- Results-driven

- Action-oriented

- Surface-level

Intent: Explore new ways to perceive, think, and act in relation to an issue.

Premise: One's *existing way of being* is sufficient to generate the desired results and outcomes.

What is Transformational Coaching?

Transformation has become a popular term in business, leadership, and coaching circles. Unfortunately, when a word is used so freely, we often lose touch with its true meaning and use it to describe something it is not. This can happen when the words 'change' and 'transformation' are used interchangeably. We make changes all the time to the way we look, think, feel, and act. If we have intentionally set about on a course of action to learn or grow—to communicate better, to manage our emotions more effectively, to be a better friend or partner—we have likely grown and changed, but have we necessarily transformed? All transformation is change, but not all change is transformation. As Alice said in her Wonderland experience, "at least I know who I was when I got up this morning, but I think I must have been changed several times since then."

This confusion spills over into the coaching world as well, with some coaches calling what they do 'transformational coaching' when it is, often by their own definition, something else. Take, for instance, this definition which I came across: "Transformational coaching involves interactions with a coach for the purpose of increasing a coaching client's effectiveness, performance, personal development, and growth." This is an accurate description of *all* coaching; there is no form of coaching that does not endeavor to increase a person's effectiveness, performance, development, or growth. Here is another inaccurate definition of transformational coaching: "the art of assisting people to enhance their effectiveness in a way they feel helped." Again, this is a general description of all forms of coaching.

Transformation is, by definition, a thorough or dramatic change in form or character—a metamorphosis, of sorts. Although we change all the time, we certainly do not transform all the time. The grand cycle of life and death offers to each of us the greatest transformational experience possible, yet within a person's lifetime true transformation is a relatively rare occurrence. Think back for a moment across the span of your life and identify how many times you can honestly say you 'transformed,' in that you went through a period of thorough or dramatic change in form or character—a metamorphosis on an external or internal level. My guess is you can count them on one hand. These are instances of 'human transformation,' and it's helpful to clarify what we mean by that phrase (we'll go into this further in the next chapter) because the meaning influences how we define transformational coaching.

In simple terms, transformational coaching is focused on enabling *self-actualization*. Far more than 'options-strategy-action' to attain goals or clarity or to get better at something, transformational coaching dives deep into an individual's psyche, focusing on who that person is and desires to *become*. Transformational coaching is therefore an ontological approach because it is about 'being' rather than 'doing.'

This understanding highlights a key distinction between transactional and transformational coaching approaches: each has a very different fundamental premise. Transactional coaching rests on the premise that a person will uncover what they need to and move forward in meaningful ways based on their *existing way of being*. In other words, nothing need be explored nor shifted at the level of being in order for desired outcomes to be achieved. Transformational coaching, on the other hand, rests on the premise that an *expanded or shifted way of being*—and the higher-order thoughts, perceptions, and energies available therein—is necessary to uncover what is needed.

The great transformational coaching question is therefore, *"Who do you choose to be?"* and what makes the process transformational is learning and doing what it takes to grow into the *embodiment* of that choice in being.

People will still bring their personal goals, objectives, and high dreams to the table in transformational coaching conversations; however both coach and client are aware that those function as the *context* for the deeper dive within, and are not the end game in themselves. The driving question remains grounded in a choice in being: *Who do I need to be in order for my goals or dreams to become a reality?* The 'becoming' process is the transformational path, and the end game is *the embodiment of higher than realized levels of existence.*

To facilitate this process, a transformational coach supports people to dive below the surface and immerse themselves in self-exploration, to examine their beliefs, images, and interpretations about who they are and their purpose and place in this world—it is all of these which give rise to their existing way of being, and examining them sheds light on *why* people experience life as they do.

From a coaching client it requires the willingness to face shadowy fears and beliefs in order to become free of patterns of thought and emotion that have held them captive for a lifetime. Change then happens at the core level of mind, within the person's internal operating system, and when the person grows significantly at this level it creates the impetus for equally significant shifts in their behaviors, choices, and emotions. Over time, real transformation occurs, and the necessary thoughts, attitudes, and actions which function to bring envisioned goals into existence will arise organically, as an expression of the fulfillment of their higher nature.

Transformational coaches can and will coach transactionally at times. Coaching conversations always have the potential to traverse the breadth of the coaching continuum; inevitably there will be times when it is desirable to think or act in a more transactional manner. However, the transformational coach's role is to maintain focus on the growth potentials of the deeper realm, and encourage exploration of being as precursor to taking action. Being is paramount to doing, and doing flows from being.

One of my clients, who I'll call Sam, nicely exemplifies coaching towards the transformational realm. Sam was in his late 30s, and had built a successful career as a professional consultant. When he came to me, he had recently moved to a new city and changed jobs, and was now working for one of the world's leading consulting firms. Despite his outward success, Sam was highly self-critical, and held himself to exceedingly high standards of performance, which he rarely, in his mind, ever achieved. In his new position, he found himself struggling to find his bearings, and his self-criticism had taken such a hold that it was having a detrimental impact on his entire attitude towards life. A second area he identified for coaching related to his perceived tendency towards contemplation and overthinking, which affected his ability to make decisions in a timely manner. This lack of decisiveness puzzled him greatly, and was taking a toll on his life. "It tires me out not being able to make decisions," he told me, "Everyone around me seems to have a good amount of clarity, and make decisions full of confidence and logic. Why am I not like them? Why am I so indecisive?" His objectives for coaching were to stop being so self-critical and to develop a much more positive attitude towards life, and be able to be more decisive.

As is often the case in coaching, Sam would usually come to a session with a transactional objective: "I want to explore how to be more assertive at work, especially with my boss. He drains me. I feel I should be able to stand up to him and speak my truth. I would like to explore strategies or techniques I can use to develop my confidence in his presence and to be more assertive with him." A transactional coach would pick up on the words "strategies or techniques," take them at face value, and coach the session to that outcome. Even if the conversation were to delve into the question of why a lack of confidence existed, and the beliefs or images at the root of it, in the end a transactional coach would still be coaching for 'solutions to a problem.'

What I enjoyed about working with Sam was his naturally introspective nature. In his view this was part of the indecisiveness problem; his philosophical bend and need to consider something from all angles meant he loved to analyze but rarely conclude. From my perspective as a coach, it meant he was always willing to dive deeper, to explore the core beliefs that gave rise to his daily experiences. Although he was skeptical he could actually change—years of living into expectations for his life that were never his to begin with had, despite his best efforts, stymied the fruit of change he so badly desired—he truly wanted to. In truth, Sam did not come to coaching seeking strategies and solutions to a problem, though his intellect entertained this notion, but to learn how to fundamentally shift his entire sense of self into a more enlightened state. Sessions, although beginning with a transactional objective, would rapidly evolve into a deeper conversation around a host of limiting beliefs that had long proven resistant to change yet which colored his every waking moment.

As our conversations moved into the transformational realm, the focus naturally shifted from resolving specific issues to the broader question of who Sam desired to *be* in the world, and higher truths that he was now choosing to embody: "I am good enough. I love selflessly. I express who I truly am." When you hear statements such as these from your clients, know you are standing firmly on the ground that forms the bedrock of transformational coaching. The embodiment of these emerging ideals is, however, far from 'easy' and never as linear as a transactionalist approach would conceive it to be.

One of the great challenges coaches face is what to do when confronted with a limiting core belief that is embedded so deeply into a person's inner operating system that it inhabits every cell and *defines who they are*. For Sam, one of those belief patterns was, "My purpose is to feel good, and I need to work hard and achieve to feel good. I also need to be in people's good books so that they will validate me, and I'll feel good about myself." We all have beliefs such as these, however most of the time we pay them scant attention because they are so deeply embedded in the unconscious mind that we operate through them on autopilot. However, in transformational work, those beliefs begin to rise to the surface of our conscious mind. Ultimately, they must be attended to in meaningful ways or they will continue to pose a barrier to growth. In Sam's case, from childhood he had been trying to live up to other people's high expectations, and was consistently told he was not meeting them. As a result, he continued to carry with him a profound sense of inadequacy that was alive in every cell, lurked behind every thought, and led to all kinds of behavior that would enable him to feel good enough, including the ceaseless striving for success and accomplishment.

As a coach, how do you work with this? How do you support a person to release limiting beliefs and images that are so entrenched they form the very fabric of that person's self-identity?

No matter what anyone says, this is no straightforward thing to do. Clarity-strategy-action can help create an intellectual awareness around the limiting belief and, at best, point to a solution for it, but it will not facilitate *actual releasing* of the belief. Transactional coaching reaches its limits here because an intellect-based approach is never the vehicle for *healing* limiting beliefs, which is what it means to release those mental and emotional bonds, and to live into the experience of self-actualization. What is needed is a sustainable shift at the level of being, which requires a transformational approach.

The intent of transformational coaching is to get to essence, to the heart of the matter, to explore the ground of being. This is a space of light and shadow, of fear and joy, of limitations and grand possibilities. All coaching approaches foster self-awareness, but transformational coaching goes beyond that—it enables people to attend to the structures which underlie their sense of self (who they believe they are) and then, through an exploration of being, to assume higher than realized levels of existence (who they desire to be).

Transformational Coaching in a Nutshell

Focus: Be Different

- Being-focused

- Dives below the surface

- Gets to essence

- Space of shadow and light

- Illuminates one's inner operating system

Intent: To explore new ways of being and what it takes to embody them.

Premise: An *expanded* or *shifted way of being* generates the desired results and outcomes.

The Middle Realm: Developmental Coaching

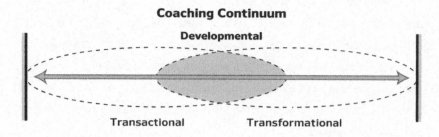

The middle of the coaching continuum is where transactional coaching becomes infused with transformational aspects. I will refer to this as 'developmental coaching,' although there is no standard definition for what developmental coaching is. We are now entering the realm where a higher level of self-awareness commingles with the way a person thinks about their goals, and the strategies and behaviors they will employ to achieve them.

People who come for developmental coaching will express a desire to align their thoughts, behaviors, and creative endeavors with their progressive ideals and values. They sincerely want to grow and develop themselves in their lives and careers, and they often exhibit a strong commitment to change on the inner plane as they recognize that their growth is an integral component of their capacity to actualize desired outcomes. They are becoming aware of themselves as capable, resourceful creators, and are acknowledging that paying more attention to their inner game will generate a positive effect on their overall life experience and trajectory.

It is the middle of the continuum where the majority of life coaching and some leadership occurs (organizational coaching tends to lean heavily towards the transactional). Developmental coaches view themselves as more than facilitators of a process in service of goal attainment, instead as essential partners in a journey of self-discovery and personal growth.

The motivations of transactional coaching to 'solve the problem,' 'figure out a solution,' or 'improve performance' still remain; however the difference from purely transactional coaching is that this *doing-level awareness* encompasses a much broader range of insight and information, stemming from questions such as:

How am I responsible for my experiences?

What are my strengths? How do I leverage my talents?

What needs to change in me to create the outcomes I desire?

At times the transformational coaching question *Who do you choose to be here?* may be asked, however more often the developmental coach is focused on helping people know more *about* themselves, commonly using an array of assessments, tools, or methodologies to expand self-awareness. Developmental coaching helps people learn about their character, strengths, perceptual truths and creative potential, and then to take action which aligns with that awareness and which develops them in meaningful ways. Thinking also expands to take in more information than the intellect alone can provide. Other forms of intelligence, such as emotional, physical, and intuitive, are accessed because they are seen to offer qualitatively different perspectives and understandings that aid goal attainment.

Perhaps the most telling identifier of the middle realm is the importance that working with one's beliefs and values takes on—there is a willingness to understand and even change one's belief system if it serves the process of goal attainment. These changes tend to be relatively specific or piecemeal, however, so as not to significantly disrupt the status quo of the deeper realm. For example, if I hunger to be successful in life because deep down I want my parents to be proud of me and to be worthy in their eyes, I can pursue a wide range of self-development initiatives to enhance my ability to be successful. I may even hire a coach to help me learn more about myself, to change my thinking patterns, to help me grow and develop as a person. But that core belief—the real reason I desire success—remains undisturbed.

The developmental coach also focuses on exploring and reframing perspectives. The underlying question driving the perspective shift would be some variation of: *What belief, perspective, or attitude would better serve you to resolve or achieve this thing that is desired?* You may notice that the transactional coaching intent to 'think and do differently' is still present, however questions such as these can go a long way towards opening up new pathways of awareness. If people are willing to look not only for new perspectives but also to look closely at what gives rise to their current perspectives, they can go deeper, to the heart of the matter, to the belief and value system that lies beneath where they will encounter their essential 'truths about life.' This is the transformational potential of the middle realm.

Four Levels of Engagement

Alan Seale, author of *Create a World That Works,* developed an insightful model called the Four Levels of Engagement which reflects the levels of awareness from which people engage with their experiences. As you study the model, you will see how the levels of engagement reflect transactional and transformational coaching approaches.

Level	Typical Questions
Drama	Whose fault is this? Who do I blame? Can you believe this happened?
Situation	How can we fix it, and how quickly?

Choice	Who do I choose to be here?
	What do I choose as my relationship to this situation?
Opportunity	What's the opportunity here?
	What wants to happen?

(Source: Alan Seale (2010), *Create a World That Works*.)

The first level is **Drama**. We all understand drama because it appears in abundance within the books, movies, and TV shows we consume daily (entertainment wouldn't be nearly so entertaining without the drama). Not only is it all around us, it's alive within us. There is drama in our relationships—He said this; she did that; then this happened; can you believe what she said; he is so infuriating; hey, this is not my fault, it's your problem; I don't understand why this is happening to me!—and there is drama within our mind: When we feel sorry for ourselves, that's drama. When we feel guilty, worried, fearful or anxious, that's drama.

From a coaching perspective, while a client may come into a session in drama, good coaches would not engage from that level. Although empathetic to the client's experience, coaches would position themselves to be objective and engage from the Situation level.

At the **Situation** level the intellect is able to clear away enough of the reactivity and emotionality to gain greater clarity and objectivity about the situation. This is level where the facts matter: Here's what's happening, this is who is involved, this is the outcome or experience we're having, here are the challenges, issues, and questions to be dealt with. Once the facts are known, as the model shows, the driving question of this level is, "How can we fix it and how quickly?" It's about finding solutions so that things can move forward or get back to normal.

At the Drama level there's as little learning as there is self-responsibility. Power is seen as outside of us, which diminishes our capacity to change things because we're essentially victims of our circumstances. As we move into the Situation level there is a significant increase in personal power, and is why coaching begins here. Learning and growth happen at this level. We recognize our capacity to resolve, improve, or attain things, and see the value in acknowledging our role in both the situation and solution. We are able to ask:

What has been my role in creating this situation?

How can I better respond to what is happening?

What do I choose as my role going forward?

Drama and Situation are for the most part where the mass consciousness lives these days. It's everywhere. And this mindset also infuses how people conceive of coaching, because coaches too are raised in a world that encourages and prizes problem-solving abilities. If something is off, feels uncomfortable, or is not working as we think it should, then it's a 'problem to be solved,' and the sooner the better. Coaches are as susceptible to this as everyone else, and is why so much coaching is transactional in nature.

It's when we move into the third level, **Choice**, that things start to change in significant ways. It's not choice as in, What are my choices of how to fix or resolve this situation? but rather:

Who do I choose to be within this situation?

What do I choose as my relationship to what's going on?

As soon as we ask the question, Who do I choose to be? we begin to step into our full power. As Alan Seale observes, "This third level invites us to recognize that although we may not be able to change the circumstances or situation right away, we can at least choose who we will be within them. And that's a huge step beyond where most people go. The door is now open for transformation and sustainable change."

And he's right, it is open; wide open. But in order to actualize the potentials inherent with that chosen way of being it must move beyond an intellectual decision into an *embodied* state. Only then are we able to step fully into the fourth level, **Opportunity**, and observe for or *sense* the opportunities inherent within the situations and events of our life:

What's the gift or message here?

What's the opportunity here?

What wants to happen?

What's trying to emerge?

Notice that these same questions can also be asked at the Situation level. However, the answers given by a person engaging at the Opportunity level will be qualitatively different because they have been *preceded by a shift being*. Once the desired way of being has been embodied, thoughts, perceptions, and emotions will *automatically* change to reflect that state of consciousness, because each state of consciousness reveals its own picture of reality.

This is an important understanding that has implications for transformational coaching. The Opportunity level is not about thinking through a range of options, searching for possibilities, or trying to reframe perspectives—that's what happens at the Situation level—it's about what happens *spontaneously* once a shift in being has occurred: opportunities and potentials will be perceived that were previously unseen, simply because new dimensions of reality have opened within the mind.

When you coach to shift ways of being you are coaching to change everything. That's what makes it transformational. *The journey of transformation itself is the movement into the embodiment of a chosen or emerging way of being.* Embodiment means to become a walking, talking personification of that way. Choice is merely the starting point. As you embody a new state of being, patterns of thought and emotion automatically reconfigure, if not transform. And that is no small thing—it has the potential to be massive and highly disruptive—yet the more you open up to it, the more its extraordinary the process becomes.

Moment of Pause

Reflect on Your Way of Being

Take a moment now to pause in your reading. Bring to mind any challenging situation or event in your life and sit with these questions:

How am I caught up in the drama of this situation?

What do I think needs to happen to resolve, fix, or handle it?

Who do I choose to be in this situation?

What is the way of being I desire to embody and express?

As the answers to the last two questions arise in your mind, gently shift into that way of being. Allow your mind and body to open to it more and more until it feels fully embodied.

When you are resting in the embodied state, notice how it invites you to step even further into your true power. Notice how you now perceive various situations and challenges in your life. Notice the opportunities and emerging potentials. Notice what it would take to become a living embodiment of this way of being, at all times, in all situations.

What you are experiencing now, is the path of transformation. There is still the question of how such shifts are sustained, however this is the path Deep Coaches support, and it is this you are here to learn.

Deep Coaching in a Nutshell

Coaching Continuum

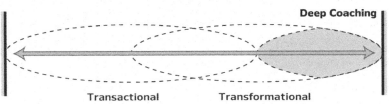

Deep Coaching is an ontological approach because it focuses on the nature of being as a manifestation of personal consciousness. Chapter 8 is dedicated to describing the Deep Coaching approach in detail, but in brief, Deep Coaching is a form of transformational coaching which 'swims at the deep end' of the coaching continuum. Deep Coaching recognizes that shifting ways of being is an avenue to shifting consciousness, and thus to enduring perceptual and behavioral change. In a Deep Coaching session, the intention is not for the person to leave with a new insight or perspective, a solution or strategy, nor a to-do action list (although all of this can happen), but rather to have experienced a core-level, 'felt shift' in being.

As I mentioned in the first chapter, when we awaken we stand at the starting point of an extraordinary journey of transformation, one that invites us to explore the edges of our existence, to know more of who we are, the true 'I' at the core of our being. In transformational coaching, the starting point is the identity question: *Who do I choose to be?* and the focus is to enable shifts into that *chosen* state. Deep Coaching also asks that question—it is a natural starting point for being-level exploration—but beyond that, Deep Coaching is interested in exploring our most essential identity question:

Who am I?

Have you ever thought deeply about this question? Have you ever sat quietly or in meditation and asked with sincerity and wonder about who you really are, the real you? This one simple question carries a powerful vibration. It not only helps you to discover the greater part of who you are, but it also helps you to see who you are not. This one question is primal to your existence and purpose. Most of us are programmed to believe a story about who we are and what we can and cannot achieve in life. We accept it as fact, and so there is little reason to question who we really are. But when you quietly and sincerely ask within, "Who am I?" you're asking for the revelation of the root cause of your being. When asking from this place you begin to strip away the story and break the spell the world has taught you to believe about who you are and what life is about. This is the place of real power.

A second intention of Deep Coaching is to support people through the *process* of transformation, enabling them to experience more and more the exquisite nature of their true Self and soul. For most people, a conscious experience of their essential Self is a rare thing, yet it is always a moment of radiant beauty, and the experience is highly transformational. At this level there is no choice, it simply *is*. No form of coaching goes deeper than this—what else is there to work with beyond experiencing who we are, at our most essential level of being?

Not all coaches will want to be versed in Deep Coaching, and not all clients are ready for a deep dive; it has to be the right fit. It's only when people are willing to question the validity of the story of who they are and to make a conscious choice in being that true transformation can occur. Deep Coaching is perfectly suited to supporting all those who are ready to grow into the truth of who they are.

CHAPTER THREE

Understanding the Journey of Transformation

Throughout our lives we change constantly. We are not the same person we were when we were a child or a teenager or a few years ago or even last week. Every experience we have leaves its mark. So the question we're working with isn't "Can I change?" but rather "How do I grow consciously into whom I desire to be?" When we make that choice of being intentional, and allow it to emanate from the core of our being, we open the door to our own transformation, which involves learning how to expand our mind into new paradigms of experience, and directing it towards higher expressions of Self and soul. (I use Self and soul synonymously through this book). We choose who we are going to *be*, and orient our thoughts, emotions, ideations, and actions towards the *embodiment* of that sense of self. But what can we expect to encounter? What happens on the journey of transformation?

In Transformation, What Is Transforming?

The journey itself is generally not well understood, yet it is a self-organizing process with distinct characteristics and stages. Later in this chapter I describe how the caterpillar's metamorphosis into a butterfly serves as a fitting metaphor for human transformation, as it tells us a great deal about the inherent dynamics of the process. Numerous developmental models have also been created (two of which I will cover in the next two chapters) which attempt to capture the stages or patterns that human beings follow as they grow or transform in their lives. For now, to ensure you have a clear understanding of what human transformation means and involves, let's explore the question:

In transformation, what exactly is being transformed?

The answer is simply this: our self-concept. We all have a mental image of who we are, an image constructed since birth from a vast range of personal and cultural circumstances, experiences, beliefs, and values. This image is our self-concept. In his book *An Overview of Self-Concept Theory for Counselors*, William Purkey provides this excellent description:

> "…of all the perceptions we experience in the course of living, none has more profound significance than the perceptions we hold regarding our own personal existence—our concept of who we are and how we fit into the world. Self-concept may be defined as the totality of a complex, organized, and dynamic system of learned beliefs, attitudes and opinions that each person holds to be true about his or her personal existence."

Our self-concept—this complex, learned, mental image of who we are—begins to form early in life. In the womb, we absorb our mother's energies and emotions. (It is likely too that certain hereditary or biological factors contained in our DNA also influence the development of our self-concept.) After birth, our self-concept develops within the family culture; the environment forms around us, shaping how we will function in the world. Children are mimics—as children we are imprinted with certain parental behaviors according to the ways our parents treat us, and more subtly by the attitudes they hold, especially their feelings towards us. Social mores, cultural beliefs, and a constellation of relationships also influence our growing self-concept.

Positive influences of love, validation, affection, acceptance, and encouragement within the family and social structures foster a healthy self-concept; as children, our growing awareness is fed with the positive images and energies necessary to develop self-esteem, and a sense of worth and value. However, when as children we do not get the love and validation we require, when there are negative influences in our life such as criticism, judgment, abuse, neglect, or trauma, we start to see ourselves as able to be hurt, and there is an impact on our self-concept. A shell of ego begins to form and we develop attack and defense mechanisms to protect ourselves, and other ego structures to project our strength and value into the world. Usually our family and social cultures are a combination of positive and negative dynamics, and as these factors come together they help construct our self-concept: our internal image of who we are.

Self-Concept and the Ego

Our self-concept is, however, a highly limited if not false rendering of who we truly are, because it is an extension of our ego. What is the ego? Simply, it is our *sense of separate self*—the belief that we are not intimately connected to, not at one with, everything in existence. Ego lives on identification and separation. Egoic consciousness says, "I am not that person. I am this body standing here. I like this but not that, look like this but not like that, believe this but not that. I am different and separate from you and you and you."

Ego expresses itself as identification with form, whether it be a thought, image, or material possession. We identify with our gender, body, sexuality, nationality, religion, profession, possessions, accomplishments, social status, and roles such as father, mother, sister, brother, spouse. We classify ourselves by the color of our skin, the color of our hair, our age, our weight, our height, our experiences and, through the savvy of marketing, our product and brand preferences. We develop a host of likes and dislikes, opinions and perspectives, and stories of 'things that happened to me,' which strengthen our sense of self as 'me and my story.' All of this combines to form an ego-based self-concept (also called our 'acquired' or conditioned self-concept), the self we have been taught we are by our culture, environment, and experiences. From the day we are born, we accumulate layer upon layer of beliefs, values, attitudes, and images that we are told are true about life and our personal existence. We see ourselves as 'other than,' fundamentally on our own in this world, struggling to survive or striving to make it. The egoic mind creates the perception of separation, the illusion of isolation, the distortions of limitation, the dream of weakness and lack, and the belief of specialness and superiority. This is all an expression of egoic consciousness.

The ego is not a 'bad thing'—it is not something to be frowned upon or disowned—it is an essential gift of life. The ego affords us the experience of being an individual in this world, and all that that entails. Until it is superseded by true Self-awareness, the ego is the solid ground beneath our feet, helping us navigate through a world of seemingly infinite form, and shaping our self-identity so that we can play out certain roles in certain situations. The ego is powerful, intelligent, and capable of unlimited creativity—and it knows just how to keep us beholden to it.

The vast majority of people completely identify with their ego-based self-concept; they perceive little if any 'I' apart from it and its concomitant thoughts and emotions, and fail to recognize it as 'not self.' This is what it means to be unawakened or to live unconsciously—we end up losing ourselves in all that we have come to identify with, all that we have been taught we are. Enormous time and energy is then spent seeking those things—possessions, associations, knowledge, ideologies, rewards, accomplishments—that strengthen how we already see ourselves or how we want to be seen.

Until, one day, something shifts. There is a moment of dis-identification from the prevailing self-concept, a shift in identity from 'self as the mental construct' to an awareness of self as something far greater. For some people this moment is experienced as a sense of liberation, or as an influx of profound joy or inner peace. This glimpse of an awareness that 'I am not my learned, mind-made I' is a point of awakening, and marks the beginning of a journey of transformation that happens at our core level of mind, within our conditioned system of belief, perception, and self-understanding. When we change our most fundamental understanding of who we are, this creates the impetus for equally significant shifts in choices, behaviors, and actions, and we 'transform.' Our mind, increasingly free from the grip of egoic consciousness, is able to perceive ourselves as we are—and the true essence of each of us is pure, unlimited spirit.

Transforming the Self-Concept

The core of all true transformational work is *facilitating a marked shift, if not a revolution, in one's self-concept*. For some people, that shift is from a disempowered state of being toward an empowered state. If we view ourselves through the lens of shame, guilt, or apathy, we will feel inadequate, unworthy, powerless, and at the mercy of life's circumstances. For instance, a woman who in childhood was regularly berated by a parent may hold a very dim view of herself and her ability to affect her life situations, and be lacking in verve because the disempowering view she holds of herself consumes considerable energy. In such a state, she is likely to find it hard to live with herself and others. However, through transformational work focused on healing her wounded self-concept, she can grow into an empowered state, where more energy is available so that she can perceive her worth and abilities, build the capacity to influence her life experiences, and move forward in meaningful ways. She may still be a long way from fully knowing herself, but will have experienced a marked shift in her self-concept toward one that is far more truthful.

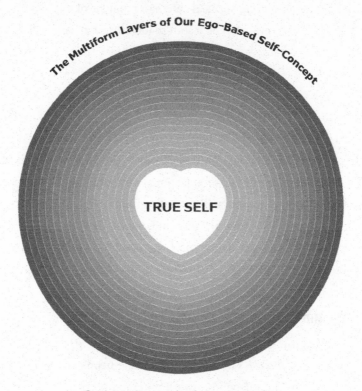

The Multiform Layers of Our Ego-Based Self-Concept

TRUE SELF

Getting to the essence of who we are is like
peeling the layers of an onion – it is a process of
stripping away all that is not who we are at the
core of our being.

For other people, the transformational shift that occurs is based on a readiness to dislodge the more firmly established self-concepts—to strip away all that does not reflect the 'I' that is at the core of being. The term 'awakening' denotes the onset of this period of profound inner development, one motivated by a desire to move from an unconscious identification with an ego-based self-concept into a higher dimension of conscious self-knowing. *The major transition we undergo in transformation is from a perception of our self that is informed by the limiting and protecting ego to knowing who we are as an evolving yet unlimited soul.* In transformation, we are restoring our mind to truthfulness and moving into our real power:

who we are beyond identification with form. Here room is made for the true essence of who we are to come forward. As we transform, we learn to perceive ourselves anew, through a lens cleared of the misperceptions and falsities that have formed our self-concept for so long. We are at last beginning to awaken from the dream of separation and identification with form that the ego has created.

True transformation is more than the normal course of change, growth, and maturation we all experience by the sheer fact of our existence. It is a *revolution of our self-concept*, a radical shift in our understanding of who we are and our purpose and place in this world. At the deepest level, to know ourselves is to be rooted in the Ground of Being, wherein lies our true Self, who we are in essence. The paradigm of our existence has shifted, and the potentials of our Self and soul have become recognized in the theater of our awakened mind.

Coaching and the Self-Concept

It's important to recognize that transactional and developmental coaching approaches aim neither to support a revolution in a person's self-concept, nor to help that person grow beyond their egoic consciousness. In fact, the reverse often happens: coaching becomes a means for *strengthening* a person's ego-based self-concept by creating new forms of association or achievement with which to identify, and which serve to enhance their prevailing sense of self.

The process unfolds like this: If coaching has helped me shift my thinking or behavior enough to succeed at a given task, and that success has satiated my inner need to feel good about myself, to be seen in a certain way, or to demonstrate my worth, my self-concept has remained anchored in the ego. It's like replacing one mask with another mask, and yet neither of them is me. I can appear to transform my persona quite effectively this way, changing one mask for another, and that is the great seduction of this approach; I can set goals and strive to make them happen, succeeding at some, failing at others, and all the while tell myself that because I know what I want out of life I know who I am. In reality, however, my false self—my ego-based self-concept—is being strengthened.

The reason for this is that if the only way I have known myself is through the distortions of the ego, then it's easy for me to get lost in a field of masks, defining myself with this label or that, and failing to recognize that I am actually living *into* the dream of my unawakened self. Transactional coaching approaches—which emphasize results, solutions, achievement, and performance improvement—highlight *doing* and *having* over being; the more I do, the more I produce, the more I achieve, the more I have, the more I am. All my accomplishments and success, bound up with the worth I believe I now possess in the eyes of others, enhances my conditioned sense of self.

Up to a point this is fine; accomplishing the goals we set is valuable in life insofar as it allows us to learn and grow, and to live a more fulfilling and meaningful life. But there is a catch: goal accomplishment can easily serve to solidify our ego-based self-concept when we become attached to or draw a sense of identity from the outcomes.

Most people spend a large part of their lives pursuing accomplishments and success in a bid to satisfy their ego's need for attainment and recognition. They spend a great deal of time and energy—including investing in coaching—chasing those things that bring attention, profit, accolades, or power. And in doing so, they live out the story they have created about who they are or what should be valued, with little if any awareness of the Ground of Being that lies beneath or the potentials of true Self-knowing that await them.

Coaching also unintentionally strengthens a person's ego-based sense of self when it helps that person to know *about* themselves. People are curious to learn about themselves, and some seek coaching for that very reason. For example, you may find personality indicators fascinating—there are many in the market, including DiSC, MBTI, Enneagram, Human Design, Social Styles, StrengthsFinder—and a helpful tool by which to better know yourself. Through these indicators you can delve into aspects of your character and gain information which reveals more of your personality. There is nothing wrong with learning about your personality; your strengths and weaknesses, your behavioral tendencies, your IQ, etcetera, are all part of the substance of your identity and play a major part in your human associations. However, you must not confuse knowing *about* yourself with knowing your Self. Is your personality all that you are? Assuredly not. The content you learn about yourself through a personality indicator or a strengths finder is not who you are in essence; there are still finer layers to your identity. At most these tools act as signposts pointing the way to the deeper, more expansive dimension of being that lies beneath.

The journey of self-actualization can be a lengthy one that is only possible if you take the time to go within and ponder the mystery of your being. Who are you? What part of you is the constant in your being? That part—the unchanging part of you, your very core—is who you are; you are so much more than your identity. So when coaching focuses on doing over being, or supports a person's unconscious effort to define himself through achievement, or takes as truth an external construct that says 'this is the type you are,' a transformation of consciousness rarely takes place—and a shift in consciousness is the necessary inner condition for a transformation of the self-concept to occur. You can certainly *change* by choosing to learn more about yourself or to grow from each experience you have, but if that knowledge and experience does not significantly shift the inner dimension of self with which you identify, your ego-based *sense of self* remains intact, and you will continue to act out its unconscious patterns of behavior.

A Lesson from the Caterpillar

Now that we've clarified what it means for a human being to 'transform,' the next step is understanding the *dynamics* of the transformational process. This and the next few chapters are devoted to shining a light upon the inner workings of the process so that you know what you are working with. The more you understand the dynamics, the more comfortable and adept you will be at coaching transformation.

The story of how a caterpillar transforms into a butterfly is a great place to start. It's more than a metaphor for transformation, it is one of the most exquisite examples of transformation in the natural world, and we can learn a great deal from it about the process itself. We first learn about this wonder of life as children, but usually without the benefit of specifics: how does the transformation actually happen? As a child, I grew up with the image that inside the chrysalis the caterpillar *morphs* into a butterfly; through shape-shifting wizardry the caterpillar slowly sprouts antennae, longer legs and wings, a proboscis, and tadah! a butterfly is formed. It wasn't until my adult years that I learned how utterly misinformed I'd been for so long.

Metamorphosis for a caterpillar is a process of death and emergence, not morphing. Wrapped in the cocoon, its body decays and disintegrates into a blob of primordial goo, a nutrient-rich stew of death cells mixed with some bits and pieces of the caterpillar's innards. Then one day something remarkable happens: in the midst of the puddle of decaying ooze, a new cell pops up—ping! These cells have been called 'imaginal cells' because they are imagining what is possible. The immune system of the dying caterpillar, taking the imaginal cell to be some sort of enemy form, attacks and kills it. Another imaginal cell then pops up—ping!—and the immune system again trounces it. Soon a number of imaginal cells pop up—ping! ping! ping!—and the immune system, although it's beginning to fail from the stress of death, continues to fight. In time, however, the imaginal cells pop up faster and in greater numbers than the fading immune system can

42

kill them off. And then, because the imaginal cells are encoded with the program to create a butterfly, they start joining together to form cell clusters: clusters of wing cells, antenna cells, digestive tract cells and others take form. The cell clusters eventually form together and the transformation is complete—the butterfly emerges as an altogether new entity.

Human beings are not nearly as simple an organism as a caterpillar, and our emergence as a 'butterfly' is not the end of our evolutionary journey—there are further periods of transformation to be experienced, mortal death being one of them—however in human transformation there too is a death and emergence process. *What is dying?* The layers of our ego-based self-concept which no longer reflect the truth of who we are. This is the unraveling of the ego's grip on the mind, the stripping away of all that is not reflective of the 'I' at the core of our being, the dissolution of our sense of separate existence. *What is emerging?* A new sense of self—our true or higher Self, the soul consciousness that is so much more authentic and real than the one we have come to identify with. Let's explore each of these dynamics further so that we can recognize their patterns and understand their role in the transformational process.

The Inner Earthquake

What happens when life breaks down, when there is systemic contradiction?

~ Ravi Zacharias

Awakening to our true nature is anathema to the ego. It views our awakened consciousness as it would an enemy approaching to destroy its world (just like the caterpillar's immune system views imaginal cells) and it will fight for its existence. To quote the poet Dylan Thomas, the ego will "not go gentle into that good night"; it will "rage, rage against the dying of the light." The collapse of our ego-based sense of self is a disruptive and often disconcerting experience; it can feel like things are breaking down and falling apart, which they are, just as they are for the caterpillar. Spiritual teacher and author Eckhart Tolle describes the moments before his leap into an enlightened state of consciousness as being filled with thoughts of death. The Roman Catholic mystic John of the Cross wrote the poem *Dark Night of the Soul* to describe the period of intense inner suffering that can precede ascension into the light and union with God. 'Dark night of the soul' sounds like an ominous experience, something to be avoided, and yet many spiritual aspirants have had to pass through the dark night in order to grow into the joy and lightness of their true nature.

Even if your personal experience of awakening is not as intense as Tolle's or John of the Cross', there are still patterns that you share with them. Awakening is often experienced as like an inner earthquake: unsettling, disorienting, even tumultuous and fear-filled. The ground upon which you have constructed your life—the acquired, mind-made self-concept—is beginning to quake and tremble, appearing far less solid and secure than it once did. If your inner world were a room, you might see pictures tilting on the wall, books falling off shelves, vases crashing to the floor, and cracks appearing in the ceiling and floor. Observing it all, you might find yourself wondering if the whole thing is going to hold up! What you have long held to be a true reflection of who you are is now being seen for what it is in the light of your awakening self.

The inner earthquake is a kind of death knell for a system of consciousness that is to be 'no longer.' Our ego does not die or disappear completely, of course—it still functions to help us experience our unique individuality and to navigate in the physical world, like a functional tool—but our relationship to it becomes altogether different. In that process of reconfiguring the ego's role in our life, however, there is a very real sense of tension and turmoil as its prevailing system of thought begins to collapse and lose its place of dominance.

The collapse of any system means significant change, and significant change always engenders some level of resistance. Resistance will be particularly acute when the emerging system is born of an altogether different consciousness, which is what happens when egoic consciousness is supplanting by soul consciousness. You will experience resistance to the passing of your prevailing self-concept. *To the ego, any movement towards a relinquishment of the status quo of cherished attitudes and beliefs is perceived as an impending death,* and you may notice it exhibits great tenacity. For example, just when you think you have grown beyond, just when your thoughts, emotions, or behavior seem to be aligning to a new way of being, wham!—you are back in its throes. Ouch. It can be a hard landing. "Why did this happen?" you cry out, "I was doing so well!" Your unawakened self will pull you down into old, unconscious patterns that serve to prolong its own existence. Until the imaginal cells of your awakened self form clusters of possibility that are far greater in strength and number than the death cells of your unconscious self, you can expect to experience varying degrees of frustration, confusion, disappointment, doubt, and uncertainty.

It is important for all those who desire to coach or facilitate true transformation to recognize and understand this inherent dynamic, because this 'passing away of the conditioned self' or 'stripping away all that is not you' process is by no means easy or comfortable. In fact, it can be so disconcerting that people will choose to turn away from this seemingly treacherous path. "What's the point of this?" they will say, "It feels so awkward, so uncomfortable. Something must be wrong with me! How can any good possibly come out of this?" Human instinct tells us to avoid discomfort; it tells us that pain is not a good thing. Our impulse is to want to move away from the tension, to declare it should not be this way or be this hard. We can become anxious with the naturally arising discomfort that signals transition from one state of consciousness into another. However, every leap has to have a platform to leap from, and the inner earthquake breaks things down to promote evolutionary leaps. As you help a person step out of identification with his old mental self-image you will, as Karlfried Dürckheim writes in *The Way of Transformation*, "help him to risk himself, so that he may endure the suffering and pass courageously through it." What it takes is the courage to face life and all that appears perilous.

Rachelle's Story

Let's meet Rachelle, a client of mine who exemplifies the discomfiture of the transformational process. She exhibits the confusion resulting from the inner earthquake as her old self-concept begins to collapse in the light of her awakening self. Notice the fear that arises when she reflects on the implications of committing fully to her transformational journey.

"It began about six years ago. I call that my formal awakening. I started going on my journey on a conscious and more formal level. At the very beginning the process was very confusing. I had no reference nearby who understood what was going on. I didn't get it either. There was this tremendous shift inside. Most of the things I had been living by were absolutely collapsing. I didn't understand the process and so I really suffered a lot internally. I felt like I couldn't share the process with anybody close to me. At times I felt as if I was going totally crazy. I questioned myself a lot.

"For quite a long time I was afraid of loving myself and expressing myself from that place. I had a lot of self-judgment because I saw the people who were in this place and either they didn't have a family or they were totally detached from the other people. The belief I had of people living in love was not a good image back then. So as part of the process I had to let go of a lot of ideas and beliefs.

"But there was something inside of me that, even in the darkest darkness, was pulling me forward and there was this very deep faith in me which I'm really proud of now because I can see everything from a new light. It's only very recently that I was able to love the past from the present. Because from this new awareness, what I used to call suffering and effort and loneliness and many others names, I can now translate into courage, into faith, into self-love, into not settling for something comfortable, but really pushing myself.

"As I talk about this from where I am now I ask, 'Why couldn't I get here before?' Because I had a lot of fear. I was really scared of what was happening. I had a lot of erroneous ideas about what the process and this place meant, and those ideas were holding me back from getting here. For example, I'm married with children and I was going on many spiritual retreats. My worst fear was that my spiritual journey would separate me from my family or the people I loved because I was spending a lot of time with myself. I was afraid that if I keep going ahead, which was really about going deeper into myself, I would lose things I love or people I love. It was a time when I was doing a lot of cleansing and releasing. It was a very deep process."

The Perfect Functionality of Dysfunction

What is a common reaction people have when things start to feel too uncomfortable or they think something isn't as it should be? They try to fix it or resolve it; they want to make it go away or right the wrongness they perceive; they hope things will return to 'the way they were' and the sooner the better. In general, we have a tendency to view discomfort, turmoil, chaos or pain as dysfunctional, undesirable states of existence rather than seeing them as essential aspects of change and growth. Whole patterns of behavior and emotional reaction emerge from the distorted belief that breakdown and dysfunction means something is wrong.

Those who experience the inner earthquake of transformation will come to coaching with this mindset, having formed an image of transformation as a relatively painless, straightforward process. ('Blink, blink, I am awake and aware of my spiritual nature. Now I will move with ease and joy from where I am today to where I want to be tomorrow.') So they come to coaching baffled and confused by, even angry with, the turmoil, stuckness, or challenge they are experiencing. In actuality, transformation is always accompanied by some degree of tension and angst, and it is rarely straightforward. Rather than being a neat, straight line from A to B, the transformational journey is more like a line a toddler would draw with a crayon on a blank piece of paper—a scribble that curves in all directions.

A primary reason people are confounded by their experience is that they have little inkling of the nature of the evolutionary (and revolutionary) process of change that is underway. Awakening and the inner earthquake which ensues shake up the status quo deep within, creating a feeling of dysfunction, as though something of great value is being lost or damaged irreparably. And if what is to replace whatever is lost is not understood or known, there can arise an even greater sense of apprehension. People then think, "This doesn't feel good, so it can't be good. Maybe I can find a solution to this so I can get back to feeling comfortable and my normal self again." Coaches who are trained transactionally and who are unschooled in the dynamics of transformation will strive alongside the coachee to find solutions to the 'problem.' Both are innocently blind to the *perfect functionality* of the inner earthquake, the pure necessity and goodness of what is happening, and therefore approach it as a problem to be dealt with.

Those unsettling feelings of dysfunction are normal and a wonderful sign, for they herald the potential for the passing of the old self-concept and the emergence of the deeper, truer I. *They reflect the perfect functionality of dysfunction.* But few people have developed the capacity to detach from the negative perceptions and emotions that arise in the midst of systemic collapse in order to simply be with and witness the perfection of what is occurring. Invariably, resistance increases towards whatever is happening, which compounds negative feelings and solidifies the perception that something is wrong and must be fixed.

In reality, there is no 'problem,' nothing that is in need of fixing. The dysfunction created by the inner earthquake is a necessary dynamic of transformation. You are on a journey to heal your self-concept, to come into contact with the ground of being that lies beyond the ego, and to know yourself for Who You Are—and to help others do the same. When you become aware of your identification with the acquired, mind-made self, it does not mean you immediately know who you are—it means you have begun to perceive and experience yourself anew, from a higher plane of reality. Your inner perception is now expanding. You begin to take more responsibility for your life experience; you will accept more, forgive more, and allow more to be as it is. Your willingness to shine the light of awareness upon your inner shadows increases, and you begin to look fearlessly upon your fears. In this light, that which is in need of healing is illuminated so that you may attend to it. The soul flourishes in this environment as it is no longer stifled by the layers of the old self-concept.

As Karlfried Graf Dürckheim observes in *The Way of Transformation*, you have to be willing to risk yourself, face your fears, and "encounter all that is most perilous in the world. Only if we venture repeatedly through zones of annihilation can our contact with Divine Being, which is beyond annihilation, become firm and stable." The inner earthquake is shaking things up, enabling a limiting self-concept to be seen for what it is, while creating space for the emergence of Self and soul consciousness. This *is* the way of transformation, and all those who awaken will experience it in one form or another. If you desire to coach or facilitate transformation, I encourage you to cultivate a deep appreciation of the inner earthquake and the dysfunction it creates. Do not resist it, do not fear it, do not try to fix it, do not avoid it, do not wish it wasn't happening, and do not push it down hoping it will go away. Accept it, lean into it, explore it, and learn from it. It's an invitation to get truly honest.

The Impulse to Transform

The inner earthquake and the 'passing away of the ego-based self' it heralds are interwoven with the second dynamic of transformation: an impulse or prompt which calls us to get in touch with our true Self and soul, and through that connection to grow into higher ways of being and new paradigms of living. You are free to define this impulse in any way that fits your understanding, however I interpret it as an evolutionary aspect of spiritual nature—an expression of the innate drive of the soul towards change and growth in attunement with our spiritual reality.

People experience the impulse to transform by the presence of life's big questions, questions for which there are no easy answers:

Who am I?

What is my purpose?

What am I doing with my life?

Is what I am experiencing all there is?

Is what I have been taught about myself and life really true?

They begin to question the foundation upon which their life has long rested. Possibly for the first time, they are giving themselves permission to self-define what is good, true, important, meaningful and necessary. It is a monumental step in life when the veil of imposed belief begins to lift and another world of possibility is glimpsed. People begin to sense that there is far more to who they are than they have come to believe, and the courageous ones choose to embark on a heroic journey of self-discovery that will shine the light of a higher truth upon the illusions and shadows of their limiting self-concept. Arising from deep within is a desire to know themselves in a way that transcends their current understanding—a new paradigm of living, one that is more integrated, real, and holistic.

Matthew's Story

"I desire to become more and more authentic. When it first came to me it sounded nice, but I had no idea what it actually meant. I didn't know what it meant to be truly authentic. I was everything to everyone else but not to myself—very much an authentic people pleaser. I thought if everyone around me was happy, I'd be happy too.

"But there was an internal discord that got louder and louder. Not a voice literally, but a feeling. And that internal feeling became stronger and stronger until I could not ignore it any more. I realized I was not being true to myself in many ways. I was trying very hard to be who other people wanted me to be. That woke me up. I started to pay more attention to finding out why I was doing it, what the reasons were behind it, how it would change me and change my relationships. It comes with many benefits but comes with many challenges as well.

"Learning to be deeply authentic is a continuing process. There is no real destination except to become more myself, aligned to who I am at the core of my being. The more authentic I am, the less the heaviness I've felt about who I am drops away. It has been heavy for a long time. I know I will never be truly joyful and happy if I do not listen and act on this inner feeling. At first it felt uncomfortable, but I've gotten signals from the Divine. I was being shown something to pay attention to. It was a tug-o-war between what I wanted to be and what other people's expectations were. Growing up, I was always prioritizing other people's needs. Now, as part of being on the authentic journey, I choose not to. Not that I ignore other people's needs. First I take care of mine and then respond as appropriate to other people's.

"I am being me, not who I thought I should be. This is a subtle but big difference there. When I reflect on who I think I should be it's constricted and boxed in. Now those walls have fallen away and there is no limit to me. There were many limitations before, what I perceived as needing to be for other people. I am being me for the first time in my life. It's about being whole."

Matthew represents the willingness to listen to and act on the inner impulse to live authentically. The feeling became so strong it could no longer be ignored. By *choosing to be* authentic, despite the tug of his old way of being, Matthew is learning what it means to live into a new paradigm of self-knowing. It's not easy, and the shift will require a truthful examination of all that is inauthentic within himself, but his decision to listen to the inner prompt and to *embody* authenticity will be hugely transformative.

LeAnn's Story

"There was this tremendous force inside of me pushing and wanting to be set free and to express in another way. And with this part I was really feeling proud, like even in the darkest moments I was respecting myself. That voice was never shushed, even if I had doubt and fear. That little voice was always saying, 'Keep on trusting, keep on trusting, keep on trusting.'

"There came a moment in which I said this is non-negotiable. I'm being pulled to this place and I'll just go no matter what. I had a deep faith in what I call God—who to me is not a person but an energy called Love or Truth or many names—who will never separate me from the things that I really love. And it has allowed me to be in this place now where I'm filled with love.

I'm so blessed at this moment, and everything is opening. It's a moment of expansion. It's a moment where all my effort is finally paying off.

"I now see this place as a blessing, and with a lot of gratitude. I feel very protected, very safe. I feel that this voice that started as a soft voice is now really a place of security, of love. It's like a sanctuary inside of me that I don't necessarily have to talk about or share with people overtly. But it's a place of total security, a place that does not shift. It's been happening to me that, no matter what happens on the outside I don't lose my center. I have tiny moments of fear, yet I can come back to my center and know that that place is always, always there. It's a very comforting experience. It's a warm place that I'm now proud of sharing.

"This process has been a time of blossoming and expansion. I keep on choosing daily to be in this place because it feels so good, so natural, so easy, so simple. And everything is starting to open up. I'm very proud of working through the process now, and everything I gained from it. I found strength inside that I was not aware of. I now know my self-worth. I don't have to prove myself to anybody because who I am is enough for me."

Both Matthew and LeAnn describe a similar experience: an inner voice 'urged' them to step into a higher level of self-knowing and being. This prompt is like our inner guide on the transformational journey and comes from that aspect of our soul that wants to express itself as it *is*, that wants us to remember that we are the lights who came to shine upon every shadow we have ever known, that we are presences capable of transmuting all that is dark, constricted, and unawakened—not by fighting it, but by recognizing and accepting it for what it is: illusions that pass through the mind like clouds through the sky. When you bring the essence of who you are—the 'I' of you that is pure spirit—and allow it to light the way, those illusionary forces will be utterly transformed. And you will step into ownership of your only reality.

Transformation Has Its Own Volition

By the time a person seeks out a transformational coach (or mentor or spiritual teacher) the inner earthquake has very likely already begun. No longer are the underlying driving questions of life, "How can I survive? How can I impress? How can I succeed? How can I manifest more [whatever]?" Instead, the inner voice invites us to explore the fundamental questions, "Who am I? What is my purpose? What is the meaning and purpose of life?"

The ego consciousness that is responsible for keeping us physically alive, that desires our survival and safety, that identifies with particular perceptions and belief structures conditioned by the schooling of our culture, is beginning to quake. Simultaneously, our soul is beginning to be heard, and with it comes a yearning to awaken further and to know the truth of who we are. All this happens without us having had to 'do' anything. Transformation is a natural process of human evolution and change, and takes place *of its own volition*.

If you desire to support transformation, it's helpful to have the mindset that transformation cannot be reduced to a goal; it's not something you 'achieve.' You don't wake up one morning and say, "Today I'm going to transform!" and then set about making a plan of action to do so. (You can certainly try, and many people will attempt to convince you that this is the way, but there is truth to the saying: Man plans, God laughs, and angels wing it!) Transformation is far more organic, far more mysterious and magical than anything you could ever plan your way through. It's a journey into the depths of being designed to strip away all that is not you, to lift the veil of illusion so that you may awaken into a new dimension of selfhood.

One of the roles of the Deep Coach is to support those who experience the inner prompt to navigate through and making sense of the journey, which is disruptive and open-ended. In the following chapters, we will continue to explore its nature, stages, and dynamics.

CHAPTER FOUR

Transformational Models 1: Six Stages of Personal Power

I encourage all students of transformation to study transformational models as a means for gaining knowledge and clarity around the stages of the process, which in turn will make you far more effective in supporting those who desire to venture down this life path. My intention here is not to provide a comprehensive list of those models; however, I would like to delve into two which I have found to be extremely helpful for my own understanding. Both of these models are *process-oriented* not *prescriptive* models, meaning that they describe the stages of change rather than instruct how to make change.

The first model comes from Janet Hagberg's book *Real Power: Stages of Personal Power in Organizations*. Many years ago I was introduced to her work, and since that time I've observed the veracity of her model over and over in those I've coached and mentored. Based on years of study, *Real Power* is a highly accessible book, filled with stories and anecdotes of people whose lives reflect the model's six stages, and is a valuable source of knowledge and inspiration for all those who desire to support people into higher levels of personal power. When I introduce this model in my programs and workshops, participants relate to it readily, seeing themselves and others within its stages. Despite the book's title, it is far from being solely about personal power in organizations; it is really about personal power in life, and its lessons apply equally to all of us.

Six Stages of Personal Power

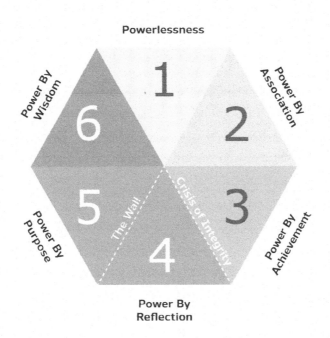

(Adapted from: Janet O. Hagberg (2003) *Real Power: Stages of Personal Power in Organizations, 3rd edition.*)

What Is Personal Power?

That some people have more 'power' than others is a fact of human existence, but what it means is open to interpretation. Janet Hagberg defines personal power as "the extent to which one is able to link the outer capacity for action (external power) with the inner capacity for reflection (internal power)." This definition of personal power does not reflect conventional images of power—authority, control, dominance, influence, or status—but instead the result of a convergence between the inner and external realms: the more we go within and allow insight and wisdom to influence our behaviors and actions, the more 'real power' we have.

In order to understand how personal power relates to our self-concept, I use this definition: *Personal power relates to that from which you draw your sense of self.* Just as you draw water from a well, from what are you drawing your sense of who you are, and your worth, purpose, and power in this world?

The Real Power model identifies six developmental stages of personal power. The first three stages reflect an *external* or outward power orientation (drawing our sense of self and personal power primarily from that which is external to us) while the latter three stages are *internally* oriented (drawing our sense of self and power from that which is internal to us). Therefore, personal power changes at each stage, with resultant positive and negative aspects that present developmental challenges which need to be resolved in order for a person to move on to the next stage.

In the book's introduction Janet Hagberg describes a number of assumptions upon which this model is based:

- "The stages of personal power are arranged in a developmental order."

- "People can be in different stages of power in different areas of their lives…However, each of us has a "home" stage that represents us more truly than the others."

- "You do not necessarily proceed to new stages merely with age or experience, although both are factors."

- "The development of one's ego and then the release of one's ego are central tasks inherent within this model."

As you read through the descriptions of each stage given below, understand that higher stages of power are not 'better' than lower stages. They are developmental: each holds a learning key that opens the door to the next stage. Not everyone progresses through all six stages in this lifetime; some people can get stuck and others don't want to move. But when people do continue, they take on the strengths of each stage, and this supports growth into the next.

Stage One: Powerlessness

At this stage people do not believe they possess much, if any, personal power. It is characterized by low self-esteem, feelings of helplessness and dependency, disempowerment and victimhood. Undoubtedly you will have experienced times in your life where you felt powerless, totally dependent on others or unable to influence the people or events in your life.

When we believe that we have no power of our own, we can retreat into blame, critical judgment, complaint, and resort to more devious forms of manipulation to get what we want: externally, a thing or outcome; internally, a sense of control. Movement into the next stage happens when we develop self-esteem, a sense of our own worth and value, and start to feel good about ourselves. We become empowered, more willing to learn new skills, and aware of our creative capacity to affect things in our life in meaningful ways.

Stage Two: Power by Association

Once we advance to Power by Association, we are beginning to recognize that we are not powerless victims of life—a realization which is itself hugely transformative. We now understand that we can influence the course of our life and, by taking personal responsibility for our attitudes, choices and actions, we can influence things towards our desired outcome. This is a stage characterized by the willingness to learn about ourselves and the world, to 'learn the ropes.' As Janet Hagberg observes, "People at Stage Two usually want to be like someone else. They frequently have a role model or at least identify themselves with more powerful people."

At this level, power is attained by associating with a person or thing that is seen to have more personal power. In other words, at this stage you will draw your sense of self from your relationships: who you know, who is on your side, who you resemble. We join teams, clubs, gangs, companies, religions, cliques and form other associations, thereby gaining personal power by association with the group or organization and what it symbolizes. Stage Two is also the realm of mentorship, where a person can learn, grow, and develop their sense of self through association with more powerful or experienced people, hoping that some of that power will rub off.

The developmental importance of Stage Two is that we develop confidence in ourselves and in our abilities. We learn new skills, get involved with projects, take bigger risks, and learn how to navigate the all-important world of relationships. As this is attained, and our level of self-esteem and confidence grows, movement into Stage Three becomes probable.

Stage Three: Power by Achievement (or Symbol)

In this stage power is experienced through connection with what we have accomplished in life, and the symbols and trappings of those accomplishments. We strive to attain things—a position, wealth, influence, goals, a nice new car or home, clothes—and when we attain them we think, "I've made it!" and "Now people will see my worth, that I am somebody!" Competition and ambition thrive here; it is the realm of winners and losers, haves and have-nots, success and failure. We work hard at this stage to gain what we desire, believing that achievement leads to validation—the more we achieve, the more the world recognizes and rewards our worth.

This stage is not only about financial or competitive success. Anytime you notice yourself *drawing a sense of self-identity and worth* through an external *thing* that you have attained or created you are operating in Stage Three. This stage is, for better or worse, a bastion of the ego. Here the ego struts its stuff, showing the world that it is worthy, possibly exceptional.

The developmental importance of this stage is that achievement is an innate human need. We benefit greatly from a healthy sense of accomplishment in our lives, particularly when we are able to make our aspirations and goals a reality. So much value is gained as we learn how to utilize effectively the creative power of will, intention, and attention.

The great challenge to movement out of Stage Three is that the vast majority of humanity has been socialized to this stage: from a young age we are taught the value of material possessions and wealth, and to strive for success in school, sports, and beyond. Our intrinsic worth and sense of self naturally becomes a reflection of our external achievements. As a result, people get stuck at this stage, continually striving to attain more and more, life reduced to an endless climb for status, primarily because they are completely unaware of the power potentials that lie beyond Stage Three. As Janet Hagberg points out, people at this stage get stuck because they don't know they're stuck—they believe they will 'make it,' or that they already have.

The Crisis of Integrity

Then one day, sometimes right out of the blue, something shifts within. Janet Hagberg calls this moment the "crisis of integrity," and it marks the movement from Power by Achievement to Power by Reflection: from externally-oriented to internally-oriented sources of personal power (real power).

The trigger for the crisis can either be internal—people can literally wake up one morning asking, "What the heck am I doing with my life?"—or external: a traumatic event or the sudden loss of a loved one. Either way, the crisis of integrity prompts the person to question how important the trappings and values of Stage Three living really are, and to ask the question: 'Is what I have been taught to believe is true about life, really true?'

Then confusion sets in. But that confusion, which feels so dysfunctional, so unsettling at its onset, is the perfect functionality of transformation at work: the inner earthquake has begun, and something deep within is stirring.

Stage Four: Power by Reflection

Stage Four is one of intense introspection and potential transformation. Here people ask the big questions of life, questions for which there are no easy answers:

Who am I?

What am I here for?

What do I really value?

What is truly important here?

What else is there to life?

What is my life purpose or mission?

These questions forge the path of internal reflection, one that leads to previously unexplored and unknown aspects of selfhood. In this stage, we are compelled to know who we are, who we are not, and our purpose and place in the world, if not the universe. The journey through Stage Four and beyond, if allowed to flower into its fullness, will bring us face-to-face with our darkest shadows and our brightest light, and transform the very nature of our ego-based self-concept.

The reflective nature of this stage means that people in Stage Four—although they often appear outwardly to be models of competence and integrity—will have inner unresolved dilemmas that create a sense of unbalance, uncertainty, and concern, particularly because the norms by which they have so long lived their lives are coming into question. In varying degrees, they will feel a sense of insecurity as they move beyond the known surety of Stage Three into the unknown, mysterious world of Stage Four. Deep down they will be asking themselves, "What will happen if I say yes to this prompt that is calling to me? What will people think of me? Will I be safe?"

The fear of the unknown and of what it means to question the foundation of belief upon which they have built their life and self-concept is so unsettling for some that they will 'refuse the call.' In actuality, once you move into Stage Four and sense the vast promise it holds in store, there is no going back. Oh yes, people will try. I have known people who went through the crisis of integrity only to dabble in Stage Four. They would read a self-help book or two, explore spirituality or think about their life purpose, attend some personal growth workshops, consider changing careers to do what they were passionate about doing, before realizing the magnitude of the journey and the commitment to change it would entail. For them it was like looking down a long, dark tunnel with only a few dim lights marking the way. "I hear the call," they would say, "but it's far too big a risk to take. I have no idea what's in that tunnel or where it leads, and I'm not going to risk the comfort, security, and status I've achieved to find out." Of course this decision does not mean their personal growth and development ends, and one day they may be ready to make a different decision, but for the moment they have erected a barrier of resistance to the process.

There are many people who have experienced the crisis of integrity who live this way, with one foot planted firmly in Stage Three and one tentatively in Stage Four. They do not commit fully to Stage Four because they fear the unknown, being seen as 'different,' or losing what Stage Three provides. As a result, they live with a tension that is the natural result of resisting the inner call to transform in order to maintain the security and rewards of life as experienced in Stage Three.

To live fully into Stage Four and through what Janet Hagberg calls "The Wall"—a place of transformation where the limiting ego is transcended—is to journey down the road less travelled, one which takes great fortitude and perseverance. Along the way you will experience a crisis of self-identity, face your darkest shadows and fears, move beyond your intellect, learn to let go of control, and develop your spiritual nature. *Stage Four is a stage of true transformation*, as defined in the previous chapter, where our self-concept undergoes a radical restructuring from one that is ego-based to one that is soul-based.

Despite the unsettling nature of the stage, being self-reflective and willing to explore deep within means that you keep moving towards greater personal power and influence. You start to develop wisdom, which comes from your ability to reflect on yourself honestly, and integrity, as you explore what it means to live in alignment with your higher ideals, values, and emerging truths. Less and less will you define your sense of self and worth by your associations, achievements, possessions, or from accolades and approval; more and more will you draw your sense of self from the nature of your being, from understanding who you are and your purpose in this world.

Stage Five: Power by Purpose

Once you have moved through Stage Four and into Stage Five, you will know it. Stage Five is resplendent in ways that no previous stage is. As Janet Hagberg describes it:

> "Stage Fives are different internally and externally. The guide
> for behavior in Fives is the inner intuitive voice. They are
> more congruent because they no longer have to live two

separate lives as Stage Fours do. Fives have a purpose in life that extends beyond themselves. They know what their life's calling is, where their deep gladness and the world's deep hunger meet. And they are able to wed this to their lifestyle and their work. But they receive their calling from their Higher Power, the Holy. It is not the same as life goals. You can set life goals at any stage but at Stage Five you live out what you are called to do or to be more fully."

People at this stage possess inner vision, and are driven by clarity and confidence in their life purpose. Because their sense of self and personal power comes from deep within, they are humble yet courageous, knowing that their inner power is so much greater than the power of anything external to themselves. Their ultimate purpose is always to serve and empower others; by drawing power from an infinite well within, they give power away freely and unselfishly. Stage Fives are generally calm, self-accepting, and come across as authentic and real. And they live the axiom: *It is not about me.*

Stage Fives have also moved beyond the prescripts and doctrines of religion into a personal, intimate expression of spirituality. This does not mean they all believe the same thing about God or the universe, it means they exude spiritual qualities: compassion, kindness, forgiveness, acceptance, patience, and an unwavering knowing that there is a higher power in the universe that extends far beyond themselves.

Where Fives get stuck, paradoxically, is a lack of faith in that very same higher power. Not a lack of faith in a spiritual sense—they assuredly have faith in a higher power—but lack of an abiding faith that the nature of universal intelligence is such that it arranges *all things* for our greatest good, no matter what may seem. Stage Fives are creative, passionate people who are eager to participate in the transformation of others and organizations. However, they still have a limited understanding of how life operates at its deepest levels. This makes them vulnerable to wanting to direct or control outcomes out of concern for what could be lost if they don't. This lack of faith means that, at times, they find it challenging to set aside their own personal agenda ("what I want to have happen") in order to make sufficient room for the greater universal agenda ("what wants to happen through me"). In Stage Five their will still matters, and so they hold on to it and allow it to direct things. Once the paradox is understood that, in Janet's words, "the individual no longer matters in the larger scheme of things and yet the individual is all that matters," movement into Stage Six becomes possible.

Stage Six: Power by Wisdom

Stage Sixes are characterized by a calm and quiet strength. They feel a deep connection to the universe and may often spend considerable time in solitude, connecting and reflecting. There is a transcendental quality to their being; to those who do not know them, they can appear powerless (think Yoda in *Star Wars*). Of course, to Stage Sixes none of that matters: they know and accept powerlessness, and in doing so find ultimate power. This is the realm of the 'enlightened' ones, those who exemplify an evolved state of mind and soul, and who have honed the wisdom to match. From this state of being they serve, quietly and humbly, in communities and organizations, to elevate the consciousness and awareness of all.

I have been immensely privileged to know a few people who are in Stage Six, and they are as described. Even into their 80s they are dedicated to their work, living out a higher purpose in service of others. Simply being in their presence can be a peaceful, healing experience. While you may have this image of a more enlightened existence as being dull or passive, I find Sixes endlessly curious, imaginative, and active. They are never bored or act as if they have learned all there is to know. In fact, it's just the opposite: they are almost in awe of how little they know and how much they have still to learn. And they exhibit a refreshing openness to learn from all those around them, young or old. Stage Six living is an aspiration worthy of all of us.

Moment of Pause
Reflect on the Six Stages of Power

Where do you see yourself within the six stages?

What is your current 'home' stage?

What are the symptoms or signals that you are experiencing which give evidence to that?

What are the barriers to movement to your next stage?

Coaching Transformationally vs. Coaching Transformation

Now that you have reviewed the six stages of personal power, this is a good time to highlight the distinction between 'coaching transformationally' and 'coaching transformation.'

To *coach transformationally* is to use a transformational coaching approach, which can be applied to *anyone who comes to coaching* regardless of their 'home' stage of personal power. No matter who you are working with, what the issue is, or whether the person relates more to Stage Two or Stage Five, you can always shift the focus of engagement from the Situation to the Choice level and explore the question, 'Who do you choose to be here?' For example, if an emotionally reactive leader, in a moment of clarity, recognizes how his critical outbursts lie at the root of much of the turmoil in his department, he can choose to 'be different' by learning to embody a more responsive or accepting demeanor in the face of employee mistakes. If your coaching with this leader explores the realm of being, you are coaching transformationally, but it does not signify that he is actually transforming.

Remember, all transformation is change, but not all change is transformation. To coach transformationally is not the same as coaching transformation. *To coach transformation is to coach the process or journey of transformation itself.*

The "crisis of integrity" (awakening) opens the door for a transformational journey into our real power, into a discovery of who we are beyond our identification with form and all the layers of our ego-based self-concept. Awakening produces a profound realization that something altogether new is arising, an iteration of self unlike what was known before. From the perspective of the person it will seem like everything in their inner world is coming under the microscope: beliefs, values, attitudes, emotions, energy, perspectives, relationships, spirituality, an understanding of the past, present, and future. Transformation turns our belief and value system upside down, and involves a significant alteration in how we perceive ourselves, other people, the world, and the relationships among them. True transformation is vivid, surprising, revolutionary, and enduring personal change at the level of being.

Life has the potential to be a positive transformational journey, but not all of us say 'yes' to the call and move courageously through Stage Four, embracing that potential. *The act of living does not ensure that the person we are taught to believe we are at a young age is dramatically different from the person we believe we are when we leave this world.* We all change and grow over the span of our lives, but we do not all experience the potentials inherent in transformation, the process of consciously choosing to examine and strip away all the conditioned layers that mask the 'I' at the core of our being.

I have found it beneficial to have the capacity to coach the full range of the Coaching Continuum—to coach transactionally, transformationally, and the process of transformation—from the surface to the depths, so that I can meet my clients where they are at, without reservation. (I have observed a correlation between people's readiness for a certain coaching approach and their home stage of personal power. Those who relate primarily to Stages Two and Three tend to desire a transactional or developmental coaching approach, while those who relate to Stages Four and beyond thrive under a transformational or Deep Coaching approach.) But not all coaches are comfortable coaching transformation, and one of the main reasons is that they simply don't know how. It's the unknown zone. They may have a level of comfort working down to the middle realm of the continuum using a developmental or transformational coaching approach, but are uncertain as to how to work at the deepest end: to coach profound transformation. This is what Deep Coaching endeavors to do and what this book is aiming to teach.

Deep Coaching is positioned to coach transformationally as well as transformation itself.

Coaching people through Stage Four and beyond is an extraordinary realm in which to operate, as we participate in and witness the miracle of human life unfolding into its highest potential. In considering what that might look like for a Deep Coach, I invite you to reflect on these questions:

> What is required to support a person to shift their sense of self, from one that is ego-based to one that is Self- and soul-based?

> Where would you, as the coach, ideally 'reside' within the Six Stages to support the journey of transformation within another person?

The answers to these questions will become clear as you read through the book and study the nine Deep Coaching practices. For now, let's tuck them away as questions to ponder and look at a second transformational model, one which highlights pivotal sub-stages in the movement from Stage Three through to Stage Five.

CHAPTER FIVE

Transformational Models 2: The Hero's Journey

The Hero's Journey always begins with the call. One way or another, a guide must come to say, 'Look, you're in Sleepy Land. Wake. Come on a trip. There is a whole aspect of your conscious-ness, your being, that's not been touched.' And so, it starts.

~ Joseph Campbell

The Hero's Journey is a journey narrative, of a type that has been around for millennia in stories and myths. A journey narrative typically centers on a hero (male or female) whose travels begin in one world and move into another. Along the way the hero encounters a series of trials and challenges—even facing the possibility of death—which shape and transform his understanding of himself and his purpose and place in the world.

One of the most influential works on journey narratives is American author Joseph Campbell's book, *The Hero with a Thousand Faces*. Campbell breaks down the journey into a series of stages that almost every hero goes through (few myths contain all the stages—some contain many, others only a few), and divides these stages into three categories: departure, initiation, and return. The 'departure' stage deals with the hero's story prior to his departing on the quest; 'initiation' tells the hero's story during the adventure; 'return' describes the hero, now transformed by the ordeals he has faced, returning to his original world.

Since the release of *The Hero with a Thousand Faces*, numerous writers and scholars have taken Campbell's stages and reduced or renamed them. One of those is Christopher Vogler, whose 12-stage Hero's Journey in *The Writer's Journey: Mythic Structures for Writers* forms the model we will be studying here. Like Janet Hagberg's Six Stages, the Hero's Journey provides a valuable map for understanding the nature of the human transformational process. The more we understand what it means to transform—which necessitates our having the capacity to relate to the experiences and decision points along the way—the better we can position ourselves to support the process with appropriate and effective methods.

Stages of the Hero's Journey

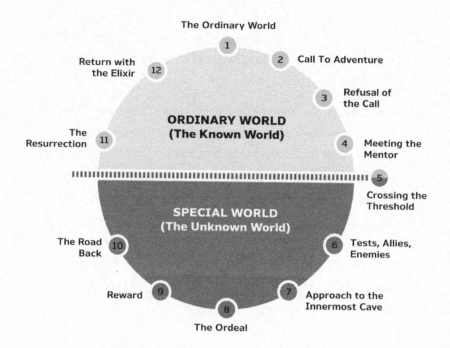

I. Departure

Stage 1: The Ordinary World

The Ordinary World is the hero's starting point, and in journey narratives it provides us with a necessary understanding of what life is like prior to departure on the quest. In *Star Wars,* a contemporary example of the hero's journey, we see Luke Skywalker as a bored farm boy working with his family on the planet of Tatooine, yet pining for far-flung adventures. In J.R.R. Tolkien's fantasy novel *Lord of the Rings,* Frodo Baggins, like most hobbits, is clearly fond of the comforts and tranquility of life in the Shire, and has no evident desire to move beyond that. Generally speaking, life in the Ordinary World is good, ordered, and relatively secure, with everything seemingly in its proper place. The Ordinary World—the world we have been raised in, taught to believe in—is *known*. But then something happens which shakes things up…

Stage 2: Call to Adventure

For the hero to be called away from the Ordinary World, there must be an event, a discovery, or a danger that stimulates him or her to depart from the safe haven. In *Star Wars*, Luke flees home with Jedi master Obi-Wan Kenobi after discovering his family has been killed; in *Lord of the Rings*, the wizard Gandalf the Grey arrives on Frodo's doorstep urging him to set out on a quest to destroy the ring he possesses. In these classic tales, the call to adventure and to embark on the quest is relatively big and dramatic—a traumatic event or a pending crisis is often the trigger—but just as easily, in life, it can be subtle, a knowing rising up from within that sets a person on the transformational path.

From the description of this stage, you can see the parallel with *Real Power*'s Crisis of Integrity: the moment that marks the movement from Stage Three, Power by Achievement (the Known World), into Stage Four, Power by Reflection (the Unknown World). In the Hero's Journey, just as in life, there is a clarion call to adventure which creates an acute awareness of the need for significant change, and we (the hero of our life story) must face what that means.

Whenever people hear that call they will be, consciously or unconsciously, asking themselves, "What will happen if I say yes? Will I be safe? What will become of me if I do?" Inherently these questions create a tension born of the need to leave that which is known and comfortable for that which is unknown and risky. And this requires the making of a grand choice.

Stage 3: Refusal of the Call

> *... you are being guided and you are participating in the Great Mystery. And it has very little to do with you except ... your 'yes' seems to be crucial. It matters. It seems that God does not operate uninvited.*

> ~ Richard Rohr

All heroes eventually say 'yes' to the call to adventure, but not without initial hesitation. Frodo is indecisive and reluctant to leave his comfortable life in the Shire, delaying his departure as long as possible; when Obi-Wan first asks Luke to become a Jedi, Luke refuses, until he learns the fate of his family. The call to adventure (or to transform) is always accompanied by the free will choice to accept or refuse the call; though greatly encouraged, it is never forced.

We don't usually hear the stories of those who refuse the call to embark on the transformational journey, however these stories exist as surely as the hero's narrative exists. I personally know a number of people who, in the face of the uncertainty and risk of saying 'yes' to the call, turned their back on it and remained in the Known World. Others I know dabble in the Unknown World, like those who straddle Hagberg's Stage Three and Stage Four; they dip their toes in but in no way commit fully to the adventure. Factoring in the unknown can create fear and insecurity. "What will it mean for me? What about my responsibilities? What will people think of me? What will I lose?" This fear makes people hesitate, or hold off accepting the call.

If you desire to support people along the transformational path, you have to be aware of their free will choice to accept or refuse the call, and the resistance that arises naturally as they contemplate the potentials and pitfalls of the journey. Their 'yes' is crucial, and people need the time and space to come to that decision on their own terms, even if that means they straddle the two worlds and live with the tension that comes from choosing not to commit fully. Life moves on, and those willing to embark on the quest will do so. Deep Coaches and others who show the way ('way-showers') can, however, play a vital role in how fear is overcome so that the threshold into the Unknown World can be crossed and the heroic journey begun.

Moment of Pause

Reflections on Refusing the Call

Have you committed to your own transformational journey, or are you hesitating or refusing the call?

Do you live straddling two worlds?

What keeps you living in the 'ordinary world,' and from committing fully to the transformational journey?

Stage 4: Meeting the Mentor

In life as in fiction, the mentor is a seasoned traveler, a way-shower of the worlds, one who has 'been there' and who is able to provide the hero with the wisdom, knowledge, and tools that aid the quest. Frodo relies considerably on the mentorship of Gandalf; Luke is guided by two Jedi masters, Obi-Wan and Yoda, who teach him how to use the power of the Force. It is often through early interactions with the mentor that our hero gains the insight, self-awareness, and courage needed to say 'yes' to the call, and cross the threshold from the Known World into the Unknown World.

The mentor does not have to be a person. The mentor can be an external inspiration such as a book or film, or an internal inspiration. For our purposes, let's change the word 'mentor' to 'coach,' because in the transformational process there is a real need for the kind of guidance a Deep

Coach provides. As people set out on the journey of transformation, navigating the tumult of the inner earthquake that signals Stage Four, Power by Reflection living, the journey is not so much an external, physical one as it is an internal, spiritual one. This inner path will contain many hurdles and obstacles, and at times people will get stuck, struggle, and find it difficult to proceed without aid. This presents a magnificent opportunity for a coach to show up as that seasoned traveler of the worlds, the one who has him- or herself faced the challenges and opportunities of 'the road less traveled.'

In truth, transformational coaching, and Deep Coaching in particular, is far deeper and more organic than transactional coaching, and seems to require a higher degree of evolved-ness, of maturity and self-mastery in the practitioner, that comes only from having travelled the path. You cannot fake being a way-shower of the worlds.

If you yourself have never explored the ground of your own being, how can you adeptly hold the space for another to do so?

The more you commit to your own transformation, the more you are capable of enabling transformation in others. Others will then perceive you as 'one who knows,' and they will seek out your support in crossing the threshold and facing the tests and ordeals which will surely arise.

Moment of Pause

Your Transformation Enables Transformation

How committed are you to your own transformation?

Are you prepared and able to be the way-shower for others to transform themselves at the deepest level of their being?

Stage 5: Crossing the Threshold

The hero's initial trepidation has now been alleviated by the mentor, to the point that he is ready to step over the threshold between the Known World and the Unknown World. In *Real Power*, crossing the threshold is signaled by a willingness to move into Stage Four and beyond. Our work as Deep Coaches is to support people to cross that threshold, to help them commit to the unknown road ahead, and to sense the rightness and goodness of the path.

Commitment does not mean that all fear and doubt has been eliminated. So much still remains unknown, and life's big questions—Who am I? What is my purpose? What else is there to life?—remain unanswered. At times people will want to give up when they face what appear to be insurmountable barriers, or when life's ordeals batter them. In these moments, the Deep Coach extends a hand of compassion and strength, helps heal the bruises, and attends to the pain and fear. The Deep Coach is a beacon of light and 'real power,' a bastion of hope and possibility, one who helps people tap into that place within where all is known and all is well, where all can be looked upon with perfect equanimity and perfect acceptance.

II: Initiation

Stages 6-8: The Road of Trials

I was born when all I once feared – I could love.

~ Rabia Al Basri

This is the meaty part of the transformational journey. Now, finally out of his comfort zone, the hero is confronted with an ever more difficult series of challenges that test him (or her) in a variety of ways. The Road of Trials is the period when the hero must face the obstacles that arise on his path, identify allies and enemies (both whom help prepare him for the ordeals yet to come), and directly confront his greatest fears, including death. Many things are experienced on this leg of the quest, among which is a descent into a kind of hell, a low point in the journey that has the hero questioning his ability to make it through. All that the hero has learned comes into play now, and each test, once passed, makes him stronger, more confident, more self-aware.

Luke Skywalker faces many trials, from his initial training in the Force through to the final showdown with Darth Vader; Frodo Baggins faces ordeal after ordeal, each one requiring him to dig deep within himself to survive and endure. These are all instances of the hero coming at last to a confrontation with his greatest fear and facing the possibility of death. Vogler calls this stage "The Ordeal," and it is a critical point in the trans-formational journey. Only through death, or appearing to die, can we be reborn, experiencing a metaphorical metamorphosis. It is a major source of the magic of the heroic myth, but also an essential aspect of the human transformational experience, as we looked at in Chapter 3.

When we make the choice to cross the threshold and move from Stage Three, Power by Achievement, to Stage Four, Power by Reflection, we too will face many tests and ordeals. The falsities and limitations of our ego-based self-concept, like the immune system of the decaying caterpillar, will not pass away without a struggle. We may even start to see them as our enemies, dark forces that thwart our efforts to live a more authentic, aligned life. But once we cross the threshold and commit to the journey of self-actualization, no more will we ignore or stuff away these shadowy aspects. We will face them head on, lean into them, attend to them, and see them not as our enemy but as our teacher, so that we may learn the lessons that need to be learned and pass courageously through.

In *Real Power*, Janet Hagberg writes:

> "One of the most profound transitions between stages is the move from Stage Four to Stage Five. At this point you hit the Wall. At the Wall we cannot move forward without embracing our own personal shadow behavior, behavior that we don't want to look at but can't seem to avoid any more. Going through it and learning the wisdom it has to teach us is life-changing. The decision to move into the Wall requires courage, for in the Wall we face our darkest selves, our shadows.

> "Going through the Wall is a process. It consists of letting go of your ego, giving up control, moving beyond your intellect, becoming intimate with a higher power, embracing your whole self with all your shadows, and facing your core with its darkness and light. The Wall is a place of transformation. Once having experienced the Wall, you will never be the same again. It is exhilarating and it is painful. It is never easy. But in it are glimpses of wisdom and light. And it is healing at a deep level, a soul level."

The journey along Stage Four, Power by Reflection, and through the Wall, is a road of trials. Here we must face the limiting manifestations of our ego and—the supreme ordeal—die to ourselves. What does it mean to die to ourselves? In *The Power of Now,* Eckhart Tolle writes, "The secret of life is to die before you die, and find that there is no death." The first "die" he refers to is the death of our ego and its false creations; the second "die" refers to physical death. The essence of who you really are is far more magnificent than the self (small 's') that your ego has created and that it projects into the world as your identity. In this sense, death is not a physical death but the stripping away of *all that is not you;* it is the mighty act of releasing and forgiving a myriad of half-baked truths that have become your internal reality. The ego creates the false self, and it is the ego, not *you*, which identifies with it. Death of the ego is when that bubble bursts and you see yourself as you truly are, and in that same moment you will know that you are much more than you have ever experienced before.

As long as we are attached to form (our thoughts, body, skin color, possessions, position, sexuality, social status, knowledge, special abilities) and identify ourselves as that, we will live with a mistaken identity and resist dying to ourselves. This resistance manifests itself as the trials of the transformational journey; the epic struggle of our ego to remain relevant, to go on running the show, to ensure today looks like yesterday.

When ego stares into the abyss of its own demise it roars, "I will not go gently into that good night, I will rage, rage against the dying of my light!" Deep down the ego works tirelessly to convince you that by letting go completely of these identity markers you will lose who you are, and you will cease to exist. (Why else do we react so badly when we feel that one is challenged or threatened?) All the tests and ordeals along The Road of Trials are designed to teach you the great secret of life: there is only life, and you exist despite the ego's own best efforts to convince you that its death is your death.

Once the hero overcomes the Ordeal, transcends the Wall, and moves from Stage Four, Power by Reflection into Stage Five, Power by Purpose, a major transformation has occurred. There has been a mystical translation in the depth of the soul, a shifting of where he perceives his sense and source of identity.

As Janet Hagberg describes this person:

> "The ultimate objective of most Fives, whether stated or not, is to empower others: to raise them up, love them, give them responsibility, trust them, learn from them, and be led by them. They feel they are merely a conduit of ideas, energy, and power to be given out or passed along. Their role is not primarily to solve the problems (of the world) but to be a powerful presence in the midst of the unsolvable situation and to work in our own way in easing pain."

Is the transformational process complete? Is this the end of the journey? Of course not; human life is endlessly progressive. Yet by this stage in our development we have come a long way in letting go of our illusory ego-based self-concept and are now grounded in a far more authentic expression of our true Self. It is now time to reap the rewards that come to those who travel this far along the road less travelled.

III. Return

Stages 9-12: Reward and the Return Home

Take a breath and smile as we celebrate the rewards of the quest. The hero has changed dramatically. He has survived the Ordeal, grown tremendously, and is ready to return home as a different person, equipped to change that world. The lessons learned have empowered the hero to effect positive change in the world; because the hero went on his journey, the world will never be the same.

At this point the hero usually takes possession of the treasure he has come seeking, his reward. In stories, the Reward stage is often symbolized by an external trophy: a kingdom, a scroll, a jewel, an honor bestowed, but it can also be greater knowledge or insight, a secret or a power. In transformational terms, the reward is a deep and abiding sense of connection with your true Self, and the clarity of knowing your purpose and place in the world. Many more lessons remain to be learned, but because of your transformative experience, you will approach these ordeals very differently than you did in the past. Now your way of being has shifted significantly, and you have been rewarded with a set of inner capacities granted only to those who have committed to the Hero's Journey. You are a master growing further in mastery each day.

The road home to the Known World presents its own unique challenges; the world has changed and so has the hero. The hero may not be welcomed or accepted back, changed as he now is. He may feel awkward with old friends and family. He may not be able to explain the wisdom he has gained to those who have not begun the journey. (This happens in real life as well as in stories. One of the most common concerns shared by those on the transformational path is that they no longer resonate with or desire to be around certain people, including lifelong friends and family, and do not know how to express what is happening within themselves.) The wisdom gained, however, supports the hero to be deeply accepting of whatever may come to pass, for he knows that he is the creator of his life experience, and this helps him transcend the difficulties of adjusting in the old world.

Be the Hero so You Can Become the Coach

In order to support others in their own transformative process, you must first have been the hero in your own. I have shared these two models so that you can begin to understand the nature and demands of the journey. Likely you already see yourself within the various stages, and hopefully this has given you a rich appreciation of what you are experiencing and why.

In *The Way of Transformation*, Karlfried Graf Dürckheim writes, "The man who, being really on the Way, falls upon hard time in the world will not, as a consequence, turn to that friend who offers him refuge and comfort and encourages his old self to survive. Rather, he will seek out someone who will faithfully and inexorably help him to risk himself, so that he may endure the suffering and pass courageously through it." Who is that someone? It cannot be a person who has not embarked on the journey themselves, or one who lives straddling the Known World and Unknown World, or one who does not truly understand the disruption to the status quo transformation creates.

Are you the hero? Are you the one who has committed fully to moving through Stage Four, Power by Reflection, into Stage Five, Power by Purpose, and beyond? Because when you do, you will become a true way-shower, a mentor, a coach for those who are 'on the Way but falling upon hard times in the world.' So many are being called to this adventure, to embark on the heroic journey that asks them to leave the comfortable home they have created for themselves and to follow the leading of the heart that calls them into a whole new paradigm of living. But it's undoubtedly challenging, and therefore coaches and mentors and others who have taken the road less traveled are needed—*you* are needed.

CHAPTER SIX
The Dual Dynamics of Transformation

In Chapter 3, and in the models explored in Chapters 4 and 5, we learned how awakening is characterized by the interplay of two forces: a disruptive inner earthquake or 'crisis of integrity' that begins to shake up the status quo, and an inner impulse or call that says: There is more to who you are than you have come to believe—it's time to know Thyself.

Each of these forces corresponds with an action that moves a person progressively down the path:

1.) Letting go: the inner earthquake precipitates the act of releasing the multiform layers of our acquired self-concept which do not align with our newly sensed, emerging dimension of selfhood.

2.) Letting come: the inner call manifests as an unshakable desire to grow into, experience, and express that emerging selfhood.

Letting go and letting come are in fact *healing acts*—together they describe what it takes to 'heal thyself'—and each person who awakens experiences the effects of these forces in varying ways and degrees.

What it Means to Heal

There are two commonly held images of healing. The first image is this:

To fix or mend that which is broken.

For instance, when you break your arm or experience a nervous break-down you receive treatment so that you mend, becoming sound or healthy again. In this image, healing is viewed as the process of returning some-thing considered broken or dysfunctional to a previously held or func-tional condition. All physical, mental, and emotional states are relevant to this image of healing whereby what is considered normal or optimal functioning breaks down, at times severely. The second image of healing is this:

To become whole and complete.

In this image of healing, we perceive ourselves as fragmented or dis-connected, and through healing we experience ourselves as increasingly whole and complete.

Although these images of healing are interrelated, in Deep Coaching we are primarily concerned with the second image. Deep Coaches recognize that each person is, at the core of their being, whole and complete. In acquiring the layers of our egoic self-concept, we lost touch with the essence of our being, and we forgot who we are. Our minds became clouded with beliefs and labels and attachments of all sorts, casting shadows that we endowed with great power. As we awaken from that dream, the dysfunctionality experienced is the result of the necessary collapse of the 'no longer' as it makes way for the emergence of 'what is to be.' It is possible not to be broken yet still be on a healing journey, an evolutionary leap into the embodiment of our true essence, which is inherently whole and complete.

As the layers of our egoic self-identity fall away, we become less and less who we thought we were and more and more who we truly are.

To transform is therefore to heal, and to heal means to know and experience ourselves as we are, as essentially whole and complete.

The Dual Dynamics of Transformation

For the purposes of learning to work with these healing forces and their effects, I put them into a frame of reference I call *the Dual Dynamics of Transformation*. In one way or another, all transformational coaching works with the dual dynamics, for the simple reason that they are inherent to the process of embodying and sustaining new ways of being. Deep Coaches focus on these forces not only to support such transformation, but also to enable people to experience themselves as they are at the core of their being; not as broken or 'less than,' but as whole and complete.

The first dynamic is personal gravity; it is that which *holds people back* from growing into more of who they are. The second dynamic is a propulsion system; it is *that which moves them forward*, enabling their transformation.

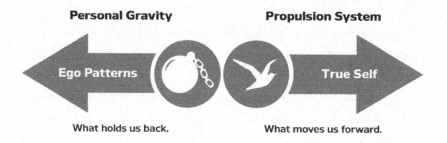

The propulsion system not only creates energy and momentum, it also heals personal gravity. *The propulsion system is the agent of healing.* The more you are able to use the propulsion system to help others to release their personal gravity, the more they can let go of the layers which mask their true identity, and the more readily will their ways of being shift and their personal consciousness expand.

Personal Gravity

Our personal gravity holds us back from growing into more of our innate potential. If our personal gravity is great, it requires much more propulsion energy to create forward movement. And if you desire to reach the heights of your human potential, you must be fully committed to looking at and releasing *all* that weighs you down and holds you back.

Your personal gravity encompasses a wide range of ego-patterns, including:

- limiting, negative, or false beliefs and stories

- unhealthy or false self-images

- fears and anxieties

- disempowering thought patterns and attitudes

- reactivity (attack and defend)

- unattended sorrow (including disappointment, trauma, abuse, shame)

- harmful behaviors and desires, including addictions

- psychological and emotional issues.

Some of our personal gravity is inherited, passed on from previous generations, yet the vast majority is conditioned into us from birth through familial relationships, our social and cultural environments, and our life experiences. As a result of our worldly conditioning, we all have a myriad of basic ego-patterns in one form or another. When we experience shame or guilt, that is our ego speaking. When we experience grief or fear, as 'natural' as these states may seem, that's our ego speaking. When we experience greed, anger, pride, or when we have the need to attack, defend, control, win, be right or dominate, that too is our ego. And when we strive to be valued, accepted, perfect, successful, powerful, or to be seen as having it all together, that too is our ego. Altogether this forms what I refer to as our personal gravity, because it holds us back from experiencing and expressing more of our inherent potentials.

In Deep Coaching we direct considerable energy towards working with personal gravity, because in order to transform we must undergo a *period of undoing*: the passing away of the acquired, ego-based self-concept that is becoming seen as less than truthful. Transformation is a process whereby much of what has been learned and held to be true is relinquished so that a greater truth can emerge. This is what it means to heal. And to heal our personal gravity is to dismantle the fear constructs that grip the mind, to let go of distorted value systems, unhealthy states of mind and harmful behaviors, to shed the baggage of our conditioned past, and to release inaccurate understandings of how reality is. This does not happen overnight, but when we do this we grow into the world of truth, how things actually are beyond the veil of the ego-based self.

Think for a moment of a time when you released a limiting belief, an unhealthy self-perception, or a deeply rooted fear. Did it not in that moment feel like you were free? Wasn't there a distinct sensation of lightness and liberation? That was a healing moment: you let go of a mental construct or painful emotion that was no longer true or necessary for you.

As I've mentioned, this period of undoing, as healing as it is, is often experienced as tension-filled, a disquieting inner struggle that can feel difficult and uncomfortable, such as you might expect when asked to give up an essential part of your self-identity. And the tension will continue until the struggle ends, until the resistance to the process ends.

"When will it end?" you might ask. It ends when you understand that nothing real could ever be threatened, and nothing of true value can ever be lost. The truth of who you are is real and unassailable; only that which you are not can feel threatened by the desire to let it go. Your greatest hope for ending the struggle—and this is a primary objective of the Deep Coaching approach—is to live in complete acceptance of what is, and to allow more space in your mind and heart for compassion, forgiveness, and abiding self-love. This is what gives you the strength and courage to face your personal gravity, take on the tests, challenges, and ordeals of your heroic journey, and ultimately heal. And when you do, your personal gravity will no longer act as the determiner of your sense of self.

Attending to and releasing your personal gravity inherently moves you towards wholeness and completion, and towards a new dimension of Self-knowing. When you strip away all that is not you, the truth of who you are will be revealed. The truth has always been there, but you have been captivated by an illusion which has seemed to hold great power over you. But you can dissipate that apparent power; real power has been given to you to remember and to recognize only what is real and true. This too is the work of Deep Coaching, to help ourselves and others experience that power, the movement which carries the mind to a new level of reality. The more your mental, emotional, and spiritual baggage has been released, the more awake and clear your mind becomes, and the more will you know the reality of who you are and your purpose for being.

Core Limiting Beliefs

Core beliefs, whether positive or negative, are fundamental beliefs about ourselves, other people, and the world we live in. They are things we hold deep down to be absolute truths, underneath all our 'surface' thoughts and beliefs. Because they are assumed to be true, core beliefs often go unnoticed and unchallenged, and toil away tirelessly in the recesses of our mind affecting our moment-by-moment experience and choices. Among the myriad of core beliefs we hold, some are *core limiting beliefs*. These beliefs and false self-images are a fundamental barrier to growth because they directly affect our sense of self-worth, and their identification and healing forms a significant part of Deep Coaching work. They come in a variety of guises, but they usually boil down to one or more of the following:

I'm not good enough.

I'm defective.

I'm not worthy.

I'm not important.

I'm not lovable.

I'm helpless.

I don't belong.

I am not safe.

This is heavy stuff, and forms a considerable part of the weight of our personal gravity. Are these true? They can certainly seem so, and that is why we act on them. However, they are merely *thoughts* resulting from the convergence of childhood experiences, environmental factors, and our innate consciousness. But we believe these thoughts so strongly that we cannot see them as untruths. They are like a pair of invisible glasses through which we perceive ourselves and the world, and after a lifetime of peering through those lenses we no longer see them as separate, something we *have,* but as part of us, something we *are.* This makes them difficult to perceive and to change. The question is then:

How do you release a belief that is alive in every cell in your body, that is wedded to the very fabric of your self-identity?

Seth's Story

"I am scared that people, especially those I work with, will say something to me or behind my back which will reinforce my greatest fear that I am not good enough. In order to avoid that situation, I must serve them and not disobey them, at all costs, even if that means I need to sacrifice many things that matter to me. The 'I'm not good enough' belief is the root cause, and I know this. And because I live through 'I'm not good enough' it makes me lose control of choice. I say yes to things without thought of whether it aligns with me and my values or priorities. Then I push myself to do things I don't want to do and end up feeling miserable doing it.

"This is not the only fear, there is another related one that comes up: when I think about losing or letting go of the thought that I am not good enough, I start to fear I will lose the drive to succeed and be good enough. In other words, I fear if I lose the feeling, I will also lose the driving force behind my success. My belief is, if I'm not in this cycle, I will not work or achieve. By striving to be good enough I have been successful in many aspects of my life and career.

"When I succeed I get validation, I get to hear that I'm doing a good job, and I need that to feel good about myself. If I don't get it, I'm ill at ease. So I need to achieve this or that to meet the standards of the external world, and I also need to strive and work hard to get the validation that I'm good enough. And I do feel good, for a while. But this cycle of trying to disprove the hypothesis that I'm not good enough by working hard and getting the validation I need is short lived. I recognize I have no capacity for self-validation.

"The question is what do I do with this truth, this awareness I have? I have no idea. The focus of my whole life until now has been to achieve things and succeed in order to feel good. Take that away, what do I do? I often question, what is life all about? Why do I exist? Why do I need to work?"

From Seth's story you can hear the inherent challenges to working with a core limiting belief. Firstly, he has no clear sense of how to release; despite his past efforts it's still there, as effective as ever in driving his choices and experiences. And then there is the fear which arises from the question: Who will I be and what will become of me if I let go of this belief that has been the driver of my life for so long? This fear increases the grip of the belief. It can also lead to attempts to find solutions which *manage* the effects of the belief, sometimes at the expense of facing it head on and doing the disciplined work of healing it. (As Seth once said to me, "Even if I think I am not good enough, the rest of the world should not know that I feel that way. Based on this premise, I am planning to project more confidence physiologically when interacting with my boss and co-workers.") Even when well aware of the effects of core limiting beliefs, coaches and clients alike will default to problem-solving, solution-finding mode, as it's more expedient than the longer, potentially arduous task of dissolving tenacious ego-patterns that serve our sense of self and worth.

Another challenge to working with not only limiting beliefs but all personal gravity is what happens as people begin to grasp the size and scope of what's there. They become overwhelmed and start believing that things are in a precarious state, which creates further anxiety. I've had people say to me, "Gosh, there is so much. I feel like I'm regressing because more and more stuff keeps showing up. And now I've got to let go of it, surrender it, move through it. How do I get past all of this?" In reality, it's not that there is "more" of it. It has always been there, playing away deep within the mind, but the inner earthquake brings more into conscious awareness, where it can feel vast, solid, and immovable.

The innate tenacity of our ego-patterns gives rise to a final challenge: the frustration, impatience, and lack of acceptance that can accompany the process. People blame and berate themselves for recurring patterns of negative thought and emotion. "Why am I still having this experience? I have been working on this for so long. I thought I'd moved past this, let go of this, and here it is again. I should be applying all I've learned by now." And then they become vulnerable to spiraling down into a core limiting belief. "It must be because I'm not good enough, smart enough, confident enough, trusting enough—not *something* enough." Now they are really hurting. Yet the fact of their experience and the presence of that belief is simply a sign that it has not yet been fully healed, that there is more to do to release it from the depths of the mind. This is how life works—it conspires to shower us with blessings in the form of people and situations whose role it is to highlight the ego-patterns in need of healing, and repeat as needed until healing is complete.

Healing our personal gravity takes patience and often considerable energy. This is where time factors in; if we want to embody new ways of being, we have to be prepared to put time and effort into healing that which holds us back from that reality. People who seek coaching tend to overlook this (conditioned as we all are to expecting near-instant results), but healing of deep seated ego-patterns is rarely instantaneous, often slow and arduous, and requires dedication and persistence. But once healing has occurred, how good it feels, like the energy drain has been plugged. Much more energy is now available, and can be channeled in new directions, focused on further healing, or used to energize shifts into even higher levels of consciousness and the creative potentials that lie within those realms.

To be clear, the reason we make room for healing in Deep Coaching is not to achieve some mystical state of consciousness or to attain the power to manifest all the material things that are desired (though this may happen along the way). We do it because it clears the pathway to our authentic Self. *To transform is to heal, and to heal is to move into wholeness and completion.* The work, for both you and your clients, is to shine the light of awareness on the mind's dark recesses and shadows, and allow healing moments. Be willing to leave no stone unturned, no corner unexplored. It will not be an easy process, but as you courageously face and attend to your personal gravity, your way of being will shift markedly, and you will step into a new paradigm of personal experience. In time, the radiance of your true Self and soul will shine brightly in the world and the whole of creation will move through you.

Your Personal Gravity

There are likely many aspects of your self-concept which need healing. Can you identify some of them, those layers of self-identity which you are beginning to see as less than truthful, limiting, as no longer reflective of who you are becoming?

> What are the limiting beliefs and perceptions you hold about yourself, how the world is, how people are?
>
> Where are you operating out of drama, self-interest, a survival instinct, the need to succeed or be seen as successful, or a winning impulse?
>
> Where are you trapped in a pattern of inhibiting thought or negative emotion?
>
> What are your addictions?

After you have thought about the question above, ask yourself:

> What is it that I feel, see, or sense is ending within me?
>
> What is ending that I am ready to let go of?

The Propulsion System: Six Engines

Healing our personal gravity is inspired and energized by the second dynamic of transformation: a propulsion system. Coaching in general is meant to propel people forward towards their goals, and to do that effectively coaches leverage a series of interrelated 'engines' which expedite awareness, growth and movement. The engines of propulsion most commonly used by coaches are:

- A safe, trusting, non-judgmental space

- Respect, empathy, and validation

- Inquiry (questions)

- Visioning—connecting with a desired future

- Possibility thinking—seeing innate potentials

- Action orientation.

As powerful as these are, they are foundational engines of propulsion. If you desire to support deep, sustained transformation, as Deep Coaches do, you will use these, but you must also be willing to move beyond them into a more expansive realm of engagement. The six critical engines of propulsion that Deep Coaches work with are:

- Spirit

- Spiritual energy

- Light of the Self

- Inner attitudes

- Environment

- Transformative practice.

The Deep Coaching approach leverages all six of these engines of propulsion, and they are interwoven throughout the nine practices which form the second part of this book. Together they forge a mighty propulsion system which helps energize corrections of mind and shifts in being that are extremely healing.

Spirit

Perhaps the single most powerful engine of transformation is also the one most overlooked in transactional coaching approaches: our spiritual nature and relationship with Spirit. (In part this is because in many societies today there is great sensitivity around it. Talking about spirituality or God can trigger negative reactions, particularly when it has the flavor of religiosity. For some people the whole subject is woo-woo, too 'out there' for application in all of life's situations.)

What is Spirit? Throughout this book I use the word (with a capital S) as an umbrella term, a label to denote the greater *consciousness, presence, or evolutionary intelligence* that guides us on our path and sustains our very existence. Depending on your belief system, Spirit could go by any of a number of names: God, the Divine, Source, Brahman, Creator, Supreme Being, Universal Consciousness or Mind, Divine Presence, Ground of Being, Breath of Life, Guiding Light, and more. All of these are generally pointing to the same thing, and so you are free to decide and define what Spirit means to you.

Now, you may not believe that Spirit exists—that there is a greater consciousness, presence, or evolutionary intelligence that guides life forward—and coaching as a field does not require you to. However, the Deep Coaching approach does rest upon a key presumption: *we are spiritual beings having a human experience* (some would even say a spiritual experience). We know that transformation itself is a healing journey which leads us ultimately to the realization of our being, of I AM—our essential identity—and our essence is spirit (with a small s). Therefore, it makes perfect sense that in deep transformational work the *presence and action* of a vast evolutionary intelligence and organizing life force, what I am labeling Spirit, is not only accounted for but leveraged in support of personal evolution.

In the movie *The Secret*, Michael Beckwith describes Spirit this way:

> "Regardless of what has happened to you in your life, regardless of how young or how old you think you might be, the moment you begin to think properly, there's something that is within you, there's a power within you that's greater than the world. It will begin to emerge. It will take over your life. It will feed you. It will clothe you. It will guide you, protect you, direct you, sustain your very existence…if you let it."

This is a excellent description of the greater intelligence which nudges if not propels us forward. It is "a power...greater than the world," a life force that is the eternal Ground of Being, the way-shower to our highest potential, the sustainer and container of life. Spirit is life-breath, the animating force in our being. Spirit is not born of our beliefs but the shaper of them—*when we let it*. Each of us is intimately connected to Spirit, this infinite life force and source of intelligence, love, wisdom, and energy. Accessed wisely, it helps us direct our thoughts and actions toward personal integration and inner harmony. Spirit knows who you are and holds this truth in store for you within its infinite mind, awaiting the day when you are able to perceive it for yourself.

Moment of Pause

Reflect on Spirit

Notwithstanding my description here, it is important that you give thought to what the term 'Spirit' means for you. I invite you to reflect on these questions:

What does Spirit mean to you?

What, if any, is the role of Spirit in your life?

How do you work with Spirit to enable your
own transformation?

In Deep Coaching we recognize the reality of Spirit and the role it plays in the process of calling forth the magnificence of our true Self and soul. What is happening deep within when the inner earthquake begins and our acquired self-concept begins to crumble is not an existential quirk of an individual personality, it is the function of a vast system of consciousness which enables human life to become Self and Spirit aware. Spirit is the alpha and the omega, the space where all possibilities are contained, and it is the essential catalyst and driver of evolutionary transformation. In Deep

Coaching this engine of transformation stands at the very center of our work, and so we *make room for the presence of Spirit* to help dissolve the manifold layers of ego-based thought and energy that we have allowed to inhabit our mind.

Spiritual Energy

Everything in the universe is made up of energy, and energy is what connects it all. Our thoughts, beliefs, attitudes and emotions are all forms of energy, vibrating away at different frequencies, influencing our moment-by-moment experience. Quantum physics has shown that as we go deep into the workings of the atom, we see that there is nothing physical there, just energy waves. The physical world you perceive—this book you are reading, the room you sit in, everything your eyes take in—while appearing solid, is pure energy in motion. It's quite the paradox, isn't it? We are so in love with, so attached to, a world that is in reality completely immaterial.

Aura, soul, spirit, consciousness—these too are forms of energy or energy fields. As spiritual beings, we are part of a unified field of consciousness that can be likened to a vast web of vibrating energy that connects bodies, minds, the world, and everything in the universe. In other words, energy and consciousness manifest themselves as the undivided power of the universe. All things are so utterly connected, so intimately one, that they are *of* each other. This is why learning to work with spiritual energy to support transformation is an essential Deep Coaching practice, as we will cover in Chapter 10. Spiritual energy is no less real than any other energy—electrical or thermal, for example—but it is vastly more important in healing. In yogic traditions, spiritual energy is referred to as Prana, the master form of all energy working on the level of mind and body, carried by pure love. Spiritual energy is a creative force of unbounded, unlimited Spirit, and functions as the *action of Spirit* within the mind and body. Spiritual energy is the fuel of life, and a powerful engine of transformation.

**Spiritual Energy as the Light and
Action of Spirit**

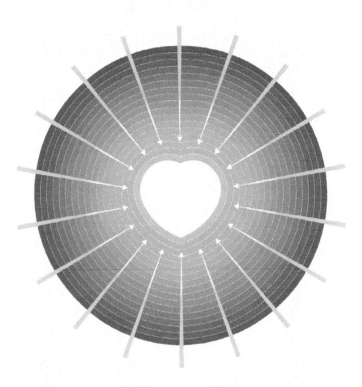

As you learn how Spirit acts to empower human evolution, as you open to and receive its manifold gifts—one of the greatest being spiritual energy healing—and as you align your life to partner with Spirit, your being and presence will be transformed radically. The consciousness of Spirit and its life force energy will pour into the reservoirs of your mind and soul, which are quite capable of receiving it, and integrate with your human life force to create and reveal a unique form of infinite expression: you. And when spiritual energy, which is infinite intelligence and perfect love, flows unobstructed through you, it transmutes anything unlike itself and manifests as truth, beauty, and goodness.

Light of the Self

Light is one way to understand our spiritual potential. We all have a certain light within us; we are born with it. (It may be why infants can give us a feeling of joy.) It is the light of the Self, an animating force in our being. But our light gets covered up by a lifetime of conditioning, buried under layers of egoic construct which cause its radiance to fade from our awareness. In time, we start to see ourselves and the world through the distorted eyes of the ego.

Light of the Self

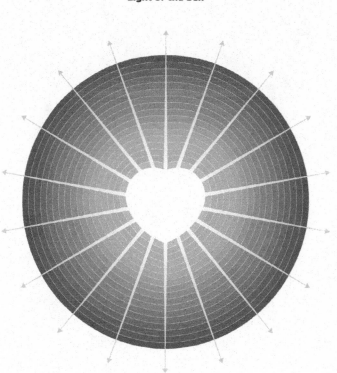

When we awaken, the light of the Self is rekindled and it brings a flow of higher consciousness into our minds, enabling us to see through life's illusions and understand more of our true nature. The light of the Self acts like a brilliant spiritual energy that shines through the earthquake's cracks upon the dark recesses of our old self-concept and illuminates them for the shadows and illusions they are. In this way our self-concept, increasingly free of distortion and falsity, is encouraged to evolve to reflect the reality of our true Self.

As transformation continues, the light of the Self begins to shine ever more brightly and the potentials increase for our self-concept to be nurtured with what it needs most: love, understanding, acceptance, forgiveness, and patience. These are the qualities that bring our soul to life and which form the foundation of our emerging self-concept. This light is a mighty enabler of transformation. It is, in essence, YOU shining through.

Our personal light of Self relates directly to the light of Spirit. The light of Spirit (the light that 'descends from above,' so to speak) works with the light of the Self (the light that 'arises from within') to guide us on the journey, expanding our consciousness, encouraging us to live a soul-nourishing life, and supporting our efforts to heal our ego-patterns, the veil between the lights. The combined action of the lights of the Self and of Spirit brings spiritual consciousness into our lives, transforms us from within, and enables us to experience our true nature. The Sufi tradition has a beautiful phrase for this dance: light upon light:

Light rises toward light and light comes down upon light, and it is light upon light.

~ Najm al-Din Kubra

Light Upon Light

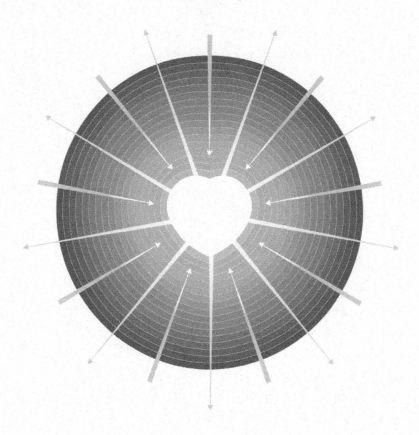

What is coming into existence is not a reiteration of past patterns but a new paradigm, a new expression of selfhood, and we can actively foster its emergence by tapping into the light of the Self and Spirit. As we dedicate ourselves to the inner work, our light shines ever more brightly, dissolving and transmuting the distortions of our personal gravity. Now we find ourselves readily able to leave behind patterns that no longer serve and anything else that is antithetical to the Self. The light of the Self and soul then becomes a dominant force of progression for those who willingly make the choice to become 'enlightened' beings.

Inner Attitudes

When an airplane has a nose-high attitude, it climbs; when it has a nose-down attitude, it falls. The same holds true for people. Thoughts and opinions create feelings, and both of them together create attitudes—positive and negative. Transformation progresses when favorable attitudes and orientations of mind are in place. What are the inner attitudes which support positive growth and change? Which ones inhibit it? With the correct attitudes in place, life offers limitless possibilities; when negative or undesirable ones are in place, potentials are lost and realizing potentials becomes unlikely.

If we are truthful with ourselves we will discover disagreeable, self-centered attitudes and impulses within. This does not make us bad people, but it can drain energy and make life feel more like a struggle for survival. The willingness to acknowledge and eliminate attitudes and thinking patterns which reflect pride (superiority), greed, jealousy, malice, cruelty, spite, selfishness, and fear will go a long way towards preventing energy from leaking out. This is like plugging the holes in a milk pail so that we can collect the milk. We can then cultivate the inner attitudes and dispositions which are so conducive to transformation: truthfulness, open-mindedness, openheartedness, responsibility, acceptance, forgiveness, commitment, perseverance, and devotion. It is these which fuel the journey through and beyond whatever may arise on the path.

Environment

Maslow's Hierarchy of Needs highlights a great truth of our human experience: when we are in survival mode, each day a quest to make ends meet, put bread on the table and keep a roof over our heads, there is little if any energy left for pursuing self-actualization, the pinnacle of the human experience. If our basic external needs for sustenance (food, water, sleep) and security (of body, mind, resources) are not sufficiently met, we cannot direct energy to the pursuit of happiness and fulfillment. The external environment in which we live has a direct effect on our inner capacity to grow; people whose basic human needs are fulfilled are better able to act based on their desire to change and grow, rather than being motivated by gnawing primal demands.

The journey of transformation is a function of the quest for self-actualization, and it too is influenced by our environment. Although people are awakening all over the world, it is not uncommon for a person to feel quite alone in the process. Some people even live within a family or community whose beliefs and culture prohibit the expression of the emerging selfhood. Therefore, a commonly expressed need of those in transformation is for association with kindred spirits who are also on the path. The ability to connect and be in an environment with like-minded people is highly rewarding and conducive to personal and spiritual growth.

Knowing that one's environment does influence progress, the question for Deep Coaches becomes:

> What is the nature of an environment that propels
> transformation?

In simple terms, it is a healing space. A healing space creates the optimal conditions in which transformation can unfold naturally and organically, with the greatest amount of ease and joy. As Dr. Esther Sternberg describes in her book, *Healing Spaces:*

> "A healing space is your own place of peace created through
> what you see and feel and smell and hear—through all your
> senses. We need to allow ourselves the time to see the sun
> glinting off the surface of the leaves, to listen to the sounds
> of silence and of nature. We need to stop and inhale the smell
> of ocean salt or the fragrance of honeysuckle on a summer's
> night. We need to feel the gentle touch of a spring breeze."

Once a person begins to de-stress and detox mind and body, and configure their life and environment to promote access to healing spaces, they facilitate transformation at the deepest levels. Now the light of Self and action of Spirit can do its best work, in a mind open and aware, at ease and in the flow of the natural rhythms of life.

Transformative Practice

Transformative practice is deep practice. It is intentional activity committed to for extended periods of time with the purpose of empowering transformation. Transformative practice gives us greater awareness of our habitual behaviors and personal gravity (that which holds us back). It promotes access to our spiritual depths and helps reveal more of the nature of our true Self (that which moves us forward). Far more than a hobby or something we dabble in, *transformative practice is a way of living, of engaging with life each day.*

Within transformative practice as a whole, there are many individual practices designed to facilitate fundamental shifts in patterns of thinking and perceiving, and to enable profound growth through the cultivation of new attributes and ways of being. The form of each practice can vary greatly and may include: meditation, breath work, movement practices such as tai chi or yoga, prayer, self-observation, sacred ritual, artistic pursuits, time in nature, forgiveness work, journaling, healing arts and more. However, any one practice only becomes *transformative* through focused intention and a persistent will to keep practicing it.

For example, say you are a person who does not feel or express much gratitude, and you wish to develop a greater appreciation of all that is in your life. For starters, you already have the *awareness* that you desire to cultivate the 'attitude of gratitude.' From this awareness, you identify one or more *practices* which align with you and the cultivation of gratitude. For the first week or two you maintain the practice and you make progress. But by week three it becomes less regular, and by week six it's intermittent at best. Old habits and routines may have gotten in the way, maybe you're tired of the practice, and fairly confident that you've 'got it,' or perhaps at some level you've decided it wasn't that important to develop anyway—a little more gratitude is good enough for now—and the next thing you know you find yourself back in familiar territory, feeling not so grateful once again and a little deflated by the whole process.

What was missing? You were aware of the need to cultivate more gratitude in your life, and you identified and were working with a practice designed to do just that. But your practice was not transformative because you did not develop the *discipline* needed to support you in achieving this goal. This is what differentiates transformative practice from sporadic practice, from dabbling. When I use the word 'discipline' I do not mean an inflexible, militaristic type of discipline (in general, rigidity and the human process do not go well together). What I am referring to is the *will*, the commitment, the deep intention and motivation to keep repeating the practice consistently in order to actualize what you desire. This notion of discipline is dynamic, spacious, and is wedded to joy—some have called it 'blissipline'—for it arises from a purposeful, creative, self-expressing place within, and its constancy helps sustain deep, lasting change.

Each of the nine Deep Coaching practices introduced later in the book is a transformative practice. Each one, by itself, has the capacity to radically shift your inner state of awareness and engagement. If you practice just one of them with great intention and attention each day for three months or more, your life will change in meaningful ways. The nine practices were selected with a specific objective in mind: *to create the optimal conditions in which transformation unfolds naturally and organically, with the greatest amount of ease and joy.* In Deep Coaching, we are learning to create a healing space so that whatever wants to happen within the transforming self can happen, and whatever wants to emerge can emerge—the nine practices are the threads with which you will weave the cocoon holding that space, the cocoon within which the dual dynamics of transformation play out.

Josephine's Story

"Every time my ego-mind is talking I choose to question it and go to my heart and anchor there. I know I can trust my heart because it has never let me down, but many of my thoughts let me down on a daily basis. So I've come to realize my heart and my mind are like two friends. The friend I call heart has never ever let me down and it has always taken me to a place of more love for myself and for the people around me. And this other friend, my mind, is a kind of pact with the devil, because it is a friend that's often deceiving me, letting me down, confusing and complicating things.

"So I said okay, why on earth would I listen to this friend who is so often crapping on me. For years I have been listening to this friend, who was a false friend but whom I believed was the right one. It kept taking me to a place of suffering or self-doubt, and seeing what's not real. So I tell myself to choose my heart, and she always leads me to the right place.

"Lately I've been having a lot of visual and physical experiences that are helping me to come back to my heart, all the time. It's becoming easier to recognize which of the two paths I want to walk. I think it also has to do with the fact that my self-love and self-worth are really in place now, so I feel the energy of love. It's like an energy field around me, a kind of shield. When I connect to my heart, the energy and the vibration is so high that even when an old habit or something is trying to get in, it's automatically pushed away because it cannot resist so much love. I'm consciously nurturing that place of love. The only thing I'm doing is keeping and nurturing that place because I know that if the energy and vibration is high enough, there's no way that something can affect me or can decenter me. And it feels lovely to have that realization and to make that choice. I'm preserving my love and my light at whatever cost because I'm loving myself so much and its becoming so important. Anything that could be harmful for me I release automatically because there's no place for punishing or hurting myself anymore."

Josephine has discovered the power of the heart. This is a wonderful example of the intentional use of a transformative practice: she returns to her heart center time and time again, anchoring in to gain the strength, energy and motivation she needs to transcend the gravitational pull of her thoughts and to grow as she desires.

All good coaches are adept at working with the foundational engines of propulsion I mentioned earlier. No matter which form of coaching you engage in, there is a need for visioning and goal setting, creating intent and generating motivation, exploring issues through inquiry, shifting perspectives, designing action, and maintaining commitment to the process. These are all forms of propulsion which enable positive, forward-moving change.

As we've learned, however, transformation itself is far more than the normal process of change; it is sweeping change, a stripping away of all that is not who we are, a *revolution* in our self-concept designed to usher in new ways of being and a new paradigm of existence. Deep Coaches are therefore adept at working with six additional engines of propulsion—Spirit, spiritual energy, the light of Self, inner attitudes, environment, and transformative practice—because they are powerful enablers and accelerants of transformation. Deep Coaches learn to work comfortably with them all because they provide the essential energy, motivation, and uplift to do the healing work transformation demands. At the same time, they connect us with the higher fields of consciousness so essential for receiving all that we need to flourish into a new paradigm of self-knowing and expression.

Your Propulsion System

Take a few minutes to reflect on these questions:

> What moves you forward and enables you to grow into a higher way of being? What conditions, attitudes, relationships or practices accelerate your evolution into more of who you truly are?

> Something is alive in you that has its own volition, that is coming into being of its own accord. What is it that you feel, see, or sense wants to emerge in you at this point in your life?

Coaching as a Healing Modality

As an inquiry-based methodology of change, 'conventional coaching' (a term I use for any coaching approach that relies heavily on inquiry to drive the coaching process) has some inherent limitations. One of those limitations is that it does not have a clear means for healing personal gravity, particularly those embedded distortions of the self-concept born of past conditioning and life experiences. In conventional coaching, generally speaking, inquiry followed by action planning is the coach's response to whatever the client desires to work on. Conventional coaching excels at enabling people to increase self-awareness so that they can make better decisions or future-focused, positive change, but it doesn't really know how to support a person to *heal* their personal gravity. This stuff goes deep, has roots in the unconscious mind, is alive in every cell in their body, and the most 'powerful' questions in the world will not necessarily help them to actually heal what is there. At best, conventional coaching can support a person to get clear on how they might like to heal themselves *after* the session, but the coach plays no intentional role in the healing process itself.

From my experience, coaches who have not learned how to support healing within a coaching context, who feel uncomfortable doing so, or who believe it is not part of coaching will turn away from it, preferring to keep the conversation at a more transactional, surface level rather than dive into the murky depths.

Deep Coaching aims to void this limitation by *positioning coaching as a healing modality*. Firstly, we recognize that *to transform is to heal* (they are not separate processes) and secondly, healing is vital to ensure *sustainable shifts in being*. If coaching does not support a person to heal their personal gravity, then it will continue to weigh them down and hold them back from embodying higher states of being. Permanents shifts then become elusive, which is difficult and frustrating for those on the path.

The nine transformative practices introduced in the second part of the book are designed to enable you, the coach, to attend to the dual dynamics of transformation confidently, and possibly in ways you have not considered or experienced before. And when you leverage all six of the propulsion mechanisms available, and you create a space in which the depths of a person's personal gravity can be attended to, you will support others to heal themselves in profound ways. Miracles can and will happen.

Deep Coaches are willing and able to attend to personal gravity, and to do so in a way that keeps things within the coaching realm. Coaching is not therapy, and is generally not intended for people who are experiencing severe emotional or mental disorders; however, coaching can be highly therapeutic. And it should be, because feelings of dysfunction are a normal, functional effect of transformation. The human mind and its many patterns of operation are being restructured, and with this comes the accompanying sense that things may be falling apart. Deep Coaches do not shy away from this. Instead, we nurture a vibrant healing space which quells discomfort and supports letting go and letting come; a space in which the deepest levels of renewal can unfold.

The Dual Dynamics in a Nutshell

When coaching, a Deep Coach works with these dynamics:

- Personal gravity

- Propulsion system.

In order to transform (heal), a coachee works with these dynamics:

- Letting go (of personal gravity)

- Letting come (a new way of being or true Self-awareness).

Living Between the No Longer and Not Yet

One of the most challenging aspects of the transformational journey is how to live amid the dual dynamics. A mentor of mine once described it aptly as "living between the no longer and not yet." In transformation, your old self-concept is beginning to die away as you shed the distortions of reality which no longer reflect the 'I' of your true Self—but your old self is not entirely *no longer*. At the same time, there is a heightened sense of an emerging 'I,' a selfhood greater than you have previously known—but it is *not yet* your permanent experience.

Isn't this what is happening within the cocoon of the transforming caterpillar? As it dies and decays into a primordial goo, its immune system continues to actively thwart the emergence and clustering of the imaginal cells. The caterpillar, well on its way to being no longer, remains influential, and the butterfly, at first merely an emerging potential, is not yet.

The phrase 'living between the no longer and not yet' captures nicely what it means to experience the ebb and flow of the dual dynamics of transformation. One moment you experience movement into an exalted state of being, and soon thereafter comes a sense of shifting back into your old self and its energy and patterns of behavior. And while living between the no longer and not yet is normal and functional and a rite of passage for all on the journey, it is also one of the hardest for people to accept as necessary. Once higher states of being are experienced with some regularity, falling back hurts; it can be frustrating, painful and, for some, exhausting. "I thought I was done with this! I thought I'd moved past this!" people will cry. Apparently not. Transformation brings with it its own unique set of experiences and lessons, and the lessons will be repeated until they are learned.

Fabienne's Story

"I'm in the space between no longer and not yet. I'd like clarity on where I'm at and where I'm going. Some shifts are happening that I don't understand and they don't make sense to me. Recently I let go of a family relationship which allowed me to shift the way that I am in the world. It made me let go of the fear of being judged, fear of not being seen, heard, accepted, and a whole new me started to emerge. I started to be inspired creatively and realized I'd been blocked for so many years. It felt great, like I'd been released from prison. It was a really profound shift and I was euphoric for a while.

"Over the past year I feel like I've been waking up out of the matrix, so to speak, and looking at life on earth and looking at the systems and going, "Wow..." I'm not sure what to do with all of what I'm seeing. Part of my mind wants to go back into the matrix, forget I know all of this, and pretend I live on earth. And the other part of me says, "No, you can't go back." But I don't know what this new paradigm or construct looks like. And frankly it's a little scary operating in a different way mentally, yet still living in a society that is still largely asleep. It feels so strange to talk about this. It's disconcerting to be out of the matrix, especially when I let my mind wander about the universe. Maybe there is something larger than earth that is at play here. I'm dipping my toe into it all, and it seems so unusual, strange, and foreign.

"What do I do with all this information? Where does this want to take me? Where do I go with this? What wants to happen next with this? I've also outgrown a lot of friends and people over the past year. I'm at a place where I'm ready to enter into a new chapter. But I don't know if I'm ready. The biggest fear is staying where I'm at, in the matrix. Living this boring unconnected life and not being myself is my biggest fear. There is also a fear of, "What if it is doesn't happen? What if I'm stuck here? What if it doesn't happen on my time frame? What if God forgets me? What if the universe forgets me? What if this is not as real as it seems to be?" Then I go back to feeling disconnected."

Fabienne is describing her experience of living between the no longer and not yet. And, as it is for most everyone, she experiences it as a place of tension and uncertainty. In transformation, our propulsion system powers us forward while simultaneously our personal gravity pulls us back. Fabienne has embraced the vision that her awakened mind has revealed, yet something within her also fears and resists it. During one of our sessions she asked me with some concern, "How do I live in this place? How do I better balance the highs and the lows, the feelings of connection and disconnection?" She was worried that if the ebb and flow was expected to last for a significant period of time, how would she manage herself within it? This is a very good question that all transformational coaches should consider as well, but I will not answer it here; as we delve into the nine transformative practices the answer will become apparent. In the meantime, I invite you to give thought to the question Fabienne asked me:

"How do I live between the no longer and the not yet?"

And the Paradigm Shifts

The ebb and flow of transformation, the sense of progression followed by a sense of regression, is one of the great trials of the journey. As I've mentioned, there tends to be a natural resistance to regression, and a questioning of its need and utility. In reality, the dynamic of transformation is not linear, from where I am today to where I desire to be tomorrow, but cyclical: an upward spiral of birth, growth, actualization, deepening, disintegration, and renewal or rebirth. Like the waves falling on the shore, each time a wave hits it rises up and then ebbs, but slowly the tide moves up. It is this cyclical process that, if accepted and allowed to do its thing, enables us to grow into a whole new paradigm of self-experience.

In his book *The Structure of Scientific Revolution*, scientist and philosopher Thomas Kuhn defines a paradigm as a conceptual framework, belief system, set of assumptions, and overall perspective through which we see and interpret ourselves and the world, its chief characteristic being that it has its own set of rules and illuminates its own set of facts. In this way it becomes self-validating and therefore resistant to change. Kuhn observes that as long as a paradigm explains most experiences and solves most of the problems we want solved, it remains dominant. We also will not question it, because we are usually unaware of its existence. But, as new information begins to contradict it, the paradigm can become weakened by increasing doubt. And as that evidence accumulates, the paradigm is thrown into crisis until a new conceptual self and world view eventually replaces the old.

You can think of a paradigm shift as a significant change from one way of conceiving and thinking about yourself and the world to another. It›s a revolution, a metamorphosis of thought, perception, and experience. But what causes a paradigm to shift? The generally accepted understanding is that a paradigm is driven to change by the pressure of new evidence or a set of conditions which enable that change to happen. Essentially, a paradigm begins to shift when it is 'wrong' or no longer reflective of reality as it is known to be. And if it is wrong it *will* shift, as reality will eventually prove inconsistent with it.

It's possible to see a connection between Kuhn's concept of a paradigm shift and how transformation happens in the natural world. Remember that when the caterpillar dies and disintegrates, imaginal cells begin to appear at random in the primordial goo of death and decay. And since these cells are anomalies and not recognized by the caterpillar's immune system, it's crisis time! and they immediately move to wipe out the new cells. But as the imaginal cells grow in number and begin to link up, they overwhelm the immune system and create a new reality. And the paradigm shifts.

In human beings it is a similar process. The dominant paradigm through which each of us operates does not initially account for anomalies—we tend to resist or filter out anything which does not align with our current paradigm of reality. Over time, however, new information—in this case let's say the imaginal cells of our awakened mind—will overwhelm the system and usher in a new phase of growth and experience. Transformation is a paradigm shifting process, moving us from one way of being to another.

Gabriel's Story

"For the past while I have noticed myself in a cycle which tends to repeat itself in my life, where I'm totally tapped in and tuned in to my higher Self and all the energies that make me feel like me. And then I totally and completely disconnect. I hate it honestly, and so a big part of my days has been exploring what is going on when that happens.

"I know I have fallen into old habits, old thought patterns, and old ways of being. It's been crappy because I've been acutely aware of it happening and feeling like I have no control of it. I really struggle with this because I am very much aware when I am disconnected, and it sucks. I'm actually physically sick at the moment, which I haven't been in years, so to say I experience this disconnection with every cell of my being is quite accurate.

"I really, really don't enjoy this part of transformation that causes my old habits, old beliefs, and lack of connection to take the driver seat. How can I be in a place where either this doesn't happen anymore, or where I can be more at peace with the contrast? Because in reality, it is only my awareness and knowing that things can be and feel different that causes me to be so irritated when I'm not feeling connected.

"My question is, "How do I *be* during these times?" I'm aware that I'm not spiritually aligned, and I know what it feels like to be in alignment, so that contrast really gets to me, and yet I feel like I have no control. I'm getting better at reconnecting, but when the light switches off, I feel like it's a bigger struggle to fight it, then to just ride it out. Will I always have these sort of ups and downs?"

This is what living between the no longer and not yet, within the cyclical nature of transformation, can feel like. Because transformation is neither innately predictable nor linear, it usually involves revisiting points that we have been through many times, and encountering the same new messages and information over and over again, in different ways and seasons, until they become relevant and meaningful. We also begin to experience previously unknown states of being, and potentially in ways not experienced before. (After having such experiences, old patterns and paradigms of reality may feel like 'lunchbag letdown,' and not a little confusing and unpleasant.) What this all means is that shifting our self-concept into a new paradigm requires time and energy both to integrate the new information and to extract even further meaning from that integration, so that our emerging way of being can become embodied and sustained.

In time, as the new paradigm settles in, the cycles or swings will become less noticeable or disappear—that is, until the next wave of new information comes along. But it is incredibly helpful to recognize the value of this pattern and know that it is just a temporary state from which we will continue to move forward, so that it becomes easier to accept what is happening and to allow what wants to happen to happen. When we live in a state of acceptance and allowing, life flows with far greater ease and joy, and we can marvel at the mystery and magic of the process, trusting—despite any appearances to the contrary—that all is working for our greatest good.

CHAPTER SEVEN

Recognizing the Readiness: Five Key Signals

Not everyone who comes to coaching wants or needs transformational coaching, and not everyone is ready to explore the depths of their being. Many people come looking only for short-term solutions or support with immediate aspirations. Even though you may desire to coach transformationally, *it can't be your agenda*—a good coach meets people where they are at. For that reason, the ability to discern the signals of awakening and transformation is an essential Deep Coaching competency, so you can meet the person where they are at with an appropriate approach.

Normalize Their Experience

As people awaken and experience the inherent disruption it entails, they will not necessarily understand *why* they are experiencing that disruption, nor what to do about it. They often misread the signals, perceiving the tension and turmoil born of the process as a 'problem to be solved' rather than as the perfect functionality of dysfunction. Some will even question their sanity. I once received an email from a young woman who was in some turmoil; she wrote that while she had been hearing a lot about the power of love, she was unable to feel it herself. She said she could feel care, even a high degree of intimacy with others, but love—not romantic love but unconditional, abiding love—remained elusive. And this apparent inability vexed her greatly. She closed the email by adding, "If my friends knew what I was writing to you about, they'd think I was crazy!" But that thought, "My friends would think I'm crazy," was a projection of her own perception, "I think I might be crazy," onto a peer group. She couldn't figure out whether her desire to experience unconditional love was real or a figment of her imagination, and the uncertainty had her questioning her own sanity, and worrying that others might laugh at her. I'm glad she reached out to me so that I could normalize the experience for her, and let her know that what she was experiencing was incredibly sane.

This story exemplifies not only how the disruption inherent in transformation can leave individuals feeling perplexed, but also how being ridiculed or scorned by others can throw salt on the fire. It does happen, particularly when the desired direction of growth runs counter to the prevailing cultural norm. If love or peace or harmony is not the norm, then anything that does not align with that norm may be stifled in an attempt to defend the status quo. This mirrors what happens when the imaginal cells pop up within the primordial goo of the dying caterpillar: the caterpillar's immune system immediately moves to snuff them out as a means of self-preservation.

Imagine: you are going about your life, doing what you are supposed to do, thinking what you are supposed to think, knowing what you are supposed to know, when one day a window in your mind opens and a new light dawns upon you—ping!— and you sense the potentials of a reality that seems removed from what you know (though in some way it also feels strangely familiar). What do you do? Perhaps you question your sanity. Perhaps you decide to take a surreptitious look around to see if anyone else is feeling the same way. "Is anyone else experiencing this odd sensation, or am I the only one?" You turn on the TV, but no one is talking about it. You read the newspaper, but it's the voice of the world you already know.

You watch a TV show, play a game on your phone, check your messages, surf the internet, pour yourself into your work, hang out with friends, get some exercise, have a nice meal, do a little shopping, go to a party, see a movie, all the things you normally do, but still the niggly, far-off voice does not go away. So, you decide to share some of your experiences with a couple of friends to gauge their reaction. But they look at you funny and don't really get what you're talking about. Now you clam up, change the subject, and get back to talking about what you always talk about them. You think to yourself, "Better I carry this inside me than have people think I'm loopy. Because just maybe I really am for feeling this way."

Then one day you're hanging out online and you notice someone has posted a little sign that speaks right to you, a message that reflects perfectly your inner voice, the one that won't go away no matter how hard you try to shut it out. The little sign resonates with you so much that you decide to look further, to see if there are more signs. And there are: dozens, hundreds, thousands of little signs that signal how not alone you are in your experience. "There are others like me out there!" you cry. "I'm okay! (Or wait…am I? Maybe we're all crazy.)" No matter, this validation is empowering. Your feelings are normal. Now, these people may not live anywhere near you, nor look like you, nor live as you do, but you know they exist, and they are out there speaking openly of things like love and unity and spirit and peace and compassion. All you need to do is connect with them in some way, and so you do. Voilà; in that moment, as in the caterpillar's metamorphosis, you have joined a cluster of imaginal cells, and an evolutionary step has been taken.

Do you see why it is important that Deep Coaches recognize the signals? Within the general populace there is a dearth of awareness around awakening and transformation as a *personal process*. People do realize they are experiencing a significant internal shift, but the experience itself does not translate automatically into an understanding of what is going on or what to do about it. But Deep Coaches know. Deep Coaches are versed in the mysteries and delights, the trials and challenges of the transformational process, are at home in the spiral of its dynamics, and understand that this journey will take people to the edge of their known existence and beyond, into the light of their true Self and nature. One of our key roles is therefore to *normalize* the experience for them, to say: You are on the grandest journey life has to offer—this is what is happening for you! And this is what I can do for you and what we will do together.

Years ago, when I was moving through a particularly confusing period in my own life, I booked a session with a coach whom I'd met through a colleague. At the time, I was unschooled in the signals of transformation and unaware that I was on something that could be called a 'transformational journey.' What I did know was that the coach's questions about options and actions and commitment levels were out of alignment with what I was needing. There was no space in the conversation, no breath, no movement to a higher level of awareness, no loftier vantage point; it was all so linear and intellect-based. Our relationship lasted just one session. Even though I was not cognizant of exactly what was happening within me, I knew that what I was seeking would not be uncovered through a 'define your options and act now to make it happen' approach. In hindsight, I suspect transactional coaching was all he knew—he didn't recognize the signals and he couldn't meet me where I was at. Had he normalized my experiences or demonstrated a knowledge of the signals of transformation, things may have turned out differently.

It Can't Be Your Agenda

The same principle applies when coaching someone who is ready for or desires a transactional approach. If you've ever had a thought such as, "I'm not really interested in transactional coaching, so I'm going to try and go deeper with this person because that's what I enjoy doing. And it will be good for her too because she's so...," you need to let that go. No matter how much you enjoy transformational coaching, if the signals are not there then a person may not be ready for it. It can't become your agenda.

There will be others you meet who exhibit the signals. They may even move to the edge, appearing ready to go on a deeper dive with you, before hesitating and turning away. In fact, this may happen numerous times over long periods before they take the plunge. A certain readiness is required, a necessary mustering of courage and faith to take the road less travelled. You cannot dictate the timing. Even if the signals are there, for whatever reason, some people will only want to work on issues at a surface level. So be it. If you attempt to go deep with someone who is not ready for it, you will encounter resistance.

Remember, our clients are in the driver's seat. Our role is to meet them where *they* are at, never forcing or manipulating them to be where *we* are at. All coaching approaches have their time and place. When your approach matches what the client is ready for, that's when the magic happens—so if you would like to be a Deep Coach, stay vigilant for these signals. The absence of these signals does not mean you cannot coach *transformationally*—recall from Chapter 4, you can coach anyone transformationally, as long as there is a readiness for it—however, when you recognize the signs that a person is on the transformational journey, you can position yourself to coach *transformation*. I have illustrated some of these signals through the personal stories and in the descriptions of related stages in the models of transformation; however, this chapter highlights the five most salient. The presence of these signals implies a heightened readiness for the deep dive that Deep Coaching facilitates.

Signal #1: A Sense of Uncertainty, Confusion and Doubt around What's Happening and the Direction of Their Life

This uncertainty is often expressed through big questions, questions for which there are no easy answers:

Who am I?

What am I doing with my life?

What is my role as a human being?

What is my purpose and how can I live it?

How can I be my most aligned, integrated self?

What is my responsibility to the world, to life?

What does the world need that my talents can serve?

Here are some examples of how it can sound:

I am questioning my life and my life direction. I'm just not happy where things are at. I am questioning how I can access and grow into my best self, into my most giving self in order to be who I am and do what I love to do. I want to make a transformation; to discover who I am without the _____ [fill in the limiting self-identity piece].

I feel so lonely at a soul level. In reality, I'm out celebrating with friends, being very social, but I'm operating from a place that not many people around me really get, and I can feel lonely on a human level. And I also worry, if I become too spiritual, can I have a relationship? Can I connect with other people? But I know I'm being nudged in a certain direction, as though choices are being made deep within me, my higher Self-intentions creating and deciding for me. I just want to surrender to that inner director.

I am in the process of letting go of attachment to many things in my life. In this process of letting go I am reclaiming my life. I am reclaiming my passions, relationships, and what it means to live a full life. I'm allowing myself to look forward to things, and to not veer off path to join another person's life as a way to fulfill my own needs. It's time to stop shopping for a life and be in love with my life as it is. I want to spread love and joy, and the essential me wants to radiate through. That's how I want to live.

My work no longer feels congruent with who I am. There is a deeper calling, and it is asking me to be the embodiment of my core values. But I hesitate to say yes to it, as there is a fear of disconnection from my family and friends. I have an obligation to them. I fear that going deeper into this calling involves separating from them and taking away what I do for them. They rely on me for energy and support. I do know however, that this calling is pulling me deeper into connection to life, God, the world, other people.

In each of these examples you can hear the questioning and the underlying tension that signifies the transformational process. The light of Self is expanding, shining itself upon the distortions and patterns that are antithetical to the Self so that we can become free of all that limits and binds us. So much of what has long been believed to be true, long been given meaning and value, is starting to crack and crumble, and with that comes the sense that things are falling apart. Losing what we have valued, what has defined us, what has given our life meaning and security, is often a confusing, doubt-filled, process.

Some of us will consider making significant life changes, changes we may likely never before have considered feasible or plausible: separating from a partner or spouse; abandoning a career path; taking a sabbatical to travel the world; becoming a professional coach. As I mentioned earlier, people who make these kinds of choices are often questioned if not ridiculed by family, friends, employers. "Why would you want to do that?" they ask.

"Your job is good, you have a steady paycheck, medical, benefits—why would you give that up?" "Your partner is such a nice person and loves you so much. You're so good together—why would you give that up?" "Why travel the world when everything you need is here? Your friends and family are here! Why would you give that up?"

Questions like this compound the confusion. "It's true," you reflect, "Why am I called to walk away from this? Is it worth it? What will happen when I do? Do I really want to create all of this turmoil in my life, in their lives?" This is the experience of many who have begun the journey while living within a community of well-meaning people who voice support for the status quo and who have not yet themselves grasped the nature and scope of the inner changes that these external choices reflect.

All in all, it can be a challenging time. When the foundation upon which you have built your home begins to crack and crumble, it's only natural to feel trepidation, confusion, and to question the rightness of it all.

Signal #2: Increasing Awareness of One's Personal Gravity and Its Effect

Transformation is a dance of light and shadow. As the inner earthquake progresses, more and more of what is hidden away in the recesses of our mind will arise into conscious awareness. As I explained in Chapter 6, this is our personal gravity. When you examine it closely, you might be surprised how much is there, how much has been overlooked, stuffed away, or left unattended. Repressed pain and sorrow will arise, triggered by the opening of old wounds or hurtful experiences. Sometimes it's the frustrations of our human limitations, the rough edges of our personality, or the effects of an immature mind acting out. In one way or another it is coming to the surface to be attended to and healed. At some level we know that this stuff is to be no longer, though how exactly that will transpire is unknown.

Meredith's Story

"My family has a strong vein of insistence energy running through it. I have gotten tired of it and said it's enough. But I realized recently my saying enough had also become an insistence, and it was time for me to back down from that because it was causing pain. I think it was simply a cry from me that said, 'If you [my family] don't want to hear me, I'll smash each one of you.' I insisted on being heard, and if they wouldn't hear me I'd act out. I never had a reason to want to be listened to, that is the irony, it's just that people kept at me for not being perfect, for not doing this and not doing that. I kept saying, 'I can't, I don't have the capacity.' But nobody listened and nobody accepted that. My whole walk down this path is because I am the one member of this family who never insisted, and I got stuck in it. What the hell is going on in my life! I never want to insist; how did I get stuck in it? I want to get out of it!

"The biggest fear I live with is whether I will lose my husband and family in the bargain of releasing this energy. I don't know how I will handle this energy with my spouse, and I don't want to lose that relationship. I am very entangled in this energy with my spouse, but I cannot carry this energy of insistence forward. I'm not made that way. I don't know how to break this vicious cycle. I can't stay in it any longer, I am so exhausted. I don't have an answer for myself. And I'm scared. Am I pulling myself out of my family life because I put it out that I can't, while people continue to insist?"

At the time of our conversation, the shadow we labelled "the energy of insistence" had only just come into Meredith's awareness, yet it had been within her family for a lifetime. You can hear her perplexity at discovering how entangled in it she had become, and also her cry of anguish at both the pain it was causing and the fear of what it would mean to release it. This is not surface level stuff; it runs deep.

She came for Deep Coaching because she knew this energy of insistence was alive within her and could no longer go unattended. As painful as it was, it was time to acknowledge its presence, to lean in and do the healing work rather than give in to the old habit of distancing herself from it. This is the path of true integration, natural and organic, felt right to the core of our being, and it leads to the third signal.

Signal #3: A Request for Healing

With this signal, people are in effect saying: "I'm ready to let go of this stuff which I've long held to be true, but which is true no longer. This stuff is not who I am nor does it reflect how I wish to experience my life. I now choose to release it, but I need some help with that."

Sam's Story

"I want to work through beliefs of not being good enough, my patterns of self-sabotage, perfectionism, feeling judged by others, and other self-imposed limitations. In general, it has all made me skeptical and negative, and I'm starting to think that nothing really matters. I used to be more positive and motivated in life. So it's time to change. I'm ready to stop suffering in my head. I am ready to embrace that I am good enough. I love that thought, but I haven't made it my truth yet. I just don't know how to dislodge it. But this is so fundamental that if I don't change it, it will keep haunting me no matter what I do or where I am."

To the outside world, Sam is a successful business consultant; in private, he admitted having mastered ways to mask these limiting aspects of himself and to project an image of confidence and surety. He acknowledged that he had chased and attained success his entire career in order to feel good about himself, yet despite his worldly achievements he still did not. On the inside, he felt inadequate and unworthy, and those thoughts and feelings were draining his energy to the point of exhaustion.

I have worked with other successful leaders who have reached the same degree of insight into their personal gravity, and while they are often willing to reveal it to me in confidence, they steadfastly refuse to delve in and heal it. Why? Because that aspect of their personal gravity is so intricately wedded to their self-identity, such a primary motivation for doing what they do—a core truth of why they pursue success—that the idea of giving it up is terrifying. "What will become of me if I let this go?" So they hang on, guarding it vigilantly. But Sam had reached the point where he had no longer had the energy or the interest in maintaining a truth that was quickly becoming 'no longer,' and he surrendered to his desire to heal.

This is the beauty of transformation: the need to continue with the charade eventually falls away. Even though Sam, like Meredith, had no idea what would become of him should he let those old self-images go—he too was seeing on the horizon the necessity for sweeping change and had concerns about what it would mean for him and his family—he accepted the risk as worth it. Sam was willing to give up his entire career, trusting that wherever this journey into greater integrity and wholeness would take him was the exact place he needed to be.

Deep Coaches listen for requests for healing as signals that something profound is shifting within a person's self-concept. However, not all requests for healing signal transformation. (Remember, all transformation is change, but not all change is transformation.) For example, if someone is grieving for the loss of a loved one, they will exhibit pain and sorrow. In time, they may express a desire to attend to the sorrow so that they can release it and feel 'normal' again. But while this is a call for healing, it is not necessarily a signal of transformation. It's a bit of an art to learn to distinguish one from the other. The following story is an example of how the dilemma can appear.

Rebecca's Story

"I know I am a person of high integrity, and I care deeply about the quality of my relationships. I want to do good, meaningful work, but every day I feel I'm being asked to live out of alignment with my values. The tension is sucking the life out of me. I feel like work is a tremendous struggle and that I really don't have much choice in matters. I'm also an introvert, and it's draining for me to be around people all day, but yet that's what I'm forced to do. I have very little time to re-energize, except on the weekends, and even then I catch up on work. I feel like a fighter on the ropes struggling to break free from the blows which keep raining down on me thinking, "If I can just get a moment of space I can get back into the game." But the space never comes, and the blows keep raining down."

You can hear the struggle in Rebecca's voice as the challenges of work consume her. As with Sam and Meredith, her energy was being depleted, and each time something negative happened that touched on one of these issues, she felt even less strength to get off the ropes. What she wanted from coaching was help getting back in the game: to breathe, relax, be herself, to re-align with her values, and to regain her vital life energy. This is surely a request for healing, and all coaching can be an avenue of support for this when the desired outcome is a return to normal or optimal functioning. But is it also a signal of transformation? Transformation calls out to separate your Self from the illusions that you have allowed to make a home in your mind. Therefore, *transformation is anything but a return to the status quo*.

As our coaching progressed, it became clear that Rebecca's request for healing was about more than a return to normality so that she could 'play her best game,' as it were. The reason she had taken the job in the first place was related to a host of beliefs dating back to a rough childhood. The reason she stayed in the position, despite the daily drama, related both to those past beliefs and to a strong sense of obligation to her family's financial needs. She was exhibiting other important signals as well, which you may now recognize: "I want to do only what I'm called to do. I want to explore who I am without it all, the success, this professional persona. I want to stop pretending that that my life is great, that I love doing what I do, that I support my company's actions when I don't, that I'm okay leading as I'm asked to, that I can fix my family's problems, that I'm okay when I'm not...I'm suffocating. But I want my life to stand for a higher way." Rebecca also expressed the great concern of so many heroic journeyers: "Who am I if all this falls away, as I've been self-defined by it for so long?"

Taken together, these signals tell us that Rebecca is indeed on the pathway of transformation. Yet it was incredibly hard for her to commit to the deep dive when she was getting thumped by her work environment at the same time. She was spending many of her waking hours in the corporate boxing ring fending off blows and trying desperately to regain a sense of balance. Her perpetual exhaustion had become so debilitating that the best she could do was seek out some relief in the hope of returning to normality.

The deep dive of transformation is a healing journey requiring time, space, energy, and an appropriate environment. Even if the signals are there, when a person's life situation is not conducive to the process, healing may only be attended to superficially, or be put off for another day.

Moment of Pause

Reflect on Coaching Approaches

Given what you have heard of Rebecca's story, give some thought to how you might work with her from each of these coaching approaches:

- A transactional coaching perspective: managing the situation or finding a solution

- A developmental coaching perspective: learning about herself and her capacities

- A transformational coaching perspective: exploring who she chooses to be

- A Deep Coaching perspective: awareness of her personal gravity and her emerging sense of Self.

Signal #4: A Willingness to Talk Openly about Spirit, Soul, and Spirituality

In *Real Power,* Janet Hagberg writes about transcending the Wall, the final stage in moving from Stage Four, Power by Reflection, to Stage Five, Power by Purpose:

> "Our work is to develop or renew or transform our spirituality into an intimate relationship with our Higher Power, the Holy. So in a sense, spirituality and healing is our work. And slowly we begin to see glimpses of how the inner movement will work itself out in our lives. Psychology can take us successfully into [Stage Four] but adding spirituality to that takes us through it and out the other side. The spirituality I am talking about is not about dogma, or liturgical practices, belief systems or organizations. The spirituality that takes us into Stage Five is the development of an intimate relationship with God, our Higher Power, the Holy, Great Spirit, Ultimate Reality, Allah, or Sophia. Only this personal vulnerable trusting intimacy will allow us to face the fears and develop the courage of Stage Five. For some the real crisis [here] is facing their need for an intimate spirituality."

This has been my experience as well. People I work with often say something like, "My interest in spirituality is new for me." Even though they come from various religious backgrounds, and some remain devoted to their faith, the notion of developing a "personal vulnerable trusting intimacy" with a higher power or source, and using that relationship to advance personal evolution, is altogether new.

One of the questions I ask my clients before we begin coaching is, "What are your core spiritual beliefs?" Here are a few typical responses:

> They remain rather vague. I believe in a common source, purpose, unity, perhaps consciousness to the universe, and that we can apprehend some small sliver of that, at least to the extent that we can understand our roles. Properly knowing and playing these will bring us greater joy and tranquility.

> I'm not sure! I'm flipping between 1.) there is nothing and 2.) a higher power with helpers or spirits and all being one. Whatever spiritual beliefs I do hold have been influenced by the Zhuang Zi, the Analects of Confucius, the New Testament, Zen Buddhism, and more recently from the practice of yoga and Pranayama.

> I was brought up as a Christian, attending an all-girls' school, with religion as a backdrop in the family. I would not call our family religious. I now refer to my beliefs as spiritual. What does that mean? For me, spirituality means a connectedness within myself, being authentic and aligned with the universe. I believe in a higher power, in some form. Something holds the universe and all that we know and don't know together.

The way spirituality reveals itself in those who are traversing Stage Four is qualitatively different from the way it does so in previous stages of personal power. Awakening will do that. As we become aware of how conditioned realities and practices have defined who we are for too long, we become open to exploring new truths. Our consciousness is expanding, our inner awareness evolving, and our minds opening to progressive meanings and values. The more we ground ourselves in the essence of our being, which is spirit and soul, the more we begin to forge a relationship with Spirit in a way that is unique to us as individuals. Awakening, by its very nature, is a flowering of spiritual consciousness, as though consciousness itself suddenly begins to recognize its ultimate nature. It's only natural that people will want to talk more openly about this.

Some years ago, Tobias came to me asking for help in examining the factors that were holding him back from branching out into new directions in his career. He was keenly aware that the way he had configured his life was not sustainable, yet he was in a state of inertia, unable to enable change in a meaningful way. At no point during our early sessions did Tobias indicate a desire to talk about spirit or soul or anything even close to that. He focused primarily on his career dilemma, on the inner struggle it was causing, and on areas he thought were stagnating or debilitating. He frequently expressed how his life felt off track, and was sure it was related to an unfulfilling career that held little meaning or value. In his mind, finding the right career path would resolve many of his issues. Yet the more I listened, the clearer it became to me that his experiences were signals of a much deeper shift. And so in one session, when the time felt right, I simply asked him, "What is your heart saying?" and a little later, "What is your soul calling for?"

When people are disconnected from the intelligence of their heart and soul they often give perfunctory answers or say something like, "I'm not really sure." But Tobias, surprisingly given his predilection for the intellect, was able to answer those questions with ease and considerable clarity. From that point on, it was as though a door had opened, and he spoke freely about his soul's calling, his sense of higher purpose, and where his heart wanted to lead him. He made the connection between his desire to change careers and the call to grow into the truth of who he is. The part of himself which knew without a shadow of doubt what was good and right for him was at last being heard and honored.

Not everyone will actualize the transformative potentials inherent within the higher spectrum of their consciousness. Nor will all our clients allow love, peace, joy or other spiritual thought and energy to shape their emerging self-concept into something altogether more real and true. However, it is important that Deep Coaches create a space in which a person's personal truths about Spirit, soul, spirituality, and religion can be shared, openly and without judgment or agenda. Because as we encourage people to dedicate time and energy to nurturing spiritual consciousness in whatever way is right for them, they will increasingly glimpse their higher nature and purpose. In time, living aligned to Spirit and soul will become as essential to a life well lived as the air they breathe.

Signal #5: An Emerging Vision of Life Purpose

As we awaken we begin to sense that our existence is greater than we had realized, and a grander vision for our lives begins to emerge. Many people go off in search of the answer to the question, "What is my life purpose?" but, within the awakening mind, increasingly unconditioned and free from the illusions of ego, it reveals itself naturally and organically. Deep Coaches listen for this revelation.

When the vision is first emerging, it usually lacks specifics, particularly *how* it will come into being. This can be a source of angst for those who 'just want to get there' and who don't understand why the grand possibility they are sensing for themselves is not manifesting in a timelier manner. (One of the primary reasons for this concern and impatience is because a key lesson has not yet been learned: living your life's purpose is not about looking to the future and expecting fulfillment there, but to actualize it in each moment now.) However, the presence of the awakened vision is itself a signal of transformation, and it functions as a mighty motivator for traversing the bumpy road ahead.

As you listen for people's life vision, notice the patterns common to the collective purpose of all humanity: the desire to be of meaningful service, to do work that delights and inspires, to make a real difference in people's lives, to live in the present moment, to allow thoughts and actions to be guided by awakened consciousness, to be a channel for a more enlightened way of living to come into the world. This is our *inner purpose,* and although it will be expressed differently by each person, reflecting individual talents, interests, and personality, it is essentially the same for all humanity. Here are a few examples of what it can sound like:

I envision myself completely transformed and reborn. The old shell and limiting walls will fall away, and the true me will make a grand entrance into my life. I will finally walk out of my self-made cage and breathe in life to its fullest, with all opportunities and endless possibilities. Based on a deep connection with myself and Spirit, I will finally know who I am and what I came here to do. I will live in peace and harmony with myself and channel my energy into creating a vibrant, exciting, fun, and soulful business filled with adventure, creativity and passion that is based on my authentic soul mission and not on ideas that my mind came up with out of desperation and frustration. I am completely open to how that may look like, I just know how I want to feel, how I want to show up.

To continue to grow, and to have people help me get deeper and deeper within, becoming simpler, more loving, easy on myself, insightful and intuitive, connecting with Spirit more deeply, and being in continual service to all that's good. I desire to be financially abundant. I see myself waking up to the sun streaming into my kitchen window early in the morning as I sit at my table silently sipping tea and penning a book that would help many even when I'm gone. To have my home be a place of recovery from hurt, for people to tend to their inner garden, to meditate, to find themselves and reconnect with their spirit. And to leave when they wanted to, to return to society, back to their lives.

I want to be clear with myself and the spiritual/sacred belief I bring to my work. I want to know what is it I'm really after, in life and with people. When I am present to and appreciate all the facets of myself at the hub of who I am, magic can happen: I am able to birth my own wisdom, passion, and experience as I have never before. I want to bring all of myself to my work, and have it shine, and let the magic and mystery radiate into the world. I want to be an ally for anyone who wants to help the world. I am about soul food; I want to feed the soul. This is where the magic happens.

These are magnificent visions, and they are born of the awakening mind and emerging self-concept. Each resonates as a celebration of life and reflects a potential that transcends a goal to be achieved or a thing to be attained. You can feel the soul as it soars into the vision. If you hear anyone speak this way, you will know that you are in the presence of one who is on the path. And despite the uncertainty and doubt that can arise around whether that vision will manifest, Deep Coaches recognize that there is nothing that needs to be solved or figured out. It is all already happening—purpose is emerging of its own volition! All that is needed is to create the optimal conditions in which it can continue to emerge, a natural unfolding process of evolutionary growth.

Deep Coaches are the holders of this vision, particularly during those times when those we support cannot hold it for themselves. People will lose sight of their own vision as they get caught up in the responsibilities and demands of their daily lives. Hold the vision out for them to reconnect with as often as needed, because a vision of this magnitude is not only an indicator of transformation, it is a motivator for transformation. Our role is to foster the conditions in which they can reconnect with their emerging sense of Self and life vision, and to help them feel and embrace its power, unbridled and alive in the world.

Moment of Pause

Reflect on the Five Signals of Transformation

How do you see each of these signals appearing in your own life?

What other signals would you add to this list?

PART II

The Art and Practices of Deep Coaching

CHAPTER EIGHT
The Deep Coaching Approach

Each person has their own journey toward their essential nature, which is unlimited spirit. This is no easy road to travel; transformation is a disruptive process that dismantles cherished belief systems, limiting self-definitions, and deeply embedded patterns of perception so that we can come to know our unlimited nature. This requires a coaching approach that relies less on the intellect to assess and query, and more on the ability to sense into emerging dimensions of being.

Deep Coaching is that approach. Here we swim at the deep end, in an ocean of energy, consciousness, and Spirit, supporting others to move beyond their ego-based self-concept into the light of true Self-awareness. If you have been schooled in, or are more comfortable with, transactional or developmental coaching approaches, you will notice that Deep Coaching asks you to unlearn some of what you have been taught. In its place, you will learn how to elevate the vibrancy of your own presence to catalyze inner dimensional change in others. This is the essence of being a Deep Coach.

The Three Tenets of Deep Coaching

Deep Coaching is healing.

Deep Coaching is Spirit-based.

Deep Coaching is transformative.

Deep Coaching Is Healing

During transformation, as systems of consciousness change, the mind's patterns of operation restructure themselves. As we've learned, although this is a healing process, it is a place of discomfort for most people as they feel the internal changes and do not necessarily understand what is occurring. Deep Coaches support this by creating a space in which people work openly with all that the inner earthquake shakes loose, with all that limits them from knowing themselves as unlimited, with all the obstacles that block true Self-knowing and expression. When a person is ready to truly let go of a limiting truth about who they are, Deep Coaches do not shy away from facilitating healing moments.

Deep Coaches also facilitate opportunities for people to experience more of their emerging Self, as whole and complete. It's like getting a glimpse of the destination, that radiant state of 'I AM.' Such experiences are deeply healing, the ultimate accelerators of transformation, and the most powerful means available for energizing a person to continue down the path. Once someone has experienced themselves as free of illusion, and that energy descends into their mind and heart, they will—no matter how it fluctuates—remain forever affected by it.

Deep Coaching is not a separate discipline from healing—Deep Coaching is a healing modality.

Deep Coaching is Spirit-based

Deep Coaching operates from the assumption that we are spiritual beings having a human experience. There are two aspects to this. The first is the recognition that we are not purely material beings, but *souls*. One way to conceive of the soul's role in transformation is that our soul is constantly seeking ways to bring to the surface of our awareness those aspects of our self-concept that are not in alignment with its essence. Therefore, as Deep Coaches, part of our work is to be tuned into what is happening for our clients at the level of soul. Are they alive there? Are they tuned in or disconnected?

The second aspect, as I wrote about in Chapter 6, is that Deep Coaching acknowledges the reality of our connection with Spirit—the greater consciousness, presence, or evolutionary intelligence that uplifts, sustains, and guides each of us along our life path—and this has several implications:

- Deep Coaching recognizes that awakening and transformation are evolutionary processes designed to reveal the truth of who we are, which is unlimited spirit.

- Deep Coaching is Spirit-based, not religion-based. It is free of religious concepts and moral precepts, focusing only on highlighting the spiritual commonalities that all human beings share.

- Deep Coaching makes no attempt to ignore or downplay the role of Spirit or spirituality within the coaching context. The presence and action of Spirit is accepted as integral to the transformational journey.

- Deep Coaching recognizes the action of Spirit within the human mind as a 'healing agent' between the illusions of self we have created and the truth of who we are as spiritual beings.

I know there will be those, and you may be one of them, who are concerned as to whether the Deep Coaching approach will align with your religious or spiritual belief system. I will not attempt to convince you one way or the other. And I do not wish to suggest that you must believe in God or angels or spirit guides in order to support profound inner transformation. Not at all; there is no such requirement. Rather, I invite you to read through the nine practices with an open mind and heart. Allow the work to speak not only to your intellect, but to your highest Self and soul. I have taught Deep Coaching to people from all over the world, from many different faiths and religious backgrounds, and in all my years there has never been a conflict. The reason relates to what Mahatma Gandhi is quoted as saying: "The essence of all religions is one. Only their approaches are different." That is Deep Coaching, a Spirit-based approach designed to get to essence, to explore the Ground of Being we all share, to have us inhabit that space where all things connect as one. It is a new paradigm of coaching for a new paradigm of experience.

Deep Coaching Is Transformative

"Who do I choose to be?" is the core question upon which transformational coaching is founded. Asking the question shifts the focal lens away from the situation towards the self and into the recognition that we can, at any time, choose our way of being in the world. *Movement into the embodiment of that choice can be massively transforming.* Yet the question has its limits because it resides within the realm of choice. When the readiness is there, our desire for Self-knowing will move us beyond choice into a more expansive realm, the realm of *actualities.* In this realm, the question becomes:

Who am I?

This is the most intimate of questions you can ask, because when you ask, "Who am I?" you're asking for the revelation of the root cause for your being. When this is asked with sincerity, you begin to strip away the story and break the spell the world has taught you to believe. This is the place of real power—this is the revelation of your most essential Self as it is within the greater reality of the one, universal consciousness. At this level, *there is no longer a choice*—it is the recognition of your actual nature, as it *is.* The only choice you have now is how much of your true Self you will inhabit and express into the world. Deep Coaching is transformative because it involves creating a space in which such transcendental awareness can be experienced.

Key Roles of the Deep Coach

The three tenets—healing, Spirit-based, transformative—give rise to the primary roles of the Deep Coach. Some coaches interpret these as a departure from conventional coaching competencies such as asking questions, active listening, giving feedback, creating action, and holding people accountable, but that is not wholly accurate. It is more accurate to say that those are foundational competencies for *all* forms of coaching—they are what define coaching as a discipline—and upon that foundation Deep Coaching constructs a framework of roles that are better suited to supporting the deep dive. These roles, which build upon yet supersede conventional coaching competencies, are:

- Hold Space
- Uphold the Prime Directive (Make Room for Spirit)
- Attend to the Dual Dynamics of Transformation
- Energize Shifts in Being
- Spiritual Partnering.

Hold Space

Deep Coaches create and hold a space in which transformation can unfold, naturally and organically, with the greatest amount of ease and joy. What does it mean to hold space for someone else? One of the most encompassing definitions I have come across was written by Heather Plett:

> "It means that we are willing to walk alongside another person in whatever journey they're on without judging them, making them feel inadequate, trying to fix them, or trying to impact the outcome. When we hold space for other people,

we open our hearts, offer unconditional support, and let go of judgement and control. To truly support people in their own growth (or) transformation…we have to be prepared to step to the side so that they can make their own choices, offer them unconditional love and support, give gentle guidance when it's needed, and make them feel safe even when they make mistakes."

When holding space, the role of the Deep Coach becomes analogous to that of the cocoon in a caterpillar's metamorphosis: both act as a *container* which facilitates the natural unfolding process of transformation. A caterpillar's cocoon is made of silk or some other fibrous material that is spun around the caterpillar—so what is the Deep Coach's cocoon woven of? It is woven of all that which supports the flourishing of the soul and the elevation of human consciousness: the energies and qualities of unconditional love, compassion, trust, positivity, sincerity, forgiveness, truth, beauty, and goodness.

The image of the Deep Coach as the cocoon can make holding space seem like passive involvement—for the most part, the caterpillar's cocoon acts as a protective cover against the outside environment—but holding space is in reality an active and dynamic position. It is our capacity to *intentionally* create and energize the space that sets us apart from the caterpillar's cocoon. The nine transformative Deep Coaching practices to come will enable you to hold that space, one in which others can face their shadows and heal, grow in certainty and strength, and come to know more of the truth of who they are—not just intellectually, but within the entire fabric of their being.

Uphold the Prime Directive (Make Room for Spirit)

The term Prime Directive was first coined in the fictional world of *Star Trek* as the single most important guiding principle binding on Starfleet personnel. In Deep Coaching we too are guided by a Prime Directive, a principle which focuses our attention on that which matters most, and inspires our thoughts and actions.

The Prime Directive of Deep Coaching is to hold a space which fosters connection with one's deepest sense of Self and which makes room for the presence and action of Spirit.

The Prime Directive is an acknowledgment of the role both Spirit and our essential spiritual nature play in the restructuring of our self-concept. As Deep Coaches, we are not only learning how to partner with individuals, groups, or communities to support their transformation, we are learning how to partner with Spirit to support the evolution of our collective consciousness. Spirit is the ultimate uplifter, the ultimate energizer, the ultimate source of knowledge and wisdom, the ultimate way-shower. Spirit is evolutionary consciousness in action. And we are human beings learning how to walk the spiritual path, which means we are actively and consciously co-creating with Spirit to enable personal and collective evolution.

Deep Coaches uphold the Prime Directive because it accelerates transformation. When we make room for the presence of Spirit within ourselves, Spirit is able to seed in our mind what we need to support the healing of human consciousness. And the more room we make for Spirit within ourselves, the better will we be able to discern the soul-needs of another. In other words, we make room for connection with the Source of Being in order to realize what is at the core of being.

It will never be possible for us to know all that is happening within another person. We cannot see the full spectrum of change that is unfolding across all dimensions of mind, consciousness, and soul within another human being; there are many things hidden from view. But nothing is hidden from Spirit. Can you trust that? When you partner with Spirit in the coaching space, you will be guided, your clients will be guided, and what needs to be known will be made known.

Attend to the Dual Dynamics of Transformation

In Chapter 6 we learned about the Dual Dynamics of Transformation: that which holds us back and that which moves us forward. Conventional coaching approaches also work with variants of the dual dynamics, as they are inherent in the coaching process; but what sets Deep Coaching apart is that it is *not* focused on helping people live into or strengthen their acquired self-concept or to preserve their ego-based self-images by helping them to become 'successful' or 'perform better to feel worthy.' (The amount of human activity motivated by egoic needs is astounding, and most types of coaching invariably support that.)

Instead, Deep Coaches attend to the dual dynamics to influence how the transformational journey ultimately unfolds. Specifically, Deep Coaching enables people to shed their identity masks, to heal the perceptual wounds of their time-bound experiences, and to dismantle all that has been learned that is out of alignment with the true Self. To do this, Deep Coaches hold a space in which people can illuminate and explore what's there, and move beyond their ego's survival impulse into an experience of their essential nature.

Energize Shifts in Being

The energies (or energy fields) of egoic consciousness are marked by a slower, denser vibrational rate than the energies of the true Self or enlightened consciousness. Deep Coaches support people to elevate their vibration through an intentional shift in being so as to open their minds to new levels of consciousness, which is inherently healing. From this expanded sense of self, they have the ability to perceive more of the way life works and gain access to new vistas of opportunity and possibility (recall the Four Levels of Engagement in Chapter 2). Their raised vibration also enables them to receive clearer and more direct guidance from their higher Self and Spirit. Over time, their fundamental identity evolves, as does the energy field they generate—it vibrates consistently at a higher rate—such that they are becoming a new kind of human being, one reflective of and connected to Self and soul.

The fundamental purpose of a Deep Coaching session is therefore to *energize a shift in being*, one that facilitates either letting go (a limiting ego-pattern) or letting come (the emerging selfhood). It's not a conceptual shift ('what it would be like if they did'), it's a tangible shift *during the session itself* so that the person you are coaching experiences a higher-than-previously-realized level of existence. Such experiences help recalibrate their vibrational frequency to correspond less with their ego-based self-concept and increasingly with that of their Self and soul. Over time, lower vibrational energies reflective of basic ego-patterns begin to dissipate, allowing the higher frequencies to increase, which in turn helps heal further layers of ego-pattern and awaken untapped dimensions of being.

This is the reason why coaching conversations about a person's core values must become *experiential*. You can ask a person to talk about their value of peace, but it doesn't necessarily bring them any closer to its experience. (I'm sure you've seen how angry anti-war protestors can be when they march for peace.) Peace has to be felt and embodied in order to be transformative. Once it flows through their being, peace raises their vibration and immediately impacts their perceptions and overall quality of life. *Experience* is what instills peace (or any other core value) within the mind.

Spiritual Partnering

Some years ago a colleague sent me a document called *Conscious Evolution Through Spiritual Partnering*, authored by Elyse Hope Killoran. Even after all these years, whenever I read it, it puts a smile on my face—Elyse has captured beautifully the essence of what it is to be a Deep Coach. And her insights into what it means for two or more people to come together in the service of a higher purpose reveal an important truth about life: when we act as spiritual partners, the work we do transcends the needs of any one individual; we transcend together, serving the highest good of all simultaneously.

Spiritual partnering is recognition of our oneness, our unequivocal unity within the infinite field of consciousness and the joy of Spirit. When even one of us shifts into a higher level of personal consciousness, we all benefit. In spiritual partnering there is no separation, no divide that keeps us from each other, nothing that prevents us from sharing equally in the goodness of life that is the birthright of all. What happens for one happens for all.

Elyse's work has had a profound effect on the many Deep Coaching students who have read it, forever shaping their understanding of the perspectives, behaviors, and potentials that lie within *all* our relationships when we choose to view those relationships as sacred. I would like to share her writings with you, because spiritual partnership is what Deep Coaches aspire to in each encounter and conversation.

Conscious Evolution Through Spiritual Partnering by Elyse Hope Killoran

Spiritual Partnering refers to a conscious path of relating in which two (or more) individuals hold an intention for their relationship to serve a higher purpose.

The Elements of Spiritual Partnering

1.) Spiritual partners know that the solitary spiritual path is no longer the optimal choice for conscious evolution and that interpersonal relationships provide us with the greatest laboratory in which we can come face-to-face with the edges of our comfort zones. They recognize that insights experienced through journaling and meditation are of little value unless they can be brought into the everyday world of activity and interaction. For this reason, so many on the path are hungry for a deeper form of relationship with true alchemical power.

2.) Spiritual partners hold the awareness that they are connecting, simultaneously, on the level of personality and soul. In this way they commit to "walking between the worlds" in every area of their relationship.

3.) Spiritual partners know that at every moment we have the choice to participate in the unfolding of our lives unconsciously (as a victim of seemingly random circumstances) or consciously (as an active, co-creative participant). Spiritual partners choose the latter. From this perspective, life is a process of creation and evolution and the individual's experience is indeed a heroic journey.

4.) Spiritual partners choose to believe that our higher selves (in partnership with God/the Universe) are deliberately attracting people, circumstances and events to us so that we may have ample opportunities to grow into our best selves. Whether an event seems positive or negative at face value, spiritual partners acknowledge that our "individually calibrated Divine curriculum" is always leading us to perfectly orchestrated opportunities for the highest good of all concerned.

5.) Spiritual partners strive to create a positive energy environment. By committing to truth, trust, equality and to seeing the light in one another, spiritual partners create a safe container in which transformation can take place.

6.) Spiritual partners understand that our greatest power to shape our future lies within our intentions. In every interaction, spiritual partners must leave their ego-agendas at the door and invoke a higher path. "God please use this relationship for the highest purposes for all concerned," is a powerful, growth-enhancing intention.

7.) Spiritual partners savor the opportunities to face and heal ineffective patterns affecting careers, relationships, finances and lack of self-love. When one acts in a manner that is less than his/her highest, compassion and a commitment to healing becomes the focus of both partners.

8.) Spiritual partners use the enhanced sense of unconditional love that is modeled for them by their partners as a touchstone while they learn to find and hold their own connection to source energy, freedom, expansion and full expression.

9.) Spiritual partners recognize that the personal and spiritual growth that they enjoy as a result of their connection benefits the individual, the other partner(s) and countless others whose lives are touched, directly or indirectly. In a grand domino effect, spiritual partnering has the power to heal the world.

10.) For spiritual partners, the ultimate destination is: wholeness, authentic power, the replacement of reactivity with choice and the freedom and flexibility to become a conscious chooser even in the most challenging of circumstances.

In other words, spiritual partnership accelerates evolution.

Moment of Pause

Reflection on Spiritual Partnering

Deep Coaching invites us to create 'spiritual partnerships,' to act from the knowledge that we are all connected, simultaneously, on multiple levels of mind and soul. Because soul is beyond what our eyes can see, it's helpful to envision and feel this level of connection with another.

Take a moment and bring to mind a relationship you are having in which you desire to help that person grow in meaningful ways.

When you have that relationship in mind, see yourself taking a step back from the vision of the two of you so that you can see yourselves within a much larger context. See the two of you within a vast field or web of consciousness, one that connects you to that person and also to every other human being.

Across the strands of webbing that connect you to the person you desire to help, you can see all the ways that your mind and soul are connected and in communication with each other—an endless flow of cosmic telegrams zipping along at a speed so fast it appears instantaneous. See how your minds meet in that field, across many dimensions, with no disconnection, no disruption to the flow, no sense of separation between anyone and anything. All that you need is there in that field, vibrating away, in a kind of suspended state of altered consciousness, waiting for you to *create the conditions* that open you and all others to it.

How does this vision change your understanding of the nature of the coaching relationship? Of your role? Of what is possible?

Creating the Conditions: What It Takes to Be a Deep Coach

The nine transformative practices of Deep Coaching create the optimal conditions in which transformation unfolds naturally and organically.

Who you are *being* plays an integral role in creating those conditions, and in determining your personal readiness to support the deep dive. The following insights will help you to reflect on your own internal readiness:

- Your transformation enables transformation
- It begins with who you are being
- Transformation is not about doing but about allowing
- People heal in the presence of love.

Your Transformation Enables Transformation

If you want to awaken all of humanity, then awaken all of yourself. If you want to eliminate the suffering in the world, then eliminate all that is dark and negative in yourself. Truly, the greatest gift you have to give is that of your own self-transformation.

~ Lao Tzu

I am often asked what makes for a great transformational coach. My answer is as the Lao Tzu quote states: the greatest gift you can bring to the transformation of another is that of your own transformation. The great transformational coaches have reached a level of maturity that comes from having committed unwaveringly to the journey of their own transformation. In doing so, they have readied themselves to be the way-showers for others not through the attainment of degrees or certifications, but by having passed through the fire of *experience*.

Does this mean you must be 'fully transformed' (whatever that means) to support another along the path? Not at all. You can be in the throes of your own transformation and still be of help to others simply because you exemplify the awakened one, 'warts and all.' You may have heard the saying: You do not need to be a master to speak of mastery. This is true. You do not need to be a master to speak of mastery, just as you do not need to be a master to hold space for transformation. However, it behooves those who choose to speak of mastery to be actively walking the path of the master, even if mastery has not yet been attained. The further down the path you venture, the more you take on the characteristics and qualities of masterhood, until one day it is so.

If you desire to be a great transformational coach, you cannot fake this stuff. If you believe that because you have achieved a certain level of material or professional success in life, or have a diploma or certification testifying to your educational status, that you are by default capable of facilitating deep transformation, you are deceiving yourself. You can surely try, but at best you will only scratch the surface of what is possible, probably without even knowing you are doing so. If you have never attempted to dive to the ocean floor, it's not possible to guide someone else to do so while standing firmly on the beach.

Those who live rooted in Stage Three, Power by Achievement, are inadequately prepared on the inner plane to coach or guide someone through Stage Four, Power by Reflection, over the Wall and into Stage Five, Power by Purpose. If you have never or only superficially explored the realm of being, swum in the murky rivers of your shadow side, lived beyond the constructs of your intellect, attempted to heal yourself of the myriad of false identifiers you have owned for a lifetime, or explored the vast potential of your spiritual nature, you are indeed standing on the beach, or at best playing in shallow waters. A therapist may be equipped to deal effectively with psychological issues without needing to have personally experienced those disorders, just as a transactional coach has the means to create awareness and action without needing a significant degree of understanding about the human condition, but Deep Coaching requires a level of 'evolvedness' that comes from having walked the walk. It's not book smarts that enable you to do this work, it's personal experience.

Every step you take along your own transformational path, each layer you heal of your own distorted self-concept, each time you allow your consciousness to expand into new paradigms of being and awareness, takes you closer to embodying the way of mastery. *Your transformation enables transformation.* This is your power position, greater than anything else you have ever done or could ever bring to the coaching table.

It Begins with Who You Are Being

As you transform your consciousness expands, and the quality of your presence changes. You begin to vibrate at a higher rate, you become 'lighter,' and this change to your energy signature has a mighty impact on the coaching space—your presence itself becomes transformative. The more transformative your presence, the less you have to *do* to facilitate transformation. Therefore, in essence, your *being* is your doing.

How transformational is your presence?

In India there are gurus who sit meditatively in silence throughout the day and people come to sit quietly in their presence. It's a space of pure beingness. I have a friend, Jane, who also beautifully embodies the power of presence. Her presence is incredibly spacious. Being around her is like a taking a breath of life—tension and stress just fall away. When you are with her nothing *needs* to happen, nothing *needs* to be said or done, and yet so much happens. Her home and her healing center also carry this wonderfully spacious energy; it's in the walls, the air, the plants. She enjoys holding personal retreats for people to come and spend a week with her, detoxing from the pressures of life. There is never a set agenda for those retreats, nothing is forced or made to happen. The only agenda is to give attention to whatever is arising or needed in each moment. Jane then facilitates that experience in one way or another, as an *expression and extension* of her being.

One day, when Jane and I were discussing how she sees her life work, she said to me, "You know, Leon, I'm always on retreat." Isn't that an extraordinary thought, to *always* be on retreat? Retreats are usually something we *go on* once in a while, not something we *are on* all the time. However, if you really think about it, isn't that the way of the master teachers and healers? No separation of work and play, but living in integrity, being who they are, as they are, always.

It does not matter if you think yourself far from such a place, the core lesson is the same: your capacity to support deep transformation begins with who you are being—your *being* is your doing. Take a moment to reflect on this:

> Who must you *be* in order to facilitate profound shifts in
> being and evolutionary leaps in self-awareness in a person,
> group, or community?

Deep Coaching invites you to first address the question of your own beingness before exploring anything that is going on with your client. Turn your gaze inward and focus on embodying the way of being you know is most conducive to the work, and your words and actions will then flow from that state. This orientation helps ensure that anything you choose to do within a coaching conversation or in life becomes an expression and extension of your chosen way of being.

Transformation Is Not About Doing but About Allowing

In the collapse there is something being created by itself.
I don't need to know exactly what it is. I just need to allow it.

~ Anjali Mehta

You may recall from the discussion in Chapter 3 that transformation is self-volitional, it *unfolds* of its own accord. Our work as Deep Coaches is to create the conditions in which impediments to that volition are removed—to *allow* what wants to happen to happen. Transactional coaching, with its focus on striving for goals, solutions and actions, rarely considers the questions: 'What wants to happen?' 'What is trying to emerge within this situation?' These questions imply that in any given situation, even in the midst of collapse, something is being created by itself—something 'wants to happen.' Our work is to attune to that emerging potential, because it's already happening, and afford it the space it needs to come forth, on its own terms. If we do this well, nothing ever needs to be strived for or forced to happen again.

This does not mean that Deep Coaches do not encourage action-taking. If a client desires to be more at peace, a coach can assist in identifying any number of transformative practices that would enable them to experience and embody that way of being, such as meditation or walks in nature. Transformative practice *is* action, and it supports the 'becoming' process. But when I speak about the process of awakening and transformation itself, this is not something we *do*. We cannot force or strive for transformation to happen. We cannot say, "Today I'm going to transform. I'm going to make this happen, now." You can surely try—many things that people achieve in their lives come about as a result of planning, driving, forcing, striving, making happen—however the intellectualizing and linearity of that mindset runs counter to the way of transformation. Awakening is the result of an evolutionary force *unfolding* of its own volition, enabling growth into new paradigms of Self-knowing. Given that existential reality, Deep Coaches focus on how to partner with that evolutionary force, and one of the ways to do that is to learn how to allow to happen what wants to happen.

Much of the tension and struggle you will witness in a person's transformational journey is the result of resistance to what is happening: their ego-based self will not go gently into that good night without putting up a good fight. Yet even though people may understand this intellectually, they can still be tough on themselves, demanding of life, expecting things to go as they desire them to simply because they've set an intention and done some inner work. They even resist the resistance—you've probably heard someone say, "I hate feeling this way!" —which only adds to the dis-ease. But because the world has shaped most people into control freaks, it feels unnatural to let go and allow life to work its magic, trusting life's curriculum over our own.

That allowing does not mean that we allow someone to harm us, or that we relinquish the vast creative capacity of our mind, believing we have no control anyway. Allowing is about letting go: of resistance to what is, of the *need* for things to go a certain way, of *controlling* the process and determining the outcome, of the idea that we are the sole master of our fate. It's about learning what it means to allow our highest future potential to emerge, unrestricted. When we tap into and allow something to happen that wants to happen, it's akin to giving it permission to come forth, on its own terms.

Moment of Pause

Where in your life (or coaching) are you striving for or forcing something to happen?

Where do you see others or your clients doing it?

What kind of energy does it take?

The act of allowing implies that there is something already in existence and we are making room for whatever that is to appear. I do not need to conceive of Who I Am. Who I Am has already been conceived of and exists as pure spirit. What enables the emergence within me of myself as I AM is my giving permission for that which I AM to become the driver in my life. This means I let go of my ideas of how the process should go—questioning the way it is, wishing it were different, trying to make it go faster, or bending it to my will—and I *allow* this natural process of change to unfold within me. I peacefully accept that I am neither the creator nor the owner of this extraordinary process—though I take full responsibility for my role and actions within it—and I allow my transformation to be as it is.

Doubt, frustration, concern, and fear around what is happening will arise. As a Deep Coach, you will create a space in which resistance is minimized, where people can lean into what is happening, to *be* with it, and *allow* life to unfold on its own terms. It's a remarkable process, and quite different from the typical view of a coach, which is to strive alongside the client for whatever is desired. What if you stopped trying so hard, stopped striving to *do* so much within a session, stopped trying to 'create value' and prove your worth? Can you rest in trust that you are stewarding a process that unfolds of its own volition? When you're able to allow people, things and situations to be as they are—without judging them, trying to fix them or wanting to change them—you begin to tap into the immense power of allowing. And when you support people to allow themselves and situations to be as they are, you open up a space for transformation to occur.

People Heal in the Presence of Love

In his book *Power vs. Force*, Dr. David Hawkins maps the levels of human consciousness from lowest to highest. Shame, guilt, fear, desire, anger, and pride correlate with low levels of consciousness, whereas willingness, acceptance, reason, love, joy, peace, and enlightenment indicate expanding levels of consciousness. At the highest levels (love, joy, peace, enlightenment), there is greater transforming power. And, as Dr. Hawkins observes, "the influence of very few individuals of advanced consciousness counterbalances entire populations at the lower levels." This is the innate power of high consciousness—it acts as a mighty uplifter of lower levels. Higher states of consciousness radiate a healing effect as the frequency of the energy field increases, and it's possible to experience being transformed in ways that were not possible through the lower levels, where the energy fields themselves reflect attachment to ego-based perceptions and negative emotions.

One way to understand levels of consciousness is as a continuum of degrees of 'love consciousness,' from the lowest levels where love is almost imperceptible to the highest levels where love is experienced as divine: pure and unconditional. The higher up the ladder of consciousness you go, the greater the love that you experience. And the more you open to love, the higher your consciousness goes.

Love in this context is not an emotion but a way of being in the world, a state of awareness that emanates from the heart. When you let the heart take over, rather than living through the intellect or any other lower level of consciousness, you place your mind and all your talents and abilities in service to your heart. Anything that is not of love within you is illuminated and revealed, creating the opportunity for personal healing and advancement. In time, as love weaves more fully into the fabric of your consciousness, your way of relating to the world becomes forgiving, supporting, and unifying. Love will radiate through you, a mighty energy field, healing and uplifting all that is unlike itself.

Remember, your transformation enables transformation; the higher up the ladder of consciousness you go the more you become a transformational presence, the embodiment of a more peaceful, integrated, loving way. The energy field that is created when you embody the consciousness of love becomes a mighty enabler of transformation—like the great healers, you will influence others not only by what you say or do, but as a consequence of who you have become. *It is the willingness to be a loving presence which positions a coach as a healer.* This is the way of the Deep Coach because it is understood that love itself enables the healing of all that stands in the way of consciousness expansion.

Moment of Pause

Reflection on Being a Loving Presence

Love is the consciousness that unifies and heals all things. A loving presence implicitly invites others to choose to step out of identification with the mind-made 'I' and enter into being and presence for themselves. Love *transfigures*.

Are you a loving presence (in your sessions, work or life)?

What gets in the way? What diminishes or limits that capacity in you to shine forth?

I invite you now to experience yourself as a loving presence.

Take a deep breath, and feel the energy of your heart center. Feel this love as an expansive force within you, shining through every cell, until your entire being vibrates with it. Then rest in it until you are ready to continue reading.

The Nine Transformative Deep Coaching Practices

The Deep Coaching approach is centered on nine transformative practices that create the optimal conditions in which transformation unfolds naturally and organically. 'Transformative practice' itself is intentional activity committed to for extended periods of time with the purpose of empowering transformation. It is a way of engaging life each day. If you truly desire to enable being-level transformation, it's important to commit to practicing the nine practices consistently, both inside and outside the coaching space, until you embody them. Through committed and intentional practice, you heal yourself, your self-concept evolves, and more of your essential nature is revealed. You are awake; you are free—all because you have committed to the practices which support knowing yourself as you are, in Truth. In other words, you are walking the path of mastery.

And now comes the payoff. All that effort you have put into practicing, so that each day you are walking the path of mastery, results in your evolving into a way-shower for others; your presence itself becoming an energy field in which transformation can unfold. For this reason, the nine practices are first and foremost for *you*, to enable you to navigate your own path of transformation so that you can in turn enable the same in others. Following that, they are Deep Coaching practices that you will use in your sessions to hold space, make room for Spirit, and energize shifts in being, shifts that are healing in nature.

The Nine Practices

1: Slow It All Down and Sync with the Rhythm of Life and Spirit

2: Release Your Agendas; Live Your Spiritual Values

3: Nurture a Healing Space

4: Let There Be Silence

5: Coach More from the Heart, Less from the Head

6: Attune to Your Client's Deeper Sense of Self and Let That Lead

7: Expand Your Capacity to Be with Pain and Allow Healing Moments

8: Foster the Emergence of What Wants to Happen

9: Cultivate Trust in the Mystery and Magic of Transformation

There is a loose framework to the nine practices: *those that come first lay the foundation for those that come later.* It is therefore helpful to read the practices in the order they are presented.

However, when it comes to working with the practices, some will be easier for you to grasp or have more immediate appeal. It's perfectly okay to focus on those practices first. If a practice feels too 'out there,' or you are not resonating with it, let it go for now. I assure you, even if you focus on activating the full potential of just one of the nine practices, you will notice things shift significantly. Each practice alone is capable of enabling great change; taken together they form a powerful whole. Trust your intuition and start practicing those to which you are most attracted, returning to the others as your capacity with the initial practices grows. In time, you will no longer view them as separate but as holistic.

A question I am often asked is whether the people we coach or work with need to be aware of the practices: *do we need to teach or share them?* The answer is no; it is not necessary. These practices are for you the coach, and they are what you use to create the optimal conditions in which transformation can unfold, which always begins within yourself and then extends outward. Your clients do not need to be aware of how you create and hold the coaching space, nor the key roles you are living out as a Deep Coach, though they will certainly experience the effects. Of course, you are free to share anything you believe would be helpful, but you do not need to in order to be effective.

In the spirit of the first practice (Slow It All Down…), as you read the following chapters, take time to do the exercises and reflect on the questions, as these deepen your learning. Over time, as you continue working with the practices, you will discover the seemingly limitless depth of each—just when you think you have understood it or learned all there is to know, a new dimension of possibility will reveal itself. Allow this book to become a resource you return to time and time again as you explore these potentials, and as you learn the answer to the central Deep Coaching question:

> What are the optimal conditions in which transformation unfolds, naturally and organically, with the greatest amount of ease and joy?

CHAPTER NINE

Practice 1 - Slow It All Down and Sync with the Rhythm of Life and Spirit

The goal of life is to make your heartbeat match the beat of the universe, to match your nature with Nature.

~ Joseph Campbell

One of the characteristics of modern day living is that things tend to want to move fast. There is a desire to get somewhere, and the faster that somewhere is arrived at the better. Why 'faster is better' is not always understood, but collectively we seem to be buying into a meme that says it is. Have you noticed this sense of quickening, as though everything is moving faster, including the pace at which you move through the days? I certainly feel it, and I have noticed how the quickening is negatively affecting people's stress levels and ability to relax, enjoy, and be present in each moment.

As life's tempo quickens, our expectations about the time it takes to satisfy our wants and desires are also changing. We live in an age of near-instant gratification. With the touch of a few buttons, the riches of the material world—pleasurable food and drink, shopping, communication, drugs, entertainment, almost anything we want—are available, anytime we want them, with few limits or constraints. Instant gratification is the need to experience fulfillment without any sort of delay or wait. It's the mindset of 'gotta have it now,' and it is a driving force that compels us to satisfy our needs and urges as soon as possible. Even our expectation of 'instant' has become faster—the more we get what we want *now*, the more we want what we want *now*—and our ability to be patient, to wait, and to allow something to simply take time, is diminishing.

The demand for instant results has seeped into every corner of our lives. We now expect personal growth—a phenomenon long considered to be gradual—to happen overnight. So many people on the path of transformation want to 'get there'—in other areas we have the ability to make things happen without having to wait, so why should our growth process be any different? This poses a challenge for coaching, because now the coaching process is at risk of striving for a faster fix or the 'aha moment.' And if one isn't had, there can be a sense of disappointment that the desired breakthrough didn't happen. Both the coach and coachee are susceptible to this mindset. I've had coaches share with me how they fear they are not adding value or doing a good job because the moments of breakthrough are not happening regularly, or their clients appear stuck "for too long." I've had clients who, at the end of a session in which they've had to grind through a particularly tough issue, feel deflated because it wasn't resolved in that hour. Patience has become a rare commodity, even in the world of coaching and self-development, because people are not used to waiting long for what they desire.

For Deep Coaches, it's important to recognize that change within the human transformational process happens gradually, over prolonged periods of time. It is not uncommon for a person to take ten to twenty years or more to move through a period of profound inner transformation: from, for example, Stage Three, Power by Achievement to Stage Five, Power by Purpose. Dr. David Hawkins points out in *Power vs. Force* that it is a very rare thing indeed for people to transcend the parameters of their native state of consciousness (the level of consciousness they are born into), but for those who do, it usually takes dedication and perseverance over long periods of time. The vast majority of humanity does not understand this, and when coupled with the increasing need for instant gratification, we have a potent mix for frustration and disappointment when things don't happen as quickly as expected.

Does this way of living optimally support transformation and renewal at the deepest levels of self?

Practice Application

How Fast Do You Go?

Over the next few days, begin to notice in yourself:

- The speed at which you talk

- The speed at which you walk and move around

- The speed at which you eat

- The speed at which your mind moves

- The speed at which you work

- The speed at which you drive

- The speed at which you reply to text messages

- The speed at which you coach (or are coached)

- Your level of patience with people and events.

How optimal are these rhythms for you?

The Rhythm of Life and Spirit

Life has various rhythms and tempos, some optimal for our well-being and growth, and some not. When you attune to the rhythm of life and Spirit, you will notice that it has its own unique character: it's flowing, grounded, nourishing, energizing, sustaining, and more life-giving than the speed at which modern day life moves.

In my experience, the closer I get to Spirit the better I am able to connect with the rhythms of life that are optimal for the well-being of my body, mind, and soul. For others, proximity to nature and its energies and rhythms creates that same sense of well-being. When I live in harmony with those natural rhythms, from wherever I derive them, I thrive. Conversely, when I get caught up in the hustle and bustle, succumbing to the pressure to get things done, move things forward, make things happen (the faster the better, of course), or when I try to push or force things to happen that are not ready to happen, stress and tension settle in, and I am no longer in my optimal state of connection, flow, and well-being. I am effectively acting against my own desire to live at a higher level of personal consciousness.

This first Deep Coaching practice of *Slowing it all down and syncing with the rhythm of life and Spirit* is the antidote. This transformative practice acknowledges the important role that slowing down plays in harmonizing us with a tempo that supports personal well-being and transformative growth. Within the natural rhythms of life there is an inherent cadence that modulates your energy systems so that growth and transformation can unfold gracefully and more peacefully. (The din of culture can interfere with your ability to sense this rhythm.) You are then able to perceive more of what life and Spirit wish to co-create with you through your thoughts, feelings, and actions.

Moment of Pause

Your Optimal Rhythm

Reflect for a moment on your optimal life rhythm, the tempo that serves your highest well-being. How would you characterize it?

How often during the average day do you find yourself in that rhythm, and for how long?

What happens (in life or in a coaching session) when you slow down and sync with the rhythm of life and Spirit?

Where in your life do you feel most out of sync?

What keeps you out of sync or out of your optimal rhythm?

Intention of the Practice

The transformative practice of slowing it all down and syncing with the rhythm of life and Spirit has three primary objectives:

1.) To *experience* how a life slowed down is in fact a life lived with greater acceptance, ease, clarity, patience, and often joy.

2.) To create the *optimal conditions* for transformation: a healing space where room is made for the presence and action of Spirit.

3.) And to provide a *sanctuary* from stress-inducing rhythms by harmonizing with the natural rhythms that support well-being and growth.

When coaching sessions maintain a similar rhythm to fast-paced daily living, or when they take on a sense of urgency, the subtle need to 'get somewhere,' coaches tend to listen more to the babble of the mind than to the deeper, innate wisdom of their heart and soul. Spirit is active within our minds all through the day, yet it is during those times when we slow down—breathe deeply, quieten the noise, and move into greater stillness—that more of what Spirit and soul offer can rise into our awareness, be it thoughts or energies.

When people are given a space in which they can sync with the rhythm of life and Spirit, it helps their thoughts to slow down, their bodies to relax, and their energy systems to open, creating the inner space necessary to contemplate the emerging Self that is coming into being. When, in that space, the coaching conversation slows down and syncs with the rhythm of life and Spirit, people are no longer so caught up in the drama of the situation or the desire to find an expedient solution. Much of what is not meaningful then begins to fall away, their attachment to it released, while the gifts of knowing, patience, acceptance, allowing, and trust become available.

Nothing in the realm of Spirit (or nature) ever says "faster is better" or "gotta have it now." This is not the way, as both exist in an ever-present state of now. In this moment there is nowhere to get to, nothing to be achieved, nothing that must change in order for things to be 'better.' The natural rhythm of life and Spirit, anchored in the present, reflects perfectly the optimal inner state of being for healing and Self-actualization.

The true rhythm of the ocean is not experienced by standing on the beach, listening to waves crash on the shore; that is a surface-level experience only, and provides but a glimpse what lies beyond. The rhythm of the ocean is experienced in its vast depths, in the movement of the flowing currents that are its life and breath. Transformation is a journey that is essentially about accessing the deeper sources of Self. To do that, we have to be willing to leave the shore and its crashing waves and dive deep, just as we would to hear the rhythm of the ocean.

Deep Coaches do not dictate the rhythm at which others choose to live; we understand that all people are free to live at any tempo of their choosing. We are, however, responsible for creating a coaching space that reflects the optimal conditions in which *transformation* can unfold. Slowing it all down and syncing with the rhythm of life and Spirit is one of those conditions. It is an environment in which people can experience what happens within themselves when they tap into the rhythms which flow endlessly beneath the crashing waves of life's dramas and situations.

Moment of Pause

Noticing Your Rhythm

Pause again for a moment, and notice the tempo at which you are reading this book. Take a deep breath and become aware of the space you have created and the rhythm and energy you are experiencing.

Whenever you feel hurried and stressed, take a few deep breaths and attune to a better rhythm, the true rhythm of life and Spirit. Trust in this and life will take its natural course through you.

The Challenge to Slowing Down

What I have observed is that slowing things down is easy to say but not always easy to do. People will say, "Yes, I know I need to slow down in my life, and I know it will benefit me because I'm feeling the stress and pressure of needing to do more. My life is go, go, go, and it's not good for me I know, but… [fill in excuse]." Taking a break from work or making time for life's pleasures is one thing, but when it comes to slowing life down to the point where it becomes a *transformative practice*, that's another matter entirely. For most people it would require radical change to slow it all down and sync the totality of their life to the rhythm of Spirit. For starters, it requires an honest examination of one's values, and then a concerted reconfiguration of priorities, aspirations, and lifestyle to comfortably embody a slower, more natural rhythm. The reconfiguration aspect is a challenge, given how people today organize their lives and how entrenched the 'go faster, do more' meme is within our collective culture.

One of my clients, the CEO of a small company he had founded, was working with me on detoxing and de-stressing after several consecutive years of intense business-building activity. He had thrown so much time and energy into developing his business, he had reached the point where his exhaustion was becoming chronic. In working with me, he had determined that one of his objectives was to attain a sense of abiding peace within his being. As we worked on it over the months, it became clear that while he said he wanted to feel peace, there were a number of barriers in the way, one of them being an inner resistance to the idea of things slowing down. In one session he said to me, "I don't know existence without stress. If I don't feel stress, then I feel like I'm not living." Even in those moments when there was a lull in activity and an opportunity for him to relax, enjoy the moment, and feel a higher flow of peace, he would unconsciously manufacture some sort of crisis so he could go back into stress.

Through coaching, he identified that one way for him to destress and feel more at peace was a daily practice of simply doing nothing at all for 30 minutes. How incredibly hard this turned out to be for him! He would get antsy after just 5 minutes, urged on by a nagging impulse to do something and be productive. In many such ways he resisted slowing down and creating the conditions in which he could experience a higher flow of peace within his being. Even though he valued peace, his mind and lifestyle were wired for productivity, speed, and stress—a state of being to which he was firmly habituated.

Some time ago, my wife and I decided that living the practice of slowing down was of such value to our family's well-being that we uprooted from the large, densely populated Asian metropolis we'd been living in for twelve years to resettle in a much smaller city a few hundred kilometers away, a city known for its slow, relaxed pace of life. As it turned out, living in our new city was just the beginning of the recalibration process. Old

habits of thought and behavior around busyness and speed and productivity persisted, and it took considerable time to dislodge those habits and all
the stress we had accumulated over those twelve years.

While living in the bigger city, I had done what I could to stay connected
with the rhythm of life and Spirit, but it was difficult not to be negatively
impacted by the stressful energy that seven million people bustling about
in a 24-7 city can generate. Large Asian cities are vibrant, but they are also
crowded, loud, smelly, and continuously on the go, which is taxing on both
the body and the brain. (Studies have shown that people born and raised in
cities have higher rates of psychosis, anxiety disorders, and depression.)
Leaving the large city for a smaller one was a dramatic reconfiguration of
my family's lifestyle, but it enabled us to live aligned with what we valued. This is just one example of the level of personal commitment it often
takes to slow life down in a meaningful way.

Both inside and outside the coaching space, slowing it all down will be
challenging for the people you work with as well, not only for the reasons
mentioned above, but also, in particular, for those who are experiencing
the *discomfort of the tension* brought on by the transformational process.
The discomfort of the tension triggers the fight-or-flight mechanism, and
compels people to want to escape it. They think, "The faster we can find a
way forward, get clarity, or find a solution to this discomfort I'm feeling,
the faster I'll start feeling good and normal again." They will bring this
mindset into your coaching conversations, and if you are not well prac-
ticed in slowing it all down yourself, your client's need for speedy resolution can bump you out of this most optimal state of being.

For those in transformation, rather than trying to move away from the
tension or manage the situation, they can learn to lean into the tension
and be with it. Being present to, and at peace in, moments of potentially
angst-filled change is both a challenge and a wonderful opportunity for
growth. The shadowy stuff that transformation inevitably dredges up is not
a 'problem' to be solved; it is simply the remnants of our old self-concept

passing away, and it will rage against the dying of its existence. This stuff is not solved away, it is healed away.

Slowing it all down is a preliminary condition for nurturing a healing space (Practice 3) in which people can open to what is arising, lean into any pain or discomfort, explore it safely, and do the necessary inner work. *Nothing in the Deep Coaching process needs to be avoided, forced to happen, or strived for*. This means that Deep Coaches embrace slowing down, and we invite those we work with to join us in a space infused with the deeper rhythms of life and Spirit, even though we well know they may at first resist it because it is unfamiliar or uncomfortable.

Moment of Pause

Just Be

Take a few deep, slow breaths. Slow down even further whatever rhythm you are currently experiencing.

As you do this, notice what shifting to an even deeper rhythm feels like. Sense the wavelength of the new rhythm, the easing of your presence within it, the relaxation of your muscles, the dissipation of tension, the expansion of your heart, the softening of your belly.

With each breath you take, slow it all down more and more. Let go of all thoughts or expectations and simply enjoy the harmonious energy that is arising within you at this very moment. There is nowhere to go, nothing that must be attained or completed.

Just be.

This inner activity can be done at any time, no matter where you are or what you are doing.

When the Awareness Arises

It is amazing what happens when people experience themselves in a space synced to the natural rhythms of life and Spirit. They become more authentic and real, more open and vulnerable, more patient and trusting. More blessings of joy, creativity, and other fruits of Spirit come their way. And in that space, the possibility exists for openhearted conversation that has no need to get somewhere, no need to achieve something. It becomes a time to go within and to simply be with whatever is arising and allow it to reveal what wants to happen.

For those living the transformational journey, there will invariably come a time when they become acutely aware of just how out of sync with the wisdom of their Self and soul they have been, and that what they need to do more than anything else is to give themselves full permission to slow life way down, to make more time and space for the inner work, and to allow their entire being to recalibrate to life's natural rhythms and energies. What a breakthrough this is!

Should this awareness arise in a session, give the person plenty of room for contemplation. This is not a time to intellectualize the awareness with a bunch of action-oriented questions as to when and how they will actually do it—rather, the realization itself is a profound shift with lasting consequences. All you need to do is bear witness and allow the knowing to sink in. You have contributed to this realization because you created a sanctuary woven of the breath of Spirit. And whether they are aware of it or not, when two people or more come together in sync with the rhythm of life and Spirit, and open a space for inner exploration and dialogue, what is needed *will* emerge. It will emerge from within the coach or the coachee, and it matters not which it is. When people are in sync with the rhythm of life and Spirit, they are in sync with each other, in essence becoming of ONE mind and heart. This is the highest level of connection that you can share with another human being, and it is a masterful coaching state.

Practice Application

Energy Calibration

Slowing down allows the currents of your mind to be filled with the natural energies of life which support well-being.

Sit with that thought for a minute and ask for its meaning to move deeply in you, helping you access places within your consciousness which need to calibrate to those energies.

Allow yourself to savor this experience, and know that it is this slowing down of your thoughts and actions which breeds productivity, creativity, and satisfaction.

Practice slowing down each day, integrating these energies into the depths of your being, and you will thrive. For this is what life is all about!

CHAPTER TEN

Practice 2 - Release Your Agendas; Live Your Spiritual Values

During the transformational process, the major transition we undergo is moving from how we perceive ourselves vis-à-vis our limiting and protecting ego-based self-concept to knowing who we truly are, in essence. During this transition it is normal to begin questioning the foundation upon which our identity and life truths have long rested, and to seek answers to some of life's biggest questions. Possibly for the first time in their lives, people who are awakening are giving themselves permission to *self-define* what is good, true, important, meaningful, and necessary. It is a monumental step in a person's life when the veil of imposed belief begins to lift and a new paradigm of living is glimpsed.

Transformation is therefore a time of truth seeking, and truth seeking requires the courage to be vulnerable. Many people turn away from truth seeking because they fear being vulnerable and the potential harm to their sense of self it can bring. Yet those who embark on the heroic journey toward enlightened meaning, identity, and purpose must open themselves up within the world, and that same willingness to be vulnerable also makes them vulnerable to having their lives manipulated or exploited by those who claim to have the answers. This is the arena in which some religions, cults, spiritual movements, gurus from both east and west, and—yes, it's true—life coaches operate. They hold up placards saying something like, "I know the way, truth seeker. This is how to live, follow me." The issue is not that their teachings are inherently false or misleading—many of them do espouse great truths and life wisdom, and improve the quality of people's lives—the issue is when they actively seek 'followship' through a form of belief imposition and value transfer.

Deep Coaches have a responsibility not to exploit the vulnerability of the truth seeker. Rather than suggesting or imposing a way to think or act, or encouraging any form of followship, the Deep Coach creates an expansive space for exploration, contemplation of the emerging Self, and, ultimately, healing. Most importantly, in this space, we invite people to open themselves to their essential magnificence and to the greater consciousness or Presence that guides life forward. It all follows from the Prime Directive:

> The Prime Directive of Deep Coaching is to hold a space which enables a person to connect with their deepest sense of Self and which makes room for the presence and action of Spirit.

There is an incredible spaciousness to the realm of Spirit because it has no agenda, nothing that *must* be achieved, and no desire to impose a belief system or course of action. Spirit simply *is* and invites us to join it in that state of being.

Your Agenda Influences Transformation

Most coaches hold the intention to keep the coaching space as free as possible from the undue influence of their own stuff, but at the same time we have to be honest and recognize that we will have an influence. What we want to do is make that influence *positive* and *effective*, in the same way that we recognize how the influence of Spirit is positive and effective.

This is why the image of 'coach as cocoon' is so fitting. In a caterpillar's metamorphosis, the cocoon is that which shapes, holds, and protects the transformational space. The cocoon is not directing the action, nor manipulating the way the metamorphosis unfolds; rather it shapes and holds the space, allowing the natural, organic process of transformation to unfold within. Shaping and holding the space is still a form of influence—without the cocoon transformation would not be possible—yet it is positive and effective. But because we are human cocoons made up of more than material alone, there is always a chance that we will influence the transformational space in a negative or non-effective way.

What forms of influence effectively empower transformation and what forms interfere with or obstruct it?

A coach's own belief and value system is a significant influencer, as that system gives rise to a host of attitudes and behaviors, both empowering and disempowering. Any thought a coach has around what should or should not be believed or valued, or what should or should not be happening as the truth seeker embarks on her quest for self-actualization, is rarely an effective influencer because it projects an externally imposed system of thought (or agenda) upon one who is learning to discern and define her own truth about life.

Most if not all coaches have their client's best interests at heart, but in reality agendas come into it. We are susceptible to meddling, to interfering with another person's process, to imposing our own thoughts, judgments, and ideas about how things should go or the way they should think. And when that happens, we're basically saying, "I know what is right or best for you."

A Deep Coach is always aware of the necessity to let go of any such personal agenda and thus not direct the process of change that is unfolding of its own volition. (There is enough of that happening in the world around us as it is.) Otherwise, and this is what makes the coach's personal agenda an undue form of influence, it's the conditioning pattern of childhood repeating itself.

Developing Your Coaching Presence

Our belief and value system also affects another significant influencer on transformation: our coaching presence. Presence means undivided awareness, which is simply the act of being there. Presence is; it is effortless in that we don't have to make it happen. Presence is where all resistance to what is falls away. Space then arises, a space for relating to each other, so that two or more people can *be* there, to listen to that which is, to that which would like to happen. As the eminent psychologist Carl Rogers wrote in *A Way of Being*:

> "When I am at my best, as a group facilitator or as a therapist, I discover another characteristic. I find that when I am closest to my inner, intuitive self, when I am somehow in touch with the unknown in me, when perhaps I am in a slightly altered state of consciousness, then whatever I do seems to be full of healing. Then, simply my presence is releasing and helpful to the other."

The state of presence Carl Rogers describes is the way of being a Deep Coach aspires to, as it is an immensely positive and effective influencer on the transformational process. The Deep Coach not only coaches from presence, but also lives from presence. The quality of your presence enables you to be completely in the moment, to accept people wherever they are at, and to tap into what is emerging at the level of being.

How do you develop a transformative coaching presence?

All nine Deep Coaching practices show the way, however with the first part of this practice—Release Your Agendas—you are encouraged to become aware of all the ways your own belief system influences your presence. The more agenda you bring into the coaching space, the more your presence and actions will stifle the inherent capacity of the transformational process to generate meaningful self-awareness within the other person (and visa versa).

Releasing your agenda begins with upholding the Prime Directive, as it affirms that when it comes to navigating the journey of transformation, all answers and all power lie within. I recognize trusting that 'all your client's answers lie within' can be challenging, particularly when things get rocky and they get caught up in drama, struggle, or pain. Your sympathetic nature may want to alleviate that struggle or pain with a balm of your own making: "You should try…" "Have you considered…" "Let's do this…," but that would be a mistake. It is not that you should never make suggestions, but a Deep Coach's role is to create a space in which a person can attune to what is available and emerging within themselves. In transformation, people are beginning to access fields of higher awareness, of intuition and wisdom. The information is there; you need to make room for them to perceive it—and the quality of your coaching presence will impact whether or not they do.

Spiritual, Religious, and Philosophical Beliefs Impact Transformation

There are coaches, and you may be one of them, who coach through the lens or teachings of a particular religion, faith community, spiritual movement or philosophy. What you personally choose to believe, however, is not the issue; each of us is free to believe what serves us best. The issue is that your belief system can unduly influence another person's transformation if it is imposed or suggested as a course of thought or action because it is what you believe to be a better way. Deep Coaches are aware of this potential, and release the need to propose answers to anyone else's life questions. Instead, we create a space which allows others to ask the questions and to explore deeply within themselves what the answers may be.

How do spiritual, religious, or philosophical beliefs get in the way?

Many religious, spiritual, and philosophical teachings are helpful guides to understanding life, but the other side of the coin is that those same teachings (or the organizations that support them) often *prescribe* behaviors for others to live by. During transformation, any attempt to conform behavior to a belief system is like a speed bump on a train track: it has the potential to derail things. Systems of belief, whether held by the coach or coachee, can become influencing agendas, potentially muting the inner voice of Self and soul.

Let's take, for example, a situation where the coach is helping a person reframe their perspective on a situation, and asks the question: "What would Jesus or Buddha do in this same situation?" If the coach has a preconceived idea of what Jesus or Buddha would do, then the subsequent dialogue could be used to influence the person into adopting that same perspective. In other words, if the coach believes what Jesus would have done is "repent and ask for forgiveness," then this belief can, in subtle and not so subtle ways, influence the person's process for discovery of their own truth.

In transformation, the ground upon which a person has built their self-concept is quaking and cracking, and this tumult includes their spiritual, religious, or philosophical belief systems. All of it is now up for questioning and examination. How disconcerting this time can be, how vulnerable one can feel! And equally, how tempting it can be for us as coaches to proffer up personal ideals and direction that reflect what we believe is the way to think, perceive, or act. But this is shaky ground for a Deep Coach. Unless you are capable of releasing a belief or conviction as you become aware of it, it will inevitably find a way to influence your coaching process. Any preconceived idea of what ought to be thought or done is a potential interference pattern in a truth seeker's transformation (including your own).

Reflect for a moment on what can happen when you bring your personal beliefs to bear at the time when a person is questioning the foundation of their life understanding. Regardless of how well-meaning your advice, or how empowering the information may seem to you, to bring your beliefs in at a time when your client is in a vulnerable state of truth seeking is a subtle form of manipulation—even if done with care, even if done with the person's highest good in mind—because you are telling yourself something like, "If they think or perceive this way, things will be better for them." That is the way of the teacher, mentor, preacher or guru, not the way of the Deep Coach.

People on the transformational path are discovering their own truths, attitudes, and ways for living—including those which are no longer and those which are emerging—and they are consciously shaping a revitalized set of personal tenets and values. This shaping process is the 'art' of the transformation, and it can happen in a Deep Coaching space free of agenda and undue influence, where a person can quiet the mind, more clearly hear and respond to the inner direction of Self and soul, and begin to make decisions which reflect their own highest truth.

The transformational process, when allowed to run its course unimpeded by imposed belief, gives birth to a human being who is far more self-aware, soul-aligned, and integrated. People may still choose to retain spiritual or religious beliefs which they have held for a lifetime and which serve them well, just as they may choose to explore new pathways of belief; it is all perfectly okay. Deep Coaches have no vested interest in what other people choose to believe or value, just as the caterpillar's cocoon has no vested interest in what the butterfly will look like.

All of us have religious, spiritual, and philosophical beliefs in one form or another—please recognize that this is neither a judgment nor a nullification of those beliefs. Deep Coaches are, however, aware that their own beliefs can become agendas in the coaching context, and agendas can influence transformational processes in ways that do not necessarily reflect what is being called for at the deeper level of Self and soul. Since our work is to foster inner connection and allow transcendental awareness to emerge, we must honestly acknowledge where and how our agenda shows up, and find ways to release it.

Identify Your Core Spiritual, Religious, and Philosophical Beliefs

Awareness of your belief system is a good starting point for understanding how you can, deliberately or inadvertently, influence your client's transformational process. This exercise asks you to list the core religious and spiritual tenets you hold or anything that forms your personal life philosophy. Some examples include:

- We are meant to grow into Christ (Christian belief)

- Desire and attachment are causes of suffering (Buddhist belief)

- The object of life is to live in a way that is pleasing to Allah (Islamic belief)

- You can manifest everything your heart desires (New Age belief)

- It's important to stay positive and happy (life philosophy).

Take time now to reflect on and write down your answers to the following question. This will require honesty.

What are the primary religious, spiritual, or philosophical beliefs that give meaning and fulfilment to your life, that guide your choices and actions, and that you believe others would do well to hold?

    A.) List at least five, but more if possible:

        1.)

        2.)

        3.)

        4.)

        5.)

B.) When you have finished, think about how these beliefs show up when you coach, or influence the way you support the development of another person.

Identify Your Core Spiritual Values

There is a distinction between beliefs and values. We use both to form attitudes, and to guide our actions and behaviors, but they are different, and this difference lies at the heart of the second part of this practice: Live Your Spiritual Values.

Beliefs are convictions that we hold to be true; they are assumptions we make about the world, whether provable or not. Values are things that we deem important. Our values are more universal in nature and include concepts like equality, achievement, perseverance, loyalty, success, pleasure, justice, faithfulness, hard work, and many others. Spiritual values are a subset of all existing values, and are those values which are *in harmony with the consciousness and action of Spirit.* Spiritual values are not of any one religion or movement; they are universal in nature. For example, love is a spiritual value that is not of any one religion. However, "Jesus tells us to love each other as brothers and sisters" is the belief of a particular religion.

This first part of this practice is about letting go of any agenda born of your beliefs (though not the belief itself) so as to avoid unduly influencing another person's transformational process. The second part of the practice, live your spiritual values, is about *learning how to energize shifts in being* that are healing in nature, one of the key roles of the Deep Coach.

Let's first take time to determine what your spiritual values are by reflecting on these questions:

What are your core spiritual values? What do you stand for in the world that reflects the essence of Spirit, soul, or spirituality?

A.) List at least five core spiritual values:

1.)

2.)

3.)

4.)

5.)

B.) When you have finished, think about how you live or express each value in your daily life, and the effect it has on the people around you.

Turning Spiritual Values into Spiritual Energy

Science has already shown that everything is energy in motion, including you. You are a vibrational being, like a tuning fork, and every moment you radiate a frequency of energy. All the products of your mind, your thoughts, memories, emotions, and *values* are also all forms of energy.

What is the energy you radiate?

If you live habitually in a negative state of mind where you perceive suffering, fear, ugliness, ignorance, scarcity and the like, you will primarily give and receive energy of that kind because you are vibrating in that way. But if you cultivate positivity, kindness, patience, inspiration, or any other such values, then you are able to vibrate within those fields of energy.

What does this mean for the Deep Coach? One of the most effective ways to support transformation, while remaining free of agenda, is to take your spiritual values and *turn them into a current of spiritual energy* that weaves into and nourishes the coaching space. You may recall from Chapter 6 that spiritual energy is one of the six primary engines of propulsion Deep Coaches work with; here we are learning how to access and channel it in service of personal and planetary transformation.

The Sufi teacher Llewelyn Vaughan-Lee once said,

> "We often underestimate the potential of our spiritual nature. Part of the vision…is to explore and activate the transformative potential of spiritual energy, and the sense that it has a vital role to play in our own individual transformation. Many of you have been on your own journey long enough to have experienced that potential and how it can transform one's

life as it takes us into an infinitely expanding space within the heart."

This is the crux of Practice 2, and what we are learning to do:

Turn spiritual values into spiritual energy and activate its transformative potential.

With this practice, you are encouraged to live your spiritual values more holistically than you ever have before. Your values are far more than ideals or guidelines to live by, they represent *energy fields* which can be directed intentionally in order to energize shifts in being, nurture higher states of consciousness and, ultimately, heal.

Coaching becomes transformative when it focuses first on *who you are being* and then *what you do from that place of being*. (This applies both to the coach and the coachee.) Therefore, as a coach, living your spiritual values means to *be* that which you value, and to embody it so thoroughly, with such intent, that your vibration is itself healing. This is how you become a transformative presence in the world, not by word or deed alone, but by the vibrational quality and strength of your being. It's worth contemplating:

Are you the living embodiment of your core spiritual values?

Turning your spiritual values into spiritual energy and activating its trans-formative potential is so essential to Deep Coaching that if you mastered this practice alone you would have to do little else. In time, as you practice, you will become the living embodiment of your core spiritual values, and your presence will begin to radiate the healing light of enlight-ened consciousness.

In your sessions, focus on energizing the space by intentionally channel-ing those life-giving energies reflective of your spiritual values. Please understand, these energies are not 'yours,' they are of Spirit, and when you choose to open to them through the "infinitely expanding space within the heart," you become like a divining rod for the Divine: you become a channel by which the transformative potentials of spiritual energy flood the coaching space, quelling the discomfiture that comes with transformation, while uplifting and energizing the emergence of a higher way of being.

Practice Application

Turn Your Spiritual Values into Spiritual Energy

If you are new to energy work, be sure to practice Part 1 of this exercise a few times before moving onto Part 2.

Take your time with it, let go of any expectation around what should be happening or what you ought to be feeling, and it will be an enjoyable experience.

Part 1: Connecting with and Expanding Energy

1.) Choose one of your top 5 spiritual values.

2.) Hold the word or phrase in mind or, even better, visualize it in front of your heart center.

3.) Tune into and connect with the *energy* this value represents. Sense the energy field that lies beyond the word, which the word only represents.

4.) Once you feel the energy of that value, allow it to expand gently within and around you. Feel the vibration of it in every cell in your body. Hold it in this expanded way for as long as you're comfortable.

5.) When you feel complete, close it down and choose another of your top 5 spiritual values.

6.) Repeat the exercise with 2-3 more values or until you feel you're getting the hang of it.

7.) Each time you change values, notice how the energy or vibration changes. How does it feel different? You may also experience it somewhere in your body. Notice anything at all that helps you discern the unique energy signature of that value before moving on to the next value.

8.) Each time you change values, gently extend the time you hold its energy; with transformative practice there is no rush.

Part 2: Projecting Energy

1.) Choose one of your spiritual values and repeat the exercise above.

2.) At the point where you feel the energy expand, bring to mind any person in your life.

3.) Then, with the fullness of your heart, radiate the energy from your being so that it completely surrounds the person you are sending it to.

4.) Visualize or sense both of you as connected within a large energy field, one which is extending from you and holding the other person within it.

5.) Stay in a place of trust that the energy you are sending is being received on some level of mind and soul. ("Spiritual partners hold the awareness that they are connecting, simultaneously, on the level of personality and soul.")

6.) Hold the energy field around both of you as long as is comfortable, then slowly close it down.

7.) Take a few minutes to breathe and relax, then try it again with another spiritual value and another person.

It may take a while for you to be able to detect, hold, or project these energies for a full coaching session or even longer, but that is not a concern—the way of mastery is to practice in each moment, as best you can.

In time, as you become a living embodiment of your spiritual values, your capacity will grow. If kindness is one of your values, you will become more than a 'kind person'—you will radiate kindness, projecting it through the light of your presence into all areas where kindness is needed.

CHAPTER ELEVEN

Practice 3 - Nurture a Healing Space

Given all that I have shared about Deep Coaching as a healing modality, this third practice of nurturing healing spaces will come as no surprise. To transform is to heal, and for this to happen naturally and organically, a healing space is needed. In all coaching contexts, the coach is responsible for establishing a safe, supportive, respectful environment. There is, however, a qualitative difference between a healing space and a 'safe, supportive, respectful' space.

During my years as a leadership coach, I coached primarily in offices and conference rooms. These rooms rarely feel like healing spaces. Most often they are utilitarian, at times warm and inviting, but never healing. Any physical space can become a healing space, however, when the right conditions are met. This applies to coaching spaces as well. All good coaching spaces are safe, supportive and respectful; however, certain conditions need to be met in order for the space to become a healing space. There is no blackboard in the sky upon which these conditions are written, and yet, if you reflect on personal experiences you have had with healing spaces, you can discern relatively easily whether a space is a healing space or not.

Moment of Pause

Reflect on Healing Spaces

Bring to mind a few healing spaces you have experienced: a sanctuary, meditation room, a temple or church, a place outdoors or in nature, a spa or healing arts room, or anywhere else.

What made each place a healing space?

What Is a Healing Space?

A healing space is any space in which a person is capable of relaxing the stressors in their mind and body to the point where they have access to their most resourceful and optimal state.

So much dis-ease and disease is the result of stress in the mind and body. Some of this stress is genetic (generational) and some the result of life events that have created trauma, sorrow, or fearful thinking. For many people, stress is so commonplace that it has become a way of life. Stress isn't always bad: in small to moderate doses it can help you perform under pressure and motivate you to do your best; in emergency situations stress can save your life. But stress is generally a disempowering state of being, and when you constantly experience an underlying current of fear, worry, anxiety, or pressure, your mind and body pay a price: stress starts as dis-ease and ends up as disease. When this happens, stress has become part of your personal gravity, holding you back from moving into higher levels of well-being, fulfillment, and joy.

A healing space is therefore any physical or non-physical space which allows for stress release and decompression so that we can access our most resourceful and optimal state of being. A healing space is like an oasis in time where the heaviness of daily pressure and material concerns can be transcended; a space in which harmonious, integrating energies are enabled, and disempowering, disintegrating energies are disabled.

When we nurture a healing space, we activate energies that promote relaxation and inner connection, and release tension and stress. (An additional benefit is that when the stress that suppresses our naturally functioning immune system is released, the immune system is better able to do the job for which it was designed.) We are then primed to access the resources employed in healing that propel the transformational process forward.

Cultivating a Healing Space

Dr. Alex Loyd wrote in *The Healing Code*, "The deepest healing every person on earth needs is not physical or emotional, but spiritual, and it involves healing any disruption with a loving God." In Deep Coaching terms, we say that the deepest healing every person needs involves healing any disconnect with the intelligence of the heart and soul so that we can move closer to the realm of Spirit and its vast healing capacities. In order to enable that connection, Deep Coaches cultivate a healing space.

It is important to recognize, however, that the coach is not responsible for healing and does not need to be 'a healer.' *Each person chooses to heal him or herself.* The Deep Coach's role is to create the optimal conditions in which healing can occur, conditions which trigger the desire and ability to heal oneself; Deep Coaches are healing facilitators who help others locate and activate the healing power they hold within. The Deep Coach is a 'healer' only insofar as we cultivate an energized space of potentiality in which disrupted inner connections can be reestablished so that the renewing power of life and Spirit can be unleashed within the mind and body.

Each healing space has its own unique feel and energy; no two spaces are exactly alike. You are free to create whatever it is you desire, in any way you choose, as there is no prescription for how a healing space is cultivated. If you have not intentionally created a healing space before, the first two practices are an excellent starting point for how it is done: slow it all down, sync with the rhythm of life and Spirit, and infuse the space with spiritual energy. It is also helpful to start observing the qualities all healing spaces share, the defining characteristics which signify a space as a healing space, and reflect on how those can be brought to your work. These characteristics include:

- spaciousness

- breath

- calm, peace, serenity

- relaxation

- safety

- silence

- harmony and grace

- natural rhythms

- detachment from thinking

- freedom to be.

As the cultivator of a healing space, it begins with *who you are being*. If you are driven by your intellect, your capacity to nurture a healing space is diminished. A healing space opens when you tap into your heart and soul, and when you choose to be your most loving and authentic self. Becoming a Deep Coach means moving towards this creative power we experience as love and perceiving ourselves as energy fields, inseparable parts of the whole, radiating that love. As a loving presence, that energy field emanates from you, filling the coaching space, bathing it in healing light, and opening the door for others to access their healer within.

This practice, combined with Practice 7 (Expand Your Capacity to Be with Pain and Allow Healing Moments) is an invitation to recognize the healer within you. Its primary intention is to help you recognize the part of you that consistently abides in the space where all healing occurs, and then work from that place.

In time, as you practice nurturing healing spaces wherever you find your-self, you will come to recognize an extraordinary truth: *you are the space.* There will be a shift in your perception of a healing space from something that is outside of or an extension of yourself, to perceiving yourself as the healing space. You are the space! And you will carry this healing presence with you wherever you go, leaving a trail of light in your wake.

Moment of Pause

Nurturing Healing Spaces

Reflect on each of these qualities of a healing space. How do you bring these into the places and conversations you have each day?

- spaciousness

- calm, peace, serenity

- relaxation

- safety

- silence

- harmony and grace

- natural rhythms

- detachment from thinking

- freedom to be

- breath.

> What aspects of yourself can get in the way of nurturing healing spaces?

Practice Application

Visit Healing Spaces

1.) Take time this week to be in a healing space not of your
making. Find a place outside your home which exudes
healing for you. It could be a temple, church, spa, a place
in nature, wherever it may be for you.

Spend a good amount of time in that space, and while you are there,
reflect or meditate on what it means to cultivate healing spaces in your life
and work.

2.) Practice being a healing, transformative presence by
nurturing a healing space in all the places you go.
Wherever you find yourself, particularly those places
which are in need of healing or enlivening energies,
intentionally cultivate a healing space. At a minimum,
each place you find yourself is an opportunity to practice
projecting spiritual energy (Practice 2).

CHAPTER TWELVE
Practice 4 - Let There Be Silence

The Japanese have a beautiful concept called 'ma,' which has been described as a pause in time, the essential void between all things. It is the silent moment in a conversation, or the silence between the notes that make music. Ma, being filled with nothing but energy and feeling, creates peace of mind and serenity within. Author Katrina Goldsaito illustrates the concept of ma in a delightful book, *The Sound of Silence,* that tells the story of Yoshio, a boy living in big, bustling Tokyo:

> "The notes were twangy and twinkling; they tickled Yoshio's ears! When the song finished, Yoshio said, "Sensei, I love sounds, but I've never heard a sound like that!" The koto player laughed. "Sensei," Yoshio said, "do you have a favorite sound?"
>
> ""The most beautiful sound," the koto player said, "is the sound of ma, of silence."
>
> ""Silence?" Yoshio asked. But the koto player just smiled a mysterious smile and went back to playing."

The next day Yoshio is reading alone in his classroom:

"Suddenly, in the middle of a page, he heard it. No sounds of footsteps, no people chattering, no radios, no bamboo, no kotos being tuned. In that short moment, Yoshio couldn't even hear the sound of his own breath. Everything felt still inside him. Peaceful, like the garden after it snowed. Like feather-stuffed futons drying in the sun.

"Silence had been there all along."

What happens in those moments when your conversation goes silent? When silence arises not just for a few seconds but for an extended period of time? What happens in those moments when you become aware of your own breathing, the gap in the conversation, the void that fills the space? Does it begin to feel awkward, uncomfortable, doubt-filled? Is there an urge to end the silence, to say something, to shift back into the comfort of conversation? Or do you stay with the silence and just be with the person? What happens in those moments?

In any conversation there is the potential for ma, for the breath of silence to be experienced. In coaching conversations, pauses and short periods of silence are accepted as part of active listening, an integral coaching skill. Yet many people are not comfortable with even brief moments of silence in conversation, let alone prolonged periods. Rather than viewing silence as adding value to the conversation, it is avoided in favor of keeping things comfortable or moving the conversation forward.

Deep Coaching, however, is a quest of spiritual partners to reveal more of the nature of the true Self, our essential nature and personality found at the core of our being. Because the true Self gets hidden from view behind ceaseless thinking and mental noise, the path to experiencing our essential nature is not experienced through the thinking mind, but in the silence of our mind.

Moment of Pause

Reflect on Silence

Are you comfortable with silence?

Do you embrace 'ma' or silence when you are alone or with others?

When silences arise in conversation, how do you usually react?

What happens for you when you allow silent periods in your life?

Silence and Transformation

In our inner stillness is a truth that runs over our everyday identity like a great river overflowing its banks.

~ Bruce David

Let There Be Silence is a transformative practice, and transformative practices are aimed at bringing us into an experience of our deepest interior reality. In our modern world, where silence can be so elusive, the practice of silence can change our lives for the better: it encourages the inward journey, connection to Spirit, and is an important aspect of well-being. The world's spiritual teachers and avatars have all advocated periods of silence in order to contemplate the higher truths about life and to experience the essential nature of Self and our relationship with Spirit, the universe, and each other.

It is the same in Deep Coaching, and why Deep Coaching embraces silence. Looking back at the practices we have covered, you can see how silence connects to each one. Silence results naturally when we slow it all down and sync with the rhythm of life and Spirit. Silence arises when we nurture healing spaces, because deep silence *is* a healing space. And when we quiet mind and body, we open the portal to the higher realms where the frequencies of Spirit are domiciled, where we connect to the circuits of spiritual energy which heal and transform. Silence enables spiritual energy transmission.

Working with silence in coaching starts with the willingness to quieten the voice, to allow more space into conversations, knowing the mind will follow suit, that the mental chatter will slow down. Inspiration can then arise in the space between thoughts and words. Silence gives time to explore hidden thoughts and subtle feelings, to contemplate ideas, examine intentions, and integrate experiences, and to put together what we want to say before giving it voice. Contemplative silence is a refuge from the noise of the world and the drama of 'my story,' a space where we can be more centered, contemplative, and appreciative.

Within *prolonged periods of silence* there is a richness of texture and possibility that supports transformation. Prolonged silence is a necessary condition for perceiving the thoughts, energies, and images which emanate from the higher mind. Prolonged silence invites 'breath,' an aspirational process that helps us drop below the surface into a deeper realm of being. Here we may experience what appear as two selves: the self we currently live through and our emerging Self. Silence allows us to begin harmonizing these two selves as we contemplate questions like: What is emerging in me? Who am I becoming? What is no longer true for me? What am I ready to let go of, to heal?

As we move even further into prolonged periods of silence we connect with stillness. Stillness of mind is far more than the silencing of speech. In stillness we create the conditions for an intimate experience of our essence, of who I AM. This is a profound journey to take, the journey of silence into the innermost sanctuary of being.

As you overcome any discomfort with silence, you will create transformative spaces which enable others to listen within, make connections, see emerging patterns and opportunities, and, ultimately, heal their limiting self-concept. Learn to let there be silence, for it is the perfect position from which to bear witness to the natural unfolding process of change. In silence there is nowhere to get to, no result that must be achieved.

Silence Busters

Awkwardness

If you are not used to silence in daily conversation, it can feel like a void that needs to be filled. And that void can be deafening in a world consumed with thoughts and voices competing to be heard. It feels awkward, unnatural, and makes people uncomfortable. Check in with yourself for a moment: when silence enters your daily conversations, what happens? Do you become tense, expectant, waiting for something to happen? Do you start thinking of something to say? Or are you relaxed, allowing the space, listening within, remaining present?

Silence is often eliminated from the coaching conversations simply because it feels awkward to both the coach and client. Discomfort in silence makes the coach vulnerable to asking a question just to end it. ("Whew, I'm glad that's over," sigh both coach and client.) The question asked may have been perfectly appropriate in light of what was being discussed; however, the *need* to ask the question stemmed from the desire to end the discomfort of the silence. The danger here is that the question can close down the potentials of the very thing that the person needs for deeper awareness, and an opportunity may be lost.

The Need to Ask Powerful Questions

As we practice letting there be silence, we become increasingly comfortable with it and begin to recognize its inestimable value. This is particularly true with prolonged periods of silence: two, three minutes or more. Novice practitioners of silence tend to make an erroneous assumption about silence: that silence does not add the same value to the coaching process as does asking questions. The thinking goes something like this: *My role as a coach is to ask powerful questions to create value. A little contemplative silence for thinking is okay, but if I am silent for too long I am not doing anything and therefore I'm not adding value to the session.* This assumption compels the coach to avoid silence in favor of continuous inquiry and dialog. If you aspire to be a Deep Coach, however, it is helpful to relax any belief you have around the need to ask powerful questions or the assumption that questions are the driver of the transformational process.

In practice, Deep Coaches do not put much effort into thinking up questions to drive the session or its outcomes. Questions can and will arise, as this is the nature of coaching; however, our primary focus is to shift ways of being, and that which shifts ways of being is only marginally supported by the inquiry process itself. As we looked at in Chapter 8, creating the optimal conditions for transformation begins with who you are *being*, not the questions you are asking. Your role as a Deep Coach is to learn to *be* a healing presence, a presence of high consciousness, which is inherently capable of uplifting and transforming others simply by the nature of being.

I encourage you to keep this in mind and to work more towards becoming a loving presence at home in the depths of silence, rather than being a master of powerful questions—unless the intention is to use a powerful question, as master coach Alain Cardon puts it, "to lead a client into silence." Questions can be a mighty catalyst for new thought, inspiration and creativity; however, in deep transformational work they alone do not create meaningful shifts in being. Silence gives us permission to just be with another person as our own most authentic, loving self, rather than feeling the need to *do* something to create value. Our being is our doing.

The Need to Achieve Results

The final silence buster is the need to achieve results. Both coach and client are susceptible to the influence of this need, and both can end up striving to achieve results in order to feel good about or validate the work. What we are learning with this practice is that silence is extremely valuable. It challenges the idea that you have to do or breakthrough or achieve something in a session to create value. Silence holds incredible wisdom. It helps you connect with another's deepest sense of Self, so what you perceive is his essence, her soul song, his emerging potential, her wholeness. What a precious gift that is, to be seen in that way! In silence there is no pressure to fix something or get something done. Silence is a space of intimate connection where the story of the mind can drop, and when the story drops you are left with being, the only real thing. In silence profound shifts in being happen.

Do any of these silence busters describe you? If you are now aware that you bust silence because of your discomfort, the belief that your role is to ask powerful questions, or the need to achieve results, you may be surprised to find that you have molded the coaching process to be about meeting *your* needs. I encourage you to begin practicing sinking into silence, and gaining comfort within that field of potential.

Practice Application

Intentional Silence

Bring to mind a situation that would have been better served had you held back and remained silent. Instead you broke the silence. Recall as much detail from that situation as you can.

Now reimagine the experience with you holding back. See yourself simply keeping quiet. What happens? How does that feel?

Finally, revisit the situation again, this time intentionally choosing silence. You are not holding back; you are allowing the 'wisdom of silence' to enter the space.

How did your experience in these scenarios differ?

Introducing Silence into the Coaching Space

When I am silent, I hear my true self and reach my soul. When I am silent, I hear with a caring heart.

~ Thomas Merton

One of the greatest gifts you can give your clients is to demonstrate comfort and ease with silence, and to do this from the beginning of your coaching relationship. The pace of life is fast, so our clients may not be used to a slowed down conversation replete with periods of contemplative silence. When working with these people, you will need to nurture their capacity to be comfortable in silence. Doing this well can be a bit of a balancing act. On the one hand, we know to meet our clients where they are at, which can be interpreted to include the rhythm and tempo they bring to the conversation. On the other hand, we recognize that by slowing it all down, quieting the mind, and allowing for moments of silence, we are better positioning people to go deep.

In laying the groundwork for an effective coaching partnership, it can be helpful to communicate to people aspects of the Deep Coaching approach. (Not all at once, of course; just when you observe that some conceptual understanding might diminish resistance or open the mind to new possibilities.) If you understand the value of silence, communicate this to your clients. You can communicate it both *explicitly*, by explaining how you use silence as a means for deeper reflection and connection, and *implicitly*, by using it regularly and comfortably. The more your clients understand the benefits of working with you in silence, and the more they observe, from the very beginning of your relationship, that silence is a natural part of your rhythm of dialogue, just as a musical rest is in music, the more comfortable they will become.

One of the mistakes that novice practitioners of silence in coaching make is to invite clients to sit in silence without regard for whether they are actually ready for or desiring it in that moment. The person finishes speaking about her situation or issue, and suddenly, seemingly out of the blue, the coach says, "Let's just sit in silence with that for a minute or so. Would that be okay with you?" You can just hear the person's bafflement followed by a doubtful, "Okay [if you say so]." Forced silence can be problematic in that it makes silence an effort. The best moments of silence come of themselves—they are natural and flow from the rhythm of the music you are creating together.

Passive and Active Silence

What are you doing in those periods of silence?

I differentiate between two types of silence in the coaching conversation. The first type is *passive silence*. In passive silence the coach is doing little except intentionally remaining quiet in order to give the client some uninterrupted space for contemplation. (Essentially it's keeping your mouth closed, and it's relatively easy because it's a matter of will.) The coach can use that silence to reflect on the client's situation or formulate the next question to ask.

The second type of silence is *active*. Active silence is a state of being in which the coach invokes aspects of mind, energy, and Spirit which fall outside the boundaries of conventional forms of interpersonal communication. And it can facilitate such a profound sense of communion between all those privy to the space that it feels *sacred*. Active silence is sacred silence, and sacred silence enables heart and mind to communicate with the realm of soul and Spirit. This silence heals.

Practice Application

Activating Sacred Silence

Sacred silence is born of a desire to foster a partnership with those aspects of mind which reflect our spiritual nature.

Before the session begins, prepare yourself. Take deep breaths and relax. Slow your mind down as you draw attention away from the mental chatter, move through breath into the spaciousness within yourself, and step into connection with Spirit. You can even say to yourself, "I intend to create a sacred space for healing and wholeness." This establishes the necessary inner conditions to activate sacred silence in the session.

As the session proceeds, you will naturally engage in dialogue. However, you are also attuning to the rhythm of life and Spirit, a rhythm that naturally invites moments of rest. When an opportunity to rest in silence arises, you may notice discomfort or an urge to say something. Do not resist it; simply allow it to be there while you direct your mind towards the rest notes you are hearing and let there be silence.

Once a silent space has opened, here some ways you can use your mental activity to empower the healing space and its transformative potentials:

- Channel spiritual energy: compassion, strength, truth, love, or whatever energy you feel is needed (Practice 2).

- Invite in Divine Intelligence. Ask to be shown what you need to know, say, or do.

- Attune to the person's deepest sense of Self and listen for what is needed there (Practice 6).

- Give thanks to Spirit: Thank you for infusing us with right knowing and perfect guidance.

- Affirm perfect outcome: I trust the process. All things are working for our highest good.

- Declare the truth of what *is* for the person: She is infinitely resource-ful. He is alive with clarity. She is safe and secure.

- Feel self-love or self-worth or self-knowing arising in the person.

When you activate silence in these ways, silence becomes sacred. Sacred silence allows us connect to that matrix of infinite intelligence that guides, uplifts, heals, and enlightens. In such moments of connection 'a truth runs over our everyday identity,' and we experience more and more the essence of who we are.

Breaking Silence

When coaching, you may have had the experience whereby, just when you were about to break the silence, your client opened up with an inspired thought or new perspective. What would have happened if you had broken the silence? Determining when and how to break periods of silence is a bit of an art. Just because you think the silent period has reached its end does not necessarily mean that your client agrees.

Silence is fragile, and once it is broken a forming thought, or an opportunity to integrate energy change, can get lost as the mind moves in another direction. The learning challenge is that there are no fixed rules around how to break silence. For this you must sense the way intuitively.

A simple guideline is to wait until your client speaks or indicates in some way that they are ready to move on. This is especially so if they initiated the silence, because the silence then belongs to them, and for you to break that silence is to interrupt their chosen state of being. Sometimes the indication is a marked change in breath, a shifting of the body position, or a clearing of the throat.

If you do intuit that the time is right to break the silence, there are a couple of ways to do this gently and which limit the effect of the interruption. One way is to invite your client to speak: "What are you experiencing? Would you like to share what's coming up for you?" or, "I'm here if there is anything you'd like to say." Conversely, should you decide that prolonging the silence would be beneficial, you can say: "This silence feels good; shall we sit with this for a while longer?" and then return to silence. In both cases you have broken the silence, however the unobtrusive nature of the interruption will minimize any disruption to what is happening.

Moment of Pause

Silence in Your Coaching

Is your coaching approach conducive to periods of silence (contemplative or prolonged)?

Is your silence approach more passive or more active (sacred)?

How are you helping your clients become comfortable with silence?

Practice Application

Guidance in Silence

Bring to mind a question that you would like an answer to. The question can relate to any area in your life around which there is uncertainty, a lack of clarity, or a need for some guidance.

Once you have formulated the question, begin to breathe deeply and allow your mind to become increasingly still. Draw your attention away from these words, close your eyes, and allow your entire being to become like a placid lake. With each breath, silence a little more of the activity of your mind.

When your mind is sufficiently still, invite Spirit or your inner guidance to reveal to you what you need to know, and then return to stillness. Simply bear witness to whatever arises.

Stay vigilant to your mind's tendency towards expecting answers or information to arise in a certain way, and stay open to being shown what it is you need to know in any form.

If your 'monkey mind' comes in and distracts you from being present, quietly remind it to be still and again become the observer. Should you sense that you are being guided to focus your mind or direct your energy in a certain way, follow that and see where it takes you.

Stay in a place of observation and hold it for as long as you feel comfortable. When you finish, reflect on your experience of sitting in silence, stillness, and inner connection.

CHAPTER THIRTEEN

Practice 5 - Coach More from the Heart, Less from the Head

Spiritual partners use the enhanced sense of unconditional love that is modeled for them by their partners as a touchstone while they learn to find and hold their own connection to source energy, freedom, expansion and full expression.

~ Elyse Hope Killoran,
Conscious Evolution Through Spiritual Partnering

As a Spirit-based approach, Deep Coaching is grounded in the life-affirming energies and intelligence of the heart—not the physical heart but our non-physical, spiritual heart. This is our inner heart, within which we access our higher nature.

We all have the capacity to create the space for heart consciousness to awaken and grow in strength so that our minds can perceive life through its lens. An open heart is needed to fill the mind with the energies and thought-forms that flow from the heart; an open mind is needed for there to be the willingness to *allow in* what the heart has to offer. Mind and heart then form an open, stable, mutually beneficial relationship.

If the heart is hard or closed, or the connection between the heart and mind is weak, we lose our connection with the source of our being. Our mind then, having little or no input from the heart, becomes susceptible to an inflow of insubstantial, unhealthy, or unproductive messages stemming from the ego. The ego naturally opposes the innate divinity we all possess and functions to disconnect the heart and mind. And once the mind has been suffused with ego-based thought patterns and negative emotional energies, they are etched as neural pathways in the brain, making it even more difficult to awaken heart consciousness. This has a profound effect on the quality of our thinking and the vibrancy of our life experience.

To access the power to transform we must dissolve the grip of the ego on the mind, as the ego is the source of our conditioned, limiting self-concept. In its place we fashion a strong connection with our spiritual heart, that aspect of our higher mind which knows what is true, good, meaningful, and right for us. Its knowledge, wisdom, and vibrant energy can then flow freely into the mind where decisions can be made and actions taken to produce an experience that helps the soul to progress. A strong connection with the heart holds the key to the development of a healthy and evolved self-concept, and to uncovering more and more of our authentic Self.

Moment of Pause

Experience Your Heart of Service

Take a moment now and listen to the voice within you that speaks to your deepest desire and intent to be of service to other human beings.

What is at the core of your desire to support another person to grow and transform?

When you connect with the heart of your life's work, what do you feel or experience?

The true beauty of Deep Coaching is experienced when the heart of the coach meets the heart of the client, and two become as one in the unifying heart space.

The Head Thinks

The intellect and the mind are interdependent, the intellect being like a product that develops from the mind; it is the faculty for organizing, analyzing, and reasoning, and is therefore a vital source of intelligence. If you were to be deprived of your intellect you would be deprived of a primary asset for learning, achievement, and progress, for concluding what is right, for figuring out what should be done, for designing the systems that provide structure for our lives. The intellect observes a situation, assesses what is to be done, and determines a path of action. Through the intellect we gain a better understanding of the world around us and how it works.

Coaching can be a highly intellectual process. Most coach training schools teach an array of coaching methodologies and models built upon the systemizing capacities of the intellect. For example, the widely known G.R.O.W. model is meant to guide the coach through progressive stages of exploratory questions, each stage having a specific purpose. Models such as this are mental constructs which a coach can follow to engage the client in a systematic way. All such models and approaches have value, particularly as aids for learning coaching processes; however, when intellectual approaches are emphasized it can be easy for people to slip into the belief that coaching from the intellect, or the 'head,' is what coaching is primarily about, reinforcing the tendency to coach at the level of solution-finding and problem-solving.

The Deep Coaching practice of coaching more from the heart, less from the head, does not mean 'never use your intellect' or 'never explore a person's thinking process'—there is still a need to understand how people's minds function to create their life experiences. The intellect itself is not the issue; it's the tendency of both coach and client to *rely* on the intellect that is problematic, because it can interfere with the capacity to listen to the heart's intelligence. Transformation is a process of change that takes us through the pathways of the heart into the depths of our being; it is not a problem to be solved or something to be figured out (though many will try). To use a crude idiom, relying on the intellect in transformational work is like bringing a knife to a gunfight—its use for the job at hand is severely limited. Yet it does serve a purpose; the intellect is extremely useful for thinking through issues in an objective, reasoned way, for unraveling belief systems, for assessing effects of thoughts and perceptions, and for revealing ego-patterns in need of healing.

The main issue with relying on the intellect to support transformation is that the intellect is itself incapable of healing, and it can never penetrate to the essence of being. Only the pathways of the heart can do this. As an extension of egoic consciousness (our sense of separate self), the intellect's reasoning capacity analyses, compares and sees the relationships *between* things, but it is not that which relates *to* things. The heart is the place from which authentic relationship, connection, and expanded insight into the unified nature of life and Spirit arise. Only love can truly heal, as healing is the act of loving oneself into wholeness (a wholeness that was never really absent in the first place).

The Heart Knows

The head and the gut always have a story to tell, but the heart just knows.

~ Rania Bedeir

The intellect, and the range of other human intelligences, can always help illuminate the issues of our lives; however, Deep Coaches are primarily interested in what is (or is not) coming from the heart. The heart is the pathway to our center, our essence, our soul, our highest truth. As you loosen the grip of ego on your mind, the intellect's thinking can become uncontaminated and clear and serve your awakened mind, enabling you to think and act more from the heart in all avenues of life. The heart is the intelligence center toward which Deep Coaches and those with whom we work are learning to orient.

The heart is:

- the conduit to the Mind of Spirit (pure Being, pure Intelligence)

- the realm of Knowing, where wisdom abides

- the center from which unconditional love flows

- the energy source for soul growth and consciousness transformation.

Deep Coaches strive to model living the way of the heart, and Deep Coaching is always interested in revealing the heart of the matter. When we commit to coaching (and living) more from the heart and less from the head, we orient our mind towards the Knowing within ourselves. We become a loving presence. In turn, this connection with our heart center becomes a means for nurturing the emergence of that same connection within others. In other words, accessing our heart's intelligence as we coach encourages our clients to access their own hearts' intelligence, and to perceive the larger more encompassing truth being birthed within them.

Coaching more from the heart does not preclude the use of other intelligences such as body or emotional intelligence. There will always be times when the body needs to be felt into or the emotions explored for better understanding and management. These intelligences are not to be disregarded or discarded—we acknowledge their purpose and place within the coaching conversation—but with this practice we are learning to let go of any reliance on these intelligences and develop a robust conduit to our spiritual heart so that it may feed into our mind that which is supportive of transformative healing and true Self-knowing. All elements central to the journey—trust in the face of doubt, courage in the face of fear, perseverance in the face of setback, wisdom in the face of failure, tranquility in the face of turmoil, gratitude in the face of loss, love for oneself in the face of imperfection—are manifestations of the heart's capacity to support meaningful progress.

Moment of Pause

Practice Reflection

What aspects of this practice do you see within your current approach to coaching or living?

Where are you gripped by the intellect? Where do you see opportunity for movement into a more heart-centered approach in your life or work?

Take a moment now to listen within: what is your heart saying to you?

Accessing the Heart's Intelligence

The more we are present to our own heart, the more it becomes the center of our awareness. The more we rest our attention in the heart, the more we learn to trust that our thoughts, words, and actions are tapped into the evolutionary intelligence of Spirit. You can experience this for yourself as you honestly feel and meet the innermost space of your own spiritual heart.

Communication between the heart and mind is improved by clearing the mind of mental chatter and making time for silence and inner contemplation. You build the conduit by slowing down and relaxing into life. Smell the roses! Notice the beauty that surrounds you. Smile. Experience gratitude. Express your joy. Cultivate trust in life. Commune with Spirit.

Allow yourself to love and be loved. Begin doing those things that feed your soul. And follow your heart's guidance. This is your practice, as one who models the way of the heart.

This is also the inner work you will encourage in those with whom you work. Deep Coaches nurture healing spaces, and in those spaces invite others to relax into the knowingness of their own heart and to place more trust in its guiding capacities. The pathway then takes them ever deeper, through the manifold layers of their conditioned self-concept, into the essence of their being.

There are two approaches you can use: *direct* and *indirect*. The **direct** way is through invitation: you invite people verbally to connect with their heart center and listen for what is known in that field of awareness. This is a highly effective method for helping people gain greater access to inner knowledge and wisdom.

For example, say you are coaching a person who is having a dispute with a colleague. Your client is forthright in recognizing that he instigated the conflict, and believes it is his responsibility to make amends and find resolution. In a typical coaching conversation, you would likely ask your client to share what he sees as some options for doing that. His first idea might be to ask his manager to mediate a meeting with the colleague. His other idea is to write an email to his colleague apologizing for his behavior. Both ideas could potentially resolve the dispute and foster a more effective working relationship, yet because you are coaching from the heart, you recognize the ideas as 'coming from the head.'

Presuming your client is willing to work at the heart level, you may share this observation with him, saying something like, "I sense that there may be another option, one that is aligned with what your heart wants to have happen. I'd like to invite you to first take a few deep breaths with me." Then take the breaths together and open the space. "Let all other thoughts fall away and bring your awareness to your heart center. Listen for what your heart wants to have happen. What is your heart telling you? What does your heart *know* is the way forward?" Then move into silence (even passive silence will do) and hold it until the person speaks.

The **indirect** approach to supporting others to access their heart's intelligence focuses on *the state of being you are embodying*. People more readily open to their hearts when in the presence of heart-centered people, so when you embody heart-centered consciousness, this acts as an implicit (unconscious) invitation to others to join you in that state of being. Your very presence radiates that which emanates from the heart: compassion, acceptance, trust, joy, peace, wisdom. Now the spiritual consciousness you are supplying is doing the work, subtly yet powerfully, the gentle nudging of awareness towards the heart.

Through either approach, if your client is indeed able to connect with his heart center, you will notice a qualitative difference in his answers. They will be more heartfelt; more open, vulnerable, and authentic. He will also be more at ease revealing his inner life, particularly the shadowy thoughts, fears, and emotions swirling around the situation; less will his words speak to externally-focused solutions and actions which might resolve the issue but require little change within himself. When connected to his heart, any actions identified will come from a place of knowing: what I *know* I need to change within myself, and what I *know* I need to do in this situation.

Moment of Pause
Overcoming Resistance to the Heart

Those you coach may be challenged to discern the heart's intelligence or to live from it trustingly. After a lifetime relying on the intellect to pilot the ship, it can be difficult to change pilots. There are always underlying questions:

What is my heart really saying?

Can I trust what I'm sensing?

What will happen if I entrust my life to my heart?

Will it steer me well or will I crash upon the shore?

This doubt creates resistance, and resistance impedes a person's capacity to listen deeply within themselves.

As a Deep Coach, how might you handle this?

Working with the Self-Concept

Our self-concept is essentially a collection of beliefs, attitudes, and images about who we think we are and how life is. The objective of Deep Coaching is to create a space where people can illuminate and explore the falsities and distortions of their self-concept, and heal the emotional-energetic-behavioral effects of those. This is the optimal level to get to, the encoded 'operating system' we unconsciously live through.

When I speak about working with the self-concept, I frequently use the words *illuminate* (or reveal) and *explore* (or examine). Some students of Deep Coaching get confused by these words, as they interpret them to mean 'coach from the head,' thinking they must concertedly dig into a client's self-concept or belief system using intellect-based questions to discover what lies beneath. But this is not the case.

In transformation, people have a real need to perceive their encoded operating system clearly (illumination), to understand how it is comprised and the effect it is having on their life experience (exploration), and to begin questioning its validity in the light of their emerging Self-concept (examination). They will naturally intellectualize what is happening as part of sense-making. And because this mental processing is happening, and it feels heady, a coach can be easily drawn into 'coaching from the head.' However, it's not necessary; it is possible to support people to reveal and explore the limiting ego-patterns which underlie their self-concept without getting caught up intellectually in the process ourselves.

You do not *need* to ask intellect-based questions (although you may ask them). You do not *need* to use techniques or methods to create awareness (although you may use them). You do not *need* to have people delve into their emotions or issues (because 'it sure would be good for them if they did'). The elegance and simplicity of the work stems from the fact that, as people awaken, so much is already bubbling up to the surface *of its own volition*. The inner earthquake is shaking things loose and bringing into awareness, layer by layer, aspects of the self-concept in need of attention. When coaching people on the transformational path, you won't need to go 'digging for pain'; when the readiness is there, new layers will open up naturally, and whatever needs attention will reveal itself.

What people need is a coach who can hold a heart-centered, non-judgmental space in which they can relax enough to go deep within, to feel into and process their inner experiences, to listen for what is real and true, and to sense what is emerging at the core of their being. Your work is not to drive the illumination and exploration process from your intellect. It's all happening already, and despite what you may believe, your intellect is a minor player in the transformation of another person's self-concept, so be willing to relax its grip on your mind and coach from your heart.

Exploring Core Limiting Beliefs in a Session

When we allow ourselves to be open to and investigate these fears, we come to see them and our negative attachment to them, our compulsive warring with them, as a great unkindness to ourselves.

~ Steven Levine, *Unattended Sorrow*

When people begin to explore their self-concept, it is normal to first examine thoughts, emotions, and attitudes honestly and objectively in order to illuminate any limiting beliefs or images that are at play. We all have a myriad of surface-level beliefs such as, 'It's important to protect the environment,' or 'Genetically modified foods are unsafe,' or 'Children should learn to manage money.' While these beliefs affect our life experience, they are different from *core beliefs*, which are the very roots of our self-concept. Core beliefs can be positive or negative, and a person who has developed a healthy self-concept from birth will hold a more positive image of themselves than a person who has not. Even so, during transformation, as the grip of the ego begins to loosen, core limiting beliefs (which are negative and disempowering) will arise into awareness.

For many people, this will be the first time in their lives they have given voice to these painful, ingrained, and often hidden beliefs and images. But there they are, bubbling up to be attended to:

I'm not good enough.

I'm defective.

I'm not worthy.

I'm not important.

I'm not lovable.

I'm helpless.

I don't belong.

I am not safe.

These are the underlying factors which interfere with soul development. They are a key ingredient of emotional pain, and a driver of all sorts of behavior to receive love and validate worth. In transformation, these beliefs begin to reveal themselves in the mind, and we become conscious of what has long been running the show. These untruths (which feel very truthful) are being seen for what they are (less than truthful), and can now be healed.

The process is like weeding the garden of the mind. In transformation, we begin to look at the various beliefs and values and ideologies we've grown up with and challenge their validity:

Is this true?

Is this who I really am?

What happens when I believe this thought?

What is my highest truth?

Does this reflect the nature of reality?

We then begin to weed out those thoughts, perceptions, attitudes and emotions which no longer reflect the higher-order truths our mind is awakening to. Our self-concept can now begin to heal, which stimulates our soul to grow, because there is greater harmony between the self-concept and the soul, which is the truest, deepest part of who we are. 'Wholeness' takes form, as we recognize and feel that our self-concept is aligned with worthiness, and validation arises naturally from within.

When you get to a core limiting belief you and your client will know it; there will be a profound sense that you have touched on something essential. It can sound like this:

Client: I keep feeling like I'm not doing enough, and I know the feeling of not doing enough doesn't serve me.

Coach: Can you say more about that?

Client: There is a part of me that is very hard on myself, believing I'm not doing enough. I've accomplished a lot in my life, but it's always there, this thought that I'm not doing enough.

Coach: [Sensing that something is being revealed, moves into silence. Nothing needs to be said.]

Client: It's hard to admit, but in essence it's always been saying that I'm not enough.

Coach: [Rests in silence—ideally sacred silence.]

Client: This has been a driving factor for a very long time. It's helped me accomplish many things. But it's not who *I am*. It's not me at my core. I think it's something I've built over the years because of my upbringing. It's a voice that has been so loud lately. I try to separate it from me. But I know it's not *me*.

Coach: What are you sensing is true about *you*? [Again moves into silence.]

Client: I'm on the right path. I've always been on the right path. There never has been a wrong path. It's just who I have thought myself to be. My ego has made me so strong, protected me from being hurt, helped me accomplish so many things, but I want to accomplish things now without that ego.

You can hear the strength of Self that emerges when a core limiting belief is seen for what it is. That is what happens when you create a healing space woven of the consciousness of the heart—ego-patterns will surface organically and higher-order truths will reveal themselves.

And while there are things you will do as a coach to help a person increase self-awareness—point out recurring thought patterns, highlight a blind spot, identify core values, reflect back language or perspectives—Deep Coaches don't challenge people to 'see their stuff'—we trust that when given the proper space so much of value will illuminate itself. The most important understanding for working with limiting beliefs you can have is this:

Limiting beliefs naturally arise and dissolve as the mind awakens.

As the light of Self shines within the awakening mind it dissolves all that is unlike itself. A new quality of selfhood then permeates the egoic level of the mind and settles into their being.

Arriving at the Gateway

In a Deep Coaching space, the *energy* of the heart is the optimal substance from which the space is formed, and the *intelligence* of the heart is the optimal source of information (though not the only source). With this fifth practice you have opened the door to the heart and made room in your mind for Spirit to work through you. Your perceptions and actions will now begin to change as you allow into your mind a flow of higher intelligence.

It is the same for those you serve. For them to see how their mental iden-tifications create their moment-by-moment experience is a necessary first step; however, until the heart opens and healing happens, nothing changes significantly. Transformation is more than a change in attitude, belief, or perception; it is a shift in consciousness at a psychic and energy level into a new paradigm of reality.

Your clients may or may not choose to access their heart's intelligence. Or they will step in for a moment before their intellect kicks in and they are swept away in a current of thought. (There is nothing 'wrong' with that; it's only an indication of where they are at.) But you, the coach, must con-sider the heart center as the base from which you venture out, and to which you return, again and again, to connect with the energy and intelligence that is most supportive of the growth of self and soul. When you do this, you are extending an ongoing, implicit invitation to others to meet you in that space.

Now we come to a gateway. All the practices so far have brought us here. Beyond the gateway lies a healing experience, for in transformation that is what is needed above all else. The question is only:

What is the healing experience that wants to happen at the core of being?

To discover the answer, in the next chapter we will embark on a *sensing journey* where we will practice 'presencing' or 'seeing from our deepest source.'

Practice Application

Coach from the Head, Coach from the Heart

In this exercise you will practice coaching first from the head and then from the heart.

Select a person you are coaching and bring to mind a challenging situation he or she is experiencing. If you are not coaching, bring to mind a challenging situation someone close to you is experiencing, and put yourself in a coaching role (inquirer).

You will first 'put on your thinking cap.' Recall as many aspects of the client's situation as you can. Think about the story they told you, including people involved, thoughts, feelings, attitudes, and actions taken (or not taken).

Now begin to coach it from your head. Think through a range of questions you could be asking about the situation in order to coach it. For example: What are your feelings about it? What options do you have? What are you responsible for in this situation? What are you willing to do?

Spend a few minutes in thinking-cap coaching mode, coaching the situation from your head, until you feel ready to step back into an observer role.

When ready to observe, take off your thinking cap and notice what that experience was like. Notice what your thoughts had to say about the situation, the story that formed in your head, the perspectives, opinions, judgements, or solutions you have about the person or situation. Notice as well any feelings, sensations, or energies—both physical and emotional—that were present in you as you worked from your intellect.

Now move into the heart space and coach the situation again, this time from the heart. To begin, take a few breaths and rest your attention in your heart center. With each slow breath, open it up more and more, feeling the relaxation, the spaciousness, the energy, the depth of being.

When you feel ready, again bring to mind the person's situation. But this time, as you do, connect the images and story to your heart center. Visualize the entire situation and hold it within the energies of your heart. Once you sense it nestled in your heart space, begin to coach this situation from your heart.

When you are done, ask yourself:

- What was the difference between the two coaching states?

- How did my coaching approach vary with each?

- Was I challenged in any way to coach from either of those states?

- How do I think a client's experience varies with each state I embody?

CHAPTER FOURTEEN

Practice 6 – Attune to Your Client's Deeper Sense of Self and Let That Lead

The Prime Directive of Deep Coaching is to hold a space which enables a person to connect with their deepest sense of Self, and to make room for Spirit as a transformative agent in the awakening mind. One of the key reasons we uphold the directive is because it frees us from the need for others to be or do what we think is best for them. With this sixth practice, we let go even further of any personal agenda, invite our client's highest potential to speak to us, contemplate the information to be found there, and let that lead the way.

Agendas Are the Shadow Side of Caring

Generally speaking, coaches care for people. We care for their well-being, happiness, and satisfaction with their lives. We desire to see them grow in constructive ways and make choices that are truly good for them. The fact that we care, however, has both a light side and a shadow side. The light side is the tremendously positive impact a coach can have on a transforming life. Coaching is a force for good. It helps change lives for the better, and that is the intent coaches carry. The shadow side of caring, however, is that at times we may believe our clients are errant or misguided in the choices they make, and act on that belief. Our experience, knowledge, or gifts of insight allow us to foresee the outcome of a decision or to see a path overlooked, and in that moment we intervene. Because we care, and because we desire to help people to the best of our ability, we step in and begin to lead.

Whenever we choose to influence a person's thought process in a certain direction our agenda is showing. This is not a 'bad' thing, as our agenda is oftentimes an extension of our care for the well-being of another, however having an agenda can be problematic when it takes over and begins to lead. Deep Coaches forge spiritual partnerships, and as Elyse Hope Killoran writes in *Conscious Evolution Through Spiritual Partnering*:

> "Spiritual partners choose to believe that our higher selves (in partnership with God/the Universe) are deliberately attracting people, circumstances and events to us so that we may have ample opportunities to grow into our best selves."

If we can trust a person's higher Self to guide their life, we can also trust its ability to lead a session. How liberating is that! When we attune to our client's deeper sense of Self and let that lead, we can let go of our agenda, our wants, our hopes, our *will* for them. No longer do we need a particular path to be taken, a specific decision to be made, a breakthrough to happen, or something hidden to be seen. Instead, we attune to that which *knows* what is needed in any moment and foster that forth. To quote Elyse Hope Killoran again:

> "In every interaction, spiritual partners must leave ego-agendas at the door and invoke a higher path."

Each person has a different relationship with his or her deepest Self, and those who are more connected will inevitably make choices more reflective of that relationship than those who are not. *But that doesn't actually matter in the Deep Coaching process.* When our focus on upholding the Prime Directive is consistent, it does not matter where our clients are at in terms of their own inner relationship. Our role is to make room for the light of the Self and the action of Spirit to operate freely in the mind. We do this by slowing it all down, syncing with the rhythm of life, weaving in spiritual energy, opening the pathways of the heart, and listening deeply for *what wants to happen*, beneath all the drama and mental hubbub, at the core of being. This is how Deep Coaches express care, not through personal agendas.

Four Levels of Listening

In his book *Theory U: Leading from the Future as it Emerges,* Otto Scharmer describes four levels of listening. His fourth level is particularly salient for Deep Coaches, as this is the level of listening we aim for.

Four Levels of Listening

Listening 1: **from Habits**	**Downloading** Habits of Judgment	Reconfirming old opinions & judgments	
Listening 2: **from Outside**	**Factual** Noticing Differences	Disconfirming (new) data	Open Mind
Listening 3: **from Within**	**Empathic** Emotional Connection	Seeing through another person's eyes	Open Heart
Listening 4: **from Source**	**Generative** From the future wanting to emerge	Connecting to an emerging future and whole: shift in identity & self	Open Will

Level 1: Downloading – "Yeah, I know that already."

This level of listening is cosmetic—you listen for surface-level facts and information to confirm what you already know. It's pseudo-listening, and doesn't get a coach far.

Level 2: Factual Listening – "Ooh, look at that!"

The second level is conversational listening. You are listening primarily to respond as you would in a good conversation—you notice interesting things people are saying, give an opinion on something you agree or disagree with, and generally listen more objectively, which allows new information to come in beyond your own opinions, judgments, and world view. It requires an open mind, which is a prerequisite in a coach.

Level 3: Empathic Listening – "Oh, yes, I know how you feel."

This is the level of listening where good coaching resides. Through Empathic listening you step into another's shoes and become mentally and emotionally engaged with what they are saying and experiencing. It happens when you listen from outside your own boundaries and let go of your agenda, which requires not only an open mind but an open heart as well. The limitation of Empathic listening is that it still implies that 'you're over there and I'm over here, listening to you.' Deep Coaches aim to go beyond that sense of separation.

Level 4: Generative Listening – "I can't explain what I just experienced."

Otto Scharmer describes Generative listening this way:

> "I can't express what I experience in words. My whole being has slowed down. I feel more quiet and present and more my real self. I am connected to something larger than myself. It moves beyond the current field and connects to a still deeper

realm of emergence. We no longer empathize with someone in front of us. We are in an altered state—maybe 'communion' or 'grace' is a word that comes closest to the texture of this experience. You know you have been operating out of this fourth level when, at the end of the conversation, you realize you are no longer the same person you were when you started the conversation. You have connected to a deeper source—to the source of who you really are and to a sense of why you are here—a connection that links you with a profound field of coming into being, with your emerging authentic Self."

As Otto Scharmer attests to, this level of listening is challenging to express in words. You will know you are there when everything seems to slow down, as though you are becoming free from experiencing time. There is an altogether different quality of connection with one another than is experienced in daily interactions; a sense of oneness will arise, as the ego falls away, and your sense of self will merge into another as two (or more) become as one. You will no longer be listening from either your own reference point or another's viewpoint, but from a field of potentiality connected to a deeper source. Otto Scharmer has created a word for this level of connection: "presencing," a word formed from 'presence' and 'sensing.' Presencing is a form of perception, of "seeing from our deepest source." Presencing is when people "connect with a deeper source of creativity and knowing and move beyond the patterns of the past. They step into their real power, the power of their authentic Self."

Presencing is a necessary pre-condition for the Deep Coach to access the emerging potentials in another human being. As you open your mind and heart and *will* (which is to let go of any agenda), you activate your ability to perceive from your deepest source. And when you connect to the source of your being, you are able to connect to and perceive an existing whole in others: their deepest sense of Self.

This sixth practice is about learning to listen generatively and to engage in presencing. In essence, you are learning to adopt a consciousness of oneness, where you recognize that every single thing is an aspect of an infinite field of consciousness. At this level, there is no separation between coach and client, only two individuations of consciousness dancing within the unified field which connects everything in creation. As John Lennon put it, "I am he, as you are he, as you are me, and we are all together."

We Are Like Radios

What does it mean to 'attune' to the deeper Self? One analogy for conceptualizing the attunement process is that human beings are like radios; a radio receives and converts information sent out by a transmitter. But first we need to recognize that every person is a living, breathing, walking, talking transmitter. The body, mind, and soul are all 'communication devices' ceaselessly transmitting physical, mental, emotional, and spiritual information into the world. Floating around in the air is every possible attitude, idea, philosophy, mood, value, and energy, in an infinitude of frequencies and wavelengths. And since we are like radios, we receive and interpret the information being transmitted.

There was a time when the primitive peoples and tribes of the world lived in a relatively harmonious state with nature and Spirit, listening to its rhythms and cycles, adjusting their lives to align with those transmissions. Young children were taught from an early age to tune in to the nurturing heartbeat of Mother Earth, to sense in her life's essential lessons. And they were taught to listen for the voice of Spirit within themselves and in nature around them. In our fast-paced, technology-driven society this ability to attune to those subtler transmissions has all but been lost. We are inundated with information but no longer taught from a young age to listen deeply within for what is real and true.

In Deep Coaching, we are attempting to revive the dying art of spiritual attunement—with ourselves, others, and the world we inhabit. The information is there and available to us, but we need to calibrate our mind to perceive its finer frequencies amidst the onslaught of physical, mental and emotional information competing for our attention.

Begin Attuning to Yourself

The most effective method for learning the art of attuning to another person's deeper Self is to develop the ability to attune to your own. It's good to know yourself at a soul level, for soul is the essence of who you are. You are not the ego-based self, nor the personality you know through an examination of your talents and strengths and preferences; you are unlimited spirit. But your awareness of this has been buried beneath a lifetime of conditioning and erroneous self-knowledge. Now it is time to know who you are, in reality.

How do you attune to your deepest Self?

The answer is: in the quiet and stillness of your mind. Remember, you are not your thoughts nor the images of yourself that your thoughts project, and you will not be sensed within them. You will be sensed in the space between your thoughts, in the energy currents of your spiritual heart.

Sit quietly or in meditation and ask with the deepest of sincerity: "Who am I?" This question carries a powerful vibration, and opens a channel to Spirit. Here you will detect a powerful force, one that is familiar and yet altogether new. It strips away the story you have come to believe and reveals the god-like essence that you are. This is YOU. And it is arising in your awakened mind so that you may come to know the grandeur of your true nature.

Your soul has a frequency which is distinctly different from your physical and emotional energy vibrations. Do not be concerned if at first you find it difficult to attune to it or are unsure of what you are listening for. When you sit quietly with yourself, set the intention, ask the question, and attune to the frequencies of Spirit, you will start to perceive. The more you practice, the more proficient you will become at sensing this frequency.

The voice of your true Self is always there, a whisper in the mind, a love song in the heart, inviting you to know yourself as you are. Learn to monitor throughout your day what your mind is attuned to. Soon enough you will cherish the sounds emanating from the higher realms as they uplift your whole being. You will begin to perceive yourself in the way that Spirit perceives you, and to make choices which reflect the recognition of your authentic Self. In turn, this ability will enable you to better attune to the transmissions of another person's deeper Self, for at that level all is one.

Attune to Your Client's Deeper Sense of Self

When people come for transformational coaching, most likely they have not developed the ability to attune to their deepest sense of Self. Likely they will be aware that something within is shifting significantly; however, given the grip the old self-concept can have, any sense of the deeper Self can be like a whiff of smoke in the wind: something is there, but what it signals is unclear. Until they have developed this capacity for themselves (which will happen organically as you work together in this way), your role is to sense into what is happening at the deeper level and allow it to lead.

Tuning into a person's deeper Self is not the same as tuning into mental, physical, or emotional energy. Energy has different forms, and some are easier to detect than others. Emotional energy, the 'vibe' we give off, is readily detectable. It is the same with physical energy—when someone is energized or exhausted, it shows. Energy in its most subtle form is spiritual. The essence of who we are, our Self and soul, is pure energy oscillating at a certain vibrational frequency, and is experienced viscerally as an impulse to 'be Thyself.' Attuning to the deeper Self is, however, about more than attuning to its frequency—though this is where the practice begins—it's about accessing the *information* available at that level. In other words, your client's deeper Self is communicating ceaselessly what is needed and no longer needed on her quest to strip away the sheaths of her conditioned self so that she may stand soul bare. How is that possible? Because, as Elyse Hope Killoran wrote in *Spiritual Partnering*:

> "Spiritual partners hold the awareness that they are connecting, simultaneously, on the level of personality and soul."

It is helpful to trust this connection, and to learn to discern, through the pathways of the heart, the subtle transmissions emanating from that deeper realm of being. As you practice attuning, with open mind, open heart, open will, you will begin to sense what is needed, what is being called for at the soul level in another person. In time, you will develop a new ability, a 'sensing muscle,' one attuned to the energy field of potentiality emanating from a deeper source.

What Are You Listening For?

Within a session, begin by nurturing a healing space in which both you and your client are able to relax and quieten the mental chatter. Create the sanctuary and anchor in. Now listen deeply into the space of their deeper Self. If it helps, invite Spirit to show you what you need to know or perceive.

On the surface level you will be listening to the story: their words, thoughts, perceptions, attitudes and emotions. This is necessary information so that you can empathize with their current experience and begin to discern what is happening with their evolving self-concept. However, you are simultaneously attuning to their deeper Self, and listening for insight into these two questions:

> What wants to happen at the core of being?

> What experience is there a readiness for?

These are the essential 'tuning in' questions that you ask yourself throughout the session, even as you engage with the content being shared at the surface level. Can you sense wants to happen at the core of their being? And can you let that guide you as you hold a space for the person to go even deeper within themselves to explore the reality of their self-concept?

Pay attention to any insights, sensations, or energies that you perceive. It's a 'sensing journey,' a bit like going deep into a dark cave with only your hands and feet to guide you—you have to learn to trust what your other senses pick up when you cannot see clearly.

Attuning to what is happening at the core of your client's being influences how you listen to the surface level information: you become adept at noticing what is being said that could be a *doorway* to a deeper exploration. Let this question guide how you then engage with the person:

> What's the one thing you can say or do that will open them
> up a little more to their own deeper realm?

Perhaps you point out a meaningful word or phrase. Perhaps you highlight a pattern or connect contrasting thoughts. Perhaps you let there be silence.

Remember, your work as a Deep Coach is primarily to hold space for the shift in being the person is *ready* to have. But in order to do that, you have to discern what the desired experience is, and whether the person is actually ready for it. They may not be ready to move beyond mental exploration into the realm of being. It takes time and effort to unravel the workings of the mind, to see what's really going on beneath the story, to understand what the emotional experience is pointing to, and you have to be patient and provide plenty of space for that self-discovery. Although you may sense 'what wants to happen,' it cannot become your agenda that that *should* happen. Rather, the opposite is true: to attune to another person's deepest sense of Self you release your agenda, listen deeply through the pathways of the heart, and allow what you perceive to influence how you engage with them. Keep it spacious and open, so that as the session progresses, what wants to happen can reveal itself within your client's awakening mind, just as it has in yours.

Where will it lead?

Here we come face-to-face with an existential truth: the yearning of the soul is the same for all humanity. The soul yearns for love and loving experiences. Love is our natural state of being. Loving experiences are soul food. And love heals. When you listen deeply for the song of the soul, you will notice this universal pattern: it is calling for a healing experience.

To heal is to release all that stands in the way of true Self-knowing. The question is only which form the healing experience will take. Recall from Chapter 6 that healing can be experienced as an act of *letting go* (the ego-patterns which form our limiting self-concept) or an act of *letting come* (awareness of oneself as whole and complete, as I Am). In a session, as you attune to your client's deeper Self, can you discern which of these healing pathways there is a readiness for? What wants to happen on the inner plane? Is it an act of letting go, letting come, or both?

A Gateway Practice

This sixth Deep Coaching practice thus becomes a 'gateway' practice. The first five practices create the optimal conditions in which transformation unfolds naturally and organically, and lay the foundation for accessing the realm of the deeper Self. These are foundational practices, and are the bedrock of what it takes to hold space for transformation. Now with Practice 6 we sense into the deeper realm of Self and soul to help *reveal the healing experience desired in order to accelerate transformation.*

When you sense a readiness to let go of some aspect of self that is 'no longer,' you will take the gate leading to Practice 7: Expand Your Capacity to Be with Pain and Allow Healing Moments. When there is a readiness to experience more of the magnificence of the true Self, then you will take the gate leading to Practice 8: Foster the Emergence of What Wants to

Happen. In some situations, both experiences will be desired. Remember, it is not your choice to make. As you stand at the gateway, you must let go of your agenda, your 'will' or desire for people to have a certain experience because you know how good it will be for them. Remain wide open to being shown which direction to take, and then move that way slowly yet with confidence.

The shift that is ready to happen will reveal itself when you listen in the right way. This is a real challenge, as there is no neon billboard in the sky pointing the way. You are learning to attune to subtle vibrations of energy, to sense portals of possibility opening, nudging you in a certain direction. The deeper Self has its own unique energy and vibration, and you will need to get a feel for what that is. One Deep Coaching student described connecting with it this way: "When I tune into others I experience their imprints. I know I am there because my heart is filled with the most delicious feeling of love."

While this sixth practice may at first seem esoteric, it will prove to be essential for being-level transformation. There will be plenty of times when you are uncertain whether what you are picking up is 'mine' or 'theirs.' Do not be concerned, as this is normal when learning the art of attunement. You may spend some time trying to figure it out, however at some point you will need to let that go and trust whatever insight comes up. Trust is a must for this practice. Let go of concern and 'trying to figure it out' and simply allow yourself to drop back into that inner space of soul connection. You can always ask Spirit or your own inner guidance to show you the way. Then relax and trust that whenever there is an intention for a relationship to serve the highest good of all concerned, everything is already in motion, unfolding of its own volition within dimensions of mind scarcely comprehensible, and what needs to be known will be made known, *when the time is right.*

Practice Application

Three Exercises to Learn to Attune

Bear Witness

Take an object you have available, and simply begin to observe the object. See how long you can sustain a state of observation, where your sole purpose is to bear witness.

As you do this, sense the connection you have with that object, as you become aware of the energy field you share. If your mind wanders, bring it back to the point of observation.

Another form of this practice is to sit in observation of another person. In silence, connect to Spirit, and then attune to the essence of the other person. As you bear witness, notice what arises within you.

Tuning In Moments

This exercise invites you to practice attuning to the people around you by sitting in quiet observation. These 'tuning in moments' take anything from a few seconds to a few minutes, and can be done with people in your vicinity or distant from you.

Start by centering yourself so you don't feel overwhelmed. Affirm your intention to honor the person as you would a spiritual partner, to stay in a space of detachment and non-judgment with whatever you pick up. Still your mind, breathe, and focus on the person.

If the person is visible to you, begin by observing their movement, posture, or gestures. Then tune into their emotional and physical energy. Next, go a little deeper—and you may choose to close your eyes at this point—and sense into their interior: their needs, temperament, desires, expectations. Finally, drop below it all and attune to their deeper sense of Self, the voice or vibration of their soul.

What do you experience as you shift your focus? What do you pick up? What impressions come to mind?

Practice attuning to others whenever you have the opportunity. Notice the impressions you receive as well as the interpretations you make of those impressions. Attuning well takes practice, like building a little-used muscle, so keep at it.

Prepare for a Session

A few minutes before a session, close your eyes, calm your mind, connect to your heart center, and tune into your client. Do this by bringing their name to mind and holding it in your heart space. Ask Spirit to show you what you need to know. Then simply allow images and impressions to come to mind.

When you feel complete, open your eyes and let it all go. Move into your session, staying open to what is happening in the moment.

At the end of the session, notice if there was congruence between the impressions you picked up prior to your session and what happened during the session. You can even discuss this with your client.

CHAPTER FIFTEEN

Practice 7 – Expand Your Capacity to Be with Pain and Allow Healing Moments

Part I: Expand Your Capacity to Be with Pain

Heaven knows we need never be ashamed of our tears, for they are rain upon the blinding dust of earth, overlying our hard hearts. I was better after I had cried, than before…

~ Charles Dickens, *Great Expectations*

The hero's journey is by no means easy; all along the way we are tested. Challenge, frustration, doubt, fear, sorrow are constant companions, and we must overcome both inner and outer obstacles in order to prevail. The inner journey is one of Self-actualization: from fear to love, from doubt to trust, from ego to essence; to 'die before we die to know there is no death.' This transition is rarely if ever painless. Ego-patterns loom larger than ever; resistance rears its head; painful emotions long buried resurface—all creating an inner tension necessary to stimulate the evolution of our self-concept from one that is ego-based to one that is soul-based.

With this seventh practice we have arrived at the very heart of what Deep Coaching is about: facilitating *healing experiences* that shift ways of being and accelerate transformation. All previous practices have laid the foundation for this potential to actualize in a coaching session.

There are two interrelated aspects to learn, and I have devoted one chapter to each:

> **1.) Expanding your capacity to be with pain.** This is intended to help you hold space for the expression of painful emotions and energy.
>
> **2.) Allowing healing moments.** This will enable you to facilitate healing experiences of ego-patterns and core limiting beliefs.

What Is Pain?

In the Deep Coaching context, the word 'pain' encompasses more than feelings of hurt or suffering alone. Pain includes:

- the *negative emotions* experienced as a result of ego-based mental and emotional patterns

- the *negative energy field* (also known as the 'pain body') born of past negative emotional experiences long held within the mind and body

- our *'shadow'*—a Jungian psychology term for that side of our personality comprised of our most negative human impulses like greed, jealousy, hate, pride, and thirst for power or recognition.

We all have emotions; feelings are a natural part of who we are. So when emotions arise in a coaching context there is much wisdom to be gained from expressing them.

Negative emotion is a particularly strong and unpleasant feeling, and it seems obvious that if you are in pain, you know it, right? While this is often true, most people have a surprising amount of pain within themselves and their energy systems that remains covered up and hidden from view. This is our 'pain body' (or 'shadow'). The pain is there, alive and well, but it is repressed or denied in order for people to function 'normally' and get on with daily life. It also includes the unattended sorrow of past disappointments, hurt, abuse, humiliation, shame, and trauma that we have repressed, denied, or disowned, and which we carry through life like a bag of bricks until it is attended to.

In transformation, pain born of the past will present itself for that attention. This is normal, natural, and embraced in Deep Coaching, as attending to pain both heals and accelerates transformation. When we avoid or repress pain rather than attend to it, we hold ourselves back from growing into the fullness of Self at the core of our being.

It may never be possible to be free of pain completely (our ego-patterns are deeply entrenched); however, transformation has the potential to shake loose much that offers little benefit to our evolving self-concept. It is as though our soul knows that growth into a more integrated and whole human being requires acknowledgment and releasing of even the most painful personal baggage. Deep Coaches nurture a healing space so that people can be their most authentic and vulnerable selves, free to express and be with pain, as they move to release, transmute, or dissolve it.

Expanding your capacity to be with pain is an essential transformative practice. Why? Firstly, because an expansive capacity to be with pain enables you to hold space for any negative emotions and energies that arise during a coaching session. And secondly, because your capacity for being with negative emotions is naturally smaller than it is for positive emotions. Deep Coaches have as expansive a capacity for being with negative, painful emotions as they do for positive, enlivening emotions. If you are uncomfortable being with the negative emotion or energy your client expresses, in all likelihood you will find a way to shift the conversation to close it down or avoid it altogether, and opportunities will be lost. Even if you have an expansive capacity to be with another's pain, if you don't know what to *do* with it, if you are not used to attending to it, the same thing can happen. As you work with this practice, you will develop the capacity to be with the pain that invariably arises in transformation and attend to it in a healing manner.

Pain Thresholds

Each of us has an upper limit for the amount of another person's pain we are able to withstand, though that limit will vary by person and circumstance. Whenever that limit is crossed, we begin to feel uncomfortable. For example, there are people who are highly sensitive to conflict, and any conflict around them triggers a reaction of anxiety. The moment that anxiety arises, they may try to stop or resolve the conflict—not necessarily because they are concerned for the people in the conflict (though they may be), but because ending the conflict is the surest way to reduce their own inner angst.

It's helpful to get a feel for where your upper limits are and how they can be raised. That way, if you find yourself in the face of strong emotional pain, you can hold space for its expression without being triggered into running away or closing it down because it makes you feel uncomfortable.

Moment of Pause

Awareness of Your Pain Thresholds

How would you describe your capacity to be with your own pain? What do you normally do when it arises?

Are there certain people with whom your ability to withstand their pain is greater than with others? If so, why is that?

Are there situations where your limit is lower than in others? Why is that?

What is needed to expand your capacity to be with pain, in all cases?

Discomfort with Pain

Why do we become uncomfortable in the face of another's pain?

Partly, it is what we were taught by our parents and other adults. Watch a young child on the playground cry, and then observe how the other children respond. Most likely you'll see the other children simply getting on with playing, hardly fazed or affected by the child's expression of pain. Young children have a seemingly unlimited tolerance for being with each other's pain. Naturally, the child's parents will offer comfort—it's what parents are wired to do—however it is not uncommon to see an embarrassed parent try to hush their child if the expression of pain goes on a little 'too long' or a little too fervently. (This can happen with exuberant emotions as well.) Somewhere along the way, through these types of adult-child interactions, we learn to stifle our pain (or joy) because it makes adults feel uncomfortable.

Pain is also often seen as a sign of weakness, not strength. Whenever we interpret pain as a sign of weakness, it closes down our capacity to just be with that pain or allow it full expression. Experiencing and expressing our frailty is an integral part of the human growth process—we all experience moments of weakness and pain, and we must experience them in order to grow. And when we are given opportunities to express that vulnerability we come to appreciate the strength that lies within it.

Expanding your capacity to be with pain starts with the awareness that your discomfort with pain can stem from a history of stifling your own expression of pain (because it makes others uncomfortable), coupled with the belief that pain is a sign of weakness (and it's risky to appear vulnerable).

As you let go of these beliefs and see pain as a naturally occurring phenomenon that results whenever a person experiences some sort of hurt or disappointment, then the expression of pain becomes merely a reflection of the emotional body and not an indication of any kind of personal weakness or inherent flaw.

In Deep Coaching conversations, pain is seen as a gift, something to lean into and given safe quarters to be expressed. If you, the coach, exhibit discomfort with its presence, there is a chance it will be stuffed away again and go unattended. This is detrimental to the transformational process, where attending to pain is necessary for healing into wholeness.

Moment of Pause

Observe Your Triggers

Bring to mind a few situations where another person's expression of emotional pain triggered in you a negative reaction such as discomfort, anger, anxiety, annoyance, frustration, the need to escape etc.

How did you react in each of those moments?

What was the trigger? Why could you not handle it?

What does this say about your overall capacity to be with pain?

Pain Is a Call for Love

How can you support healing if you are triggered by or fear the expression of pain?

A Course in Miracles teaches that all behaviors and emotions are either a call for love or an extension of love. Pain is a call for love. And when you see that pain is neither a weakness nor something to be feared, but rather a call for love, you can meet that call through your own expression of compassion and empathy. This is how you expand your capacity to be with pain.

Allow pain the space to arise and be expressed in your sessions. Practice seeing it for what it is, a call for love, and respond not from your past conditioning but from your spiritual heart, which knows that pain is an opportunity to extend loving compassion and to draw closer to another person. In those moments, a field of unity consciousness is formed as the *call* for love meets the *extension* of love.

Be Like the Palm Tree

Whom do you choose to be in the face of another person's pain?

There is no tree better designed to withstand the tempestuous winds of a hurricane than the palm—its upper reaches flex and bend while its trunk remains fixed and well-grounded. A strong steel pole can also withstand the raging winds of a hurricane, yet there is something about the way the palm responds to the hurricane that makes it a fitting analogy for a Deep Coach. The steel pole, standing rigid and straight, wavering only slightly in the wind, seems cold, detached, almost resistant; the palm, on the other hand, flexing and bending just the right amount, seems to become one with the storm.

The analogy is not perfect—even the most resilient palm and pole will come crashing down under the right conditions—but you can see where it's going. When you're in the winds of your client's emotions you can be like the rigid pole or the flexing palm. As the pole, you may come across as unfeeling and detached; as the palm, you may appear empathetic and connected. Being unyielding in the wind can help you retain a sense of equanimity, but it is not the ideal stance of the Deep Coach. Deep Coaches are like the palm: we may come through the winds of emotion feeling a little battered, perhaps even a bit weathered, but we have learned to flex in the wind and to *be* at peace with it all.

In What Are You Grounded?

One characteristic of the palm tree that makes it particularly resilient in the face of harsh conditions is its wide network of fibrous roots. The roots grow in layers, and the layers hold a tremendous amount of soil, becoming very heavy, and forming an almost immovable anchor for the tree. This root system grounds the palm, enabling it to withstand forceful winds without being uprooted. Like the palm, regardless of the type or intensity of emotional energy around you, being grounded helps you manage your own state of being and expands your capacity to be with pain.

Envision this scenario: You are sitting across from a client who is high-strung and emits nervous energy. He sits on the edge of his chair, one leg twitching under the table, his eyes darting around the room as he speaks. He has a rapid-fire way of expressing himself; staccato bursts which convey authority and rightness. The energy and emotion he exhibits feels hard and pointed, and you notice yourself becoming tense. Your breathing becomes shallow, your neck muscles stiffen, and you feel the undeniable urge to stand up and walk out, if only to get a breath of air. Soon you become so distracted by that thought that you are no longer able to listen intently to him.

Situations like this do not bode well for a coach. When you find yourself taking on the negative emotions or energies of your clients, you can lose your grounding and be knocked off balance. The reality is, everyone is susceptible to other people's emotions and energies, even when unaware of it. (Some people are highly sensitive, or empathic, and pick up other people's feelings and energies easily.) If you are unaware that your own inner state can be influenced this way, you can mistakenly perceive someone else's stuff as your own, wondering why you suddenly feel tense, irritable, or down.

The solution to remaining free of other people's emotional and energy states is to learn to ground yourself. Grounding is an excellent self-care practice. Being in the presence of pain can wear you down, and you may feel discomfort at an emotional or physical level (some discomfort is okay; it's a signal of your learning edge, that your current threshold for pain can be moved), however when you are grounded that discomfort affects you only at a surface level, not at your core. The question is:

In what are you grounded?

In Deep Coaching we recognize that Spirit is the life force at the heart of transformation. So it follows that we would seek to ground in Spirit. Grounding in Spirit shifts reliance for our equilibrium to a power source far beyond our singular abilities. When we ground in Spirit, we connect with a vast well of life-giving energy, allowing us to be fully present in the moment rather than adversely affected by another's pain. The well of strength to which you are anchored will flow from your core up through your entire being, allowing you to flex in the wind while remaining balanced and unaffected at your core.

Learning to ground in Spirit, and by extension your own essence energy, requires conscious, dedicated effort. If you are wondering how it is done, you can always start with the first five Deep Coaching practices—they are designed to encourage you to enhance your spiritual connectivity. On the Internet you will find a myriad of other grounding practices to try, and some will work better for you than others. If ever you are unsure what to do, or your grounding feels shaky, you can always turn to your inner guidance: "I need support and I ask you to show me what I need in this moment," or, "What is the most loving thing I can do now for myself and this person?" Then sit quietly for a moment and allow yourself to receive the insight needed. This is a mighty spiritual practice to form, knowing that you are supported and guided always.

Practice Application

Conscious Breathing

The breath is a vital aspect of staying grounded and balanced no matter what kind of energy you are around. Think of the breath as that which supports the movement of your core life force energy up through your entire being. Breath flows in a continuous cycle moving energy from your depths up to the surface level and back down to the depths, unifying it all.

Deep Coaching sessions are full of breath.

- Begin to observe your breath in your coaching sessions.

- Notice how your breathing changes over the course of the session.

- Notice when you become aware of your breath, and when you lose that awareness.

'Conscious breathing' means to take some purposeful, visible breaths, the kind your client may notice. You do not have to invite them to join you, simply take a deep breath and allow your relaxed exhalation to be heard.

Do this a few times and observe how conscious breathing affects your client, the conversation, and the entire coaching space.

Heal Your Own Pain First

Being triggered by someone else's pain is always a signpost to something within yourself in need of healing. What happens when you get into a conversation and you feel anxious or tense because the person's negative energy is coming at you? What have they really done? Answer: they have acted as a catalyst to awaken you. When you look at it closely, you'll find it's not so much the other person's pain causing your discomfort as it is your own unresolved issues. What's going to help stop you from being affected by another's negative emotions and energy is to take a serious look at those issues. Everybody else's pain will be the problem until you go within yourself and start healing your own.

> "When we make peace with our shadow, our lives transform. We no longer have to pretend to be someone we're not. We no longer have to prove we're good enough. We no longer have to live in fear. Instead, as we find the gifts of our shadow and revel in all the glory of the true Self, we finally find the freedom to create the life we have always desired."

> ~ Deepak Chopra, Debbie Ford and Marianne Williamson,
> *The Shadow Effect*

Remember, the greatest gift you can give the world is that of your own transformation. Supporting others to heal their pain starts with you being willing to face your own, which means healing yourself. Whenever you feel the pull of your own ego causing you doubt, worry, turmoil, or fear, do not cut yourself off from the pain; allow yourself to be with it, to feel it without judgment, to invite Spirit into your mind so that you may see the shadows through the lens of understanding, compassion, and forgiveness.

As you heal, you become lighter in being, and your ability to be present to someone else's pain will increase significantly. There will be less for the pain to trigger in you, less for it to 'stick to.' And any urge to fix or take away their pain will too diminish, as you stand strong as a loving presence.

Practice Application
Expanding Awareness of Your Pain Threshold
There may still be a part of you which is affected by the appearance of strong or painful emotions, and that is perfectly okay. You can expand your awareness around this, and when you do so you have taken a first step in expanding your capacity to be with it.

Throughout the day, observe your reaction to people who exhibit strong emotions (positive or negative). What changes occur inside of you? What thoughts go through your head? What emotions do you feel? How does your body react?

Notice if you start feeling uncomfortable, or desire to get away from it or close it down.

What happens in those moments to your ability to stay grounded and centered in that situation? What happens to your capacity to just be with the other person's emotion?

Notice if you are resisting what is happening, and what happens when you resist.

You may also notice that something altogether different wants to happen for you, something in service of connection or healing. *What wants to happen within you that is of your deepest (or higher) Self?*

CHAPTER SIXTEEN

Practice 7 - Expand Your Capacity to Be with Pain and Allow Healing Moments

Part 2: Allow Healing Moments

A healer is not someone that you go to for healing. A healer is someone who triggers within you, your own ability to heal yourself.

~ Anonymous

With awakening comes the desire for healing into wholeness. The limiting and erroneous beliefs of the old self-concept will bubble up and present themselves in the conscious mind for attention. Possibly for the first time in their lives, those in transformation will acknowledge the limiting effect of their shadow and how it holds them back from stepping fully into their emerging selfhood. They will be open and vulnerable in ways they have never been before. And they will look to you, the Deep Coach, to support their healing process with confidence and certainty.

The first part of Practice 7 helps you develop an expansive capacity to be with pain so that it can be freely expressed, as it is—but then what? The second part, Allow Healing Moments, is how a Deep Coach supports a person to heal. The questions addressed are:

> How can you support a person to heal their ego-based self-concept?

> How do you engage with pain and core limiting beliefs?

> How do you facilitate a healing moment?

Healing moments are just that—times when healing occurs. And it is a key role of the Deep Coach to facilitate these experiences *within a session*. The capability and willingness to allow healing moments differentiates Deep Coaching from other coaching approaches. Instead of helping a person to think through and design actions to heal themselves *outside* the coaching space, we make room for healing *within* the coaching space.

Clarifying the Role of the Deep Coach

If the idea that the role of a Deep Coach is to allow healing moments causes you concern, there are two points I'd like to reiterate. The first is that you do not have to be or see yourself as a 'healer' to do this work. Your capacity to support healing begins with who you are being—*your being is your doing*. You do not need to know specific healing techniques to facilitate healing experiences (although if you do, it is possible to combine them with Deep Coaching). Deep Coaching is itself a healing modality, and *all you need to know and do lies within the nine practices*. What matters is your willingness to be a loving presence, for this alone is what positions a Deep Coach as a healer.

The second point is that Deep Coaching is not therapy, and you do not need to know any therapeutic techniques or methods. We are not treating emotional or psychological disorders, and we are not helping people to remedy, cure, or recover from anything. There is nothing 'wrong with,' nothing dysfunctional about, those with whom we are working. The arising of pain in transformation is the most natural, functional thing in the world. It may be deeply uncomfortable, but it is not dysfunction. Deep Coaches attend to pain as a way to accelerate a process that is unfolding of its own volition, so that people can move forward into a desired state of being and a new paradigm of reality.

It takes discernment to determine what is really going on for a person. People mask dysfunctions, hide addictions, or present their pain as something it's not. Some people are habituated to being in a state of pain, so much so that it becomes part of their self-concept. The parent who has lost a child, for instance, who has become so crippled by the pain that it dominates his life for years; the story becomes a preoccupation and keeps him stuck in the grieving process. Over time it takes away his own understanding of who he is: "Who would I be without this hurt I carry?" For others, talking about their pain and suffering is the end game—conversations constantly return to it, and they exhibit little will to move beyond it—and they see in their coach a sympathetic ear to turn to for comfort. It is good to be a compassionate presence for those in pain—at times people simply don't know how to grow beyond it—but it's important to recognize that although Deep Coaching can be therapeutic, it is not therapy.

The Limits of Inquiry

The great challenge all coaches face when working with core limiting beliefs and the pain body is how deep within mind and body this stuff resides.

How do you let go of a belief that has been with you since childhood, that is wedded to the fabric of your identity, encoded in your operating system, alive in every cell of your body? Is it really as straightforward as identifying the belief and then affirming something different as your truth?

Conventional coaching approaches examine belief systems through inquiry, which is a natural starting point in any change process. (As I mentioned in Chapter 13, retracing our steps to get clear on how our internal operating system has been programmed is a normal part of the revelation and exploration process.) Yet it's possible to spend years inquiring into these patterns and make little progress beyond them. Ego-patterns go deep—they are rooted in the unconscious mind and give rise to personal fields of consciousness—and this is where coaching bumps up against the limitations of inquiry. Inquiry can illuminate the patterns of the mind, bringing more into conscious awareness, but inquiry alone cannot heal them. The beliefs are too deeply encoded.

Through inquiry, Seth revealed (see *Seth's Story,* Chapter 6) the self-talk pattern that had been the subtle soundtrack to his life: "I'm not good enough if I don't meet other people's expectations of me." He also recognized the effects of that belief: he strove for career success because he had a constant need for validation that he was meeting those expectations. Although he frequently did meet other people's expectations, the validation he received was always short-lived, and soon he found himself striving for his next accomplishment just to feel good enough.

He was also able to identify an empowering belief: "I am good enough, as I am." The challenge was, as he said to me:

> "I love it, but I have not made it my truth. I'm now aware of
> the belief that I have to meet other people's expectations to be
> good enough, but I have to say, I have no idea how to release
> it. It's been with me for so long. My purpose in life has been
> to achieve to feel good. So intellectually I understand the truth
> that I am good enough even when I don't achieve, but I don't
> really feel it and I don't live it. How do I get out of this 'not
> good enough' state? How do I prove to myself that I am good
> enough? How do I change this very strong, hardwired belief?
> I have tried so many ways."

He was aware of both the core limiting belief and the pain it was causing him; he just didn't know how to release it, and he didn't feel a strong connection with the higher truth (though it was kindled). This is no small bump in the road—it is the single greatest challenge to the transformative process. Intellectually knowing 'I am good enough' is a wonderful starting point because falsity has been consciously met by truth, and the emotional release that accompanies it is cathartic, but it does not penetrate to the same depth as *releasing* the belief and *healing* the pain body.

As coaches, what then do we do, when we reach the limits of inquiry?

This is where Deep Coaching offers a path forward. Through inquiry we have brought the ego-patterns into conscious awareness and begun to question their validity. Through these actions things have already begun to unravel as the mind reorients towards a greater reality. But our work is not done. Now it is time to allow healing, and to heal we must learn to *experience* ourselves as the consciousness we are—we must be willing to move beyond inquiry and beyond examination, into *being*.

Listen for the Desired Experience

For a moment, let's return to Practice 6, where we are learning the essential practice of attuning to a client's deeper sense of Self and discerning what wants to happen at that level. Deep Coaches are always listening into the deeper realm, asking:

> What is the desired experience?

> What is there a readiness for?

Readiness means a person is receptive (open mind, open heart, open will) to experiencing a higher truth about the nature of themselves. Sometimes the readiness for a healing experience is evident; it's right there in the way the person expresses themselves to you and in the energy they emit: "I'm ready to let this go. This is no longer who I am."

Other times it will be less apparent, usually because they are not actually ready. They may lack clarity, or the intellect is still attempting to understand and make sense of things: "I'm trying to figure out where this is all coming from. Why do I think or react or feel this way?" When you hear that, it signals that the need to mentally process the situation has not been satiated, and that more layers need to be uncovered and explored before the readiness is there.

It takes practice to discern what there is an actual readiness to let go of, and then to move confidently with what you sense or hear. You are picking up information from the surface level (words, feelings, energy) down to the depths of being (soul), and that information does not always align. If you are unsure, you can always ask the person directly what they desire to experience in the session, and let that lead. In any case, whatever direction things take, it should not be 'of you;' it cannot be your agenda for that person. If things are not clear, if nothing seems poised to fall away, if there is no apparent readiness for a healing experience, continue to hold space for revelation and exploration from a place of trust: when the time is right, you *will* know.

One recognizable signal of that readiness is a palpable sense of expansive self-awareness around their pain. In those moments people can become quiet, more introspective, as though something profound has been recognized, as though all that needs to be said has been said (which, for the moment, it has). This is not a time to push the person to explore their insights by asking 'powerful questions.' Instead, join them in that quiet space and prepare yourself to facilitate a healing experience.

Facilitating Healing Experiences

Beyond illumination and exploration, when a limiting belief or pain arises in a session for healing, how do we engage? What is the role of the Deep Coach?

Although your work as a Deep Coach begins and ends with your own consciousness (your being is your doing), there are things you can 'do' to facilitate a healing experience effectively. The crucial understanding is this:

You don't need to go beyond the nine practices.

Everything you need to do lies within them. If you are ever in doubt, turn to the practices.

Noticing and releasing your subtle agendas is a good practice to begin with. Let go of any urge to change anything about the other person when they express their pain; let go of any need to work with them to shift one belief to another; let go of any impulse to feed them new perspectives or mental concepts, no matter how empowering they may seem to you. Why? Because Deep Coaches know that when a shift in being occurs, higher truths and new perspectives will arise naturally in the awakening mind.

A Deep Coach also never thinks, "Here is someone that I must heal." You are not the one doing the healing. Instead, you are recognizing the light of Self and Spirit as the ultimate actor in the healing process. This is what all nine practices point to. Your role, as a facilitator of a healing experience, is to hold a space steeped in sacred silence where people can be with and express their pain, and in that space supply spiritual consciousness.

Being with Pain Is Healing

We all have disempowering stuff that gets hidden away and left unattended, but not all of us have the capacity to be present to pain. The great gift of a Deep Coaching space is that pain can be acknowledged, expressed, and accepted, *as it is*. It is a gift to be able to speak openly to an empathetic ear: "I have carried this for so long and I am ready to let it go. I'm becoming more real, more of who I am. Yes, I have some fear of becoming the real me. I've been hiding it from the world, as it hasn't felt safe to show myself as I am. But I'm very aware of the person I am longing to be and become. I'm open and ready to release this stuff."

Expanding your capacity to *be* with pain means to embrace it without judgment, to hold it with compassion, to say to it, "I see you *as you are,* and you are welcome *as you are.*" This is how its grip on the mind begins to loosen. When the readiness to heal is there, Deep Coaches, as loving presences, and with an expansive capacity to be with pain, encourage others to embrace and be with theirs—not to fix or analyze or change it or to make it go away, but to open to it, feel it, and stay with it. This element of opening the heart, being with the pain, and supplying spiritual consciousness is at the core of a healing moment. And from a place of compassionate acceptance and love, the pain will begin to release and the limiting self-concept that is interwoven with the pain will begin to unravel *on its own.*

Moment of Pause

Be with Pain

Read through the scenario below, then close your eyes and begin. If you have a personal experience to work with, you can use that scenario instead.

Visualize yourself sitting with a person when the winds of a painful emotion begin to stir. Her body hunches over, she covers her face, and begins to weep, emitting a sorrowful cry.

Observe yourself in the winds of her pain, as it comes at you. How are you reacting? What thoughts arise? What feelings? Do you experience it physically, in your body? Observe yourself as you bear witness to the expression of her pain.

After a minute or so, shift the focus of your observation to that place within you that is peaceful, centered, and grounded. What do you notice? What changes?

Now allow yourself to inhabit the two levels simultaneously: the surface level that feels her pain viscerally, and the deeper level that is grounded and at peace.

It is possible for you to both empathize with and, at your core, remain detached from the windstorm of pain.

How does this understanding support your capacity to be with pain and allow healing moments?

Orient Your Mind to Truth

Healing in a Deep Coaching session is more than intellectually choosing to let go of a limiting ego-pattern or the pain body it has engendered. Healing takes the form of releasing the *energy* of the pain body. It's a form of energy healing.

Little, if anything, needs to be said during energy healing. The most powerful actions you can take are these:

Slow it all down.

Supply spiritual energy.

Invite in Spirit.

Let the silence do the work.

Allow the energy of the pain to be there *as it is*, held in the heart space, and the healing experience will begin to unfold on its own. Your role, as always, is to energize the space as a loving presence. When you actively supply spiritual consciousness, your own energy field is vibrating at a higher frequency, which impacts the denser, lower-vibrational energies in need of healing. In essence, the energy field of the pain body comes into contact with a larger, encompassing energy field, one born of the consciousness of Spirit. What truly needs to be said as this happens? Relax, breathe deeply, *be* the healing space, and let the silence do the work.

If the person you're working with has never experienced healing this way before, it can help to invite them to take a few breaths with you and relax into the process. You can also invite them to open their heart or to be with the pain or to just feel into the inner dimension of being, and then move into sacred silence.

As you both settle in, avoid directing the person's thinking, feeding them perspectives, or asking questions. Stay vigilant for subtle indications within yourself that you are becoming concerned or curious about what they are experiencing or thinking. These make you susceptible to busting silence and interrupting the healing moment prematurely.

As the healing experience unfolds and silence deepens, you will find yourself having thoughts. Some of these will reflect the experience you are having and some the experience the other person is having. If you are concerned about what your mind is doing, an effective way to work with this is to orient your mind towards the Truth that dissolves what is untrue. Eliminate doubt and fear from your thoughts and recognize that your client is a spiritual being. Sense the greater reality that lies beyond the pain and illusions of self that have been created; see the whole that is there, the truth of Self that is true always. You don't need to suggest anything or for the person to have a certain kind of experience. In the silence, as you hold space for the pain:

- Anchor into your own deepest sense of Self

- Channel spiritual energy

- Affirm the ultimate reality of the person (e.g. "You are worthy.")

- Realize the person as a divine being

- Visualize the person as whole and complete; as loved

- Sense the presence of Spirit in and through the person

- Express gratitude for the healing experience

- Ask Spirit for what you need to know or say.

As the energy is released, emotions will surface and people will often begin to cry (they may even apologize for this.) Simply let them know it's okay, that it is safe to *feel* the emotion and to *be* with it, and then move back into sacred silence.

There is no particular experience or sensation that either you or the person needs to have. Sometimes there is an accompanying feeling of peace or joy or lightness, but not always. Does that mean the healing experience offered no benefit? Not at all. You must learn to let expectation go completely and trust that when you plant seeds in the garden of consciousness they will sprout. They do not always sprout immediately, but at some point they will. Supply a spiritual consciousness to what was previously repressed or unconscious, and distorted beliefs, erroneous ego-patterns, and the pain intertwined with it all will begin to release on its own, in its own time.

At some point either you or your client will break the silence. Preferably it is the latter, but if it is you, it is acceptable to ask how they are feeling or invite them to share their experience. It's important to know, however, that deep healing experiences can shift people into an altered state of consciousness, and having to give voice to their experience immediately afterwards can disrupt the ongoing integration process. If it feels as though the energy is continuing to move, signaling that the healing moment is not over, or if the person is not yet ready to verbalize their experience, it is perfectly okay to either go back into the silence and hold it longer or gently bring the session to a close, inviting the person to remain where they are, as they are, for as long as it feels right.

A Final Word on Grief Work

Grief work is commonly understood as a therapeutic approach for dealing with the pain of loss. But is more than that, and has coaching applications as well. *Unattended Sorrow* by Stephen Levine is an excellent resource for learning more about grief work. In this book he expands the concept of grief work beyond dealing with bereavement by suggesting that whenever we experience any kind of hurt, from everyday sorrows to the great disappointments of unfulfilled hopes and ambitions, there is an opportunity to do grief work. When we do not do grief work, our pain goes unattended, adding to the weight of our sorrow, the shadow side we carry. When we do grief work, regularly and consistently, we learn to let go of mental and emotional patterns that no longer serve us. It's hard work at first, often emotionally challenging, yet it sweeps everything out so that a new joy or peace can find space to enter.

Grief work takes on many forms, but the ones I have found to be most valuable to coaching relate to working with acceptance, compassion, forgiveness, letting go, and surrendering. When we are compassionate and forgiving of ourselves and others we recognize that pain is truly an opportunity for growth, and it then becomes a marvelous catalyst for the transformation that we are looking to manifest. It's so important to be gentle with ourselves, to be non-judgmental, and to recognize that this is actually a beautiful part of how we are put together— even though in the moment, when we feel the pain, it seems to be working against our greater good. But once we do grief work, it clears the mind and illuminates our ability to see a more expansive picture of what is really happening. And with that understanding comes further compassion and a great deal of patience, true spiritual qualities that support transformation.

CHAPTER SEVENTEEN

Practice 8 - Foster the Emergence of What Wants to Happen

What Wants to Happen?

What really wants to happen?
Underneath what you can see
Underneath the surface
Underneath what you logically know
Underneath the story inside your head
Underneath the skin
Underneath the fear
Underneath the tears
Underneath the covering up
Underneath the anger
Underneath the tension
Underneath the pretending
Underneath the tree
Underneath the laughter
Underneath the pain
Underneath the need

Underneath the quaking
Underneath the running
Underneath the angst
Underneath the shell
Underneath the letting go
Underneath the reflection
Underneath the frown
Underneath the desire
Underneath the softness
Underneath the worry
Inside. Your. Bones.
At the very core of your BEing
What wants to happen?

~ Kim Ewell

In every human life there is something that is trying to emerge from deep below the surface level, below the drama and the conditions that enfold that life. In transformational terms, this is 'what wants to happen,' and is a natural unfolding process of change that reflects *emerging* potentials. What wants to happen, what is emerging from deep within, is what Deep Coaches listen for (Practice 6), and what we support our clients to both listen for and experience.

Where does this emerging potential lie? It lies beneath the surface, underneath the story, underneath the pain and sorrow, the hurt and anger, the doubt and uncertainty, the pride and pretense, the little thoughts and big denials. Beneath it all, woven into the marrow of your being, there lies 'what wants to happen.'

What is this potential?

It is the potential of your Self, the I Am, the truth of who you are, the soul becoming realized and expressed.

The soul is inherently evolutionary, a constant potential in motion, and is the source of our impulse to grow towards higher levels of consciousness and personality attainment. Part of awakening is learning to attune to the voice of the soul because when it is heard, and fed what it needs, the soul flourishes into its potential as though it is the most natural thing in the world…which it is.

The soul knows what it needs, and is constantly communicating that to the mind. Too often however, its voice is blanketed under layers of conditioning and ceaseless thinking which prevent it from being heard. Yet those who are undergoing a period of profound inner transformation are experiencing the shaking and rumbling of the bedrock upon which their self-concept has been built. Cracks are forming in the bedrock, and these cracks are being felt: "What am I doing with my life? There is more to it than this, and I know it. I'm being called to something wondrous, but I cannot explain it. It's a bit scary, but I know by the stirring in my heart that something is calling me forward into my greatest potential. The truth is, I Am more than I have ever thought!"

For many people connecting in a direct and intimate way with the essence of their being, with 'I Am,' is a rare if not elusive experience, and they are not sure what to make of it. They may not yet have acquired the capacity to listen deeply within or to interpret meaningfully the signals they are receiving. This is why Deep Coaching is invaluable in supporting transformative processes: when we listen to others with an open heart, attune to what is trying to emerge, and invite in a vibrant experience of I Am, we expand their capacity to do the same for themselves.

The Objective Is the Experience

Practice 6 is a gateway practice, a way of listening for what the desired experience is to be. The gateway leads to a healing experience: either to Practice 7 to release some aspect of personal gravity and its associated pain (letting go) or to Practice 8 for an exalted experience of oneself as I

Am (letting come). You are learning to facilitate both of those experiences within the coaching session, when the readiness is there.

Experiencing oneself as I Am (to whatever degree it is possible for any individual) is the single most powerful accelerator of transformational change—it establishes a whole new level of self-identity in the mind. To know yourself as I Am is to know the nature of your being as whole and complete, as it *is* in reality. For this reason alone, facilitating an uplifting, faith-building *experience* of the emerging I Am is the objective of the eighth Deep Coaching practice. It can be a challenge for coaches, trained in the art of asking powerful questions, to move beyond inquiry as the driver of change into experience itself. Yet the soul desires an experience, not a description of an experience.

When the readiness is there, a Deep Coach invites people to step into the emerging potential of Self and to *be* that.

The Generative Potential

Let's begin by looking at a relatively new field of study known as the 'generative potential.' In basic terms, the generative potential suggests that in any given situation, underneath the surface level hubbub, something is trying to happen: a 'field of possibility' just bubbling away waiting to be connected to and actualized through intent and action. The generative potential is *emergent*—it is in the process of coming into being—and is therefore also known as the *emerging potential*. In other words, in any moment, in any situation, there is an emerging potential waiting and wanting to happen, and what we can do is learn to *sense* it so that we can act on what it is trying to show us.

There are two related generative potentials:

1.) Inner Plane: What wants to happen within oneself. The generative question is:

> What wants to happen on the inner plane,
> beneath it all, at the core of my being?

Perhaps not surprisingly, what wants to happen at this level is universal in nature for all human beings. It is simply the desire to heal, which is to experience more and more of oneself as whole and complete, as I Am.

Not everyone on the transformational path is ready to step into an I Am experience—most people are not aware that it is possible to have such an experience, let alone with a coach in a coaching session—however, Deep Coaches learn to recognize readiness levels in order to facilitate the experience.

Even if a such profound shift in being does not happen in the session, a Deep Coaching space can always energize enough of a shift to expand self-awareness and orient the mind towards new levels of personal reality, where 'what wants to happen' on both the inner and the external plane can be better perceived.

2.) External Plane: What wants to happen outside oneself. The generative question is:

> What wants to happen on the external plane
> within the various circumstances of my life?

When a person tries to sense the emerging potential inherent within the kaleidoscope of their life's situations, 'what wants to happen' will appear in a wide range of forms appropriate to the situation at hand. And whatever is perceived will *reflect the state of being or consciousness of the sensor*, as each state of consciousness reveals its own picture of reality.

When coaching, first attune to what wants to happen on the inner plane (Practice 6), and when the readiness is there, hold space for a shift towards that desired state of being. Once the shift has happened, and it is *embodied*, you can gently inquire into the emerging potential on the external plane: "What's the opportunity you are now perceiving? What are you now seeing as a way forward?"

Once a person shifts to embody a way of being that is an expression of their highest Self, there will be a corresponding shift in how external events and situations are perceived—they will naturally see potentials and opportunities that may have been elusive or unfathomable prior to the shift. Why? Because the generative potential is 'of the whole,' and to perceive that emerging potential a person must be willing to listen from their deepest source, which is also 'of the whole.' When we embody the true, the real, and the whole within ourselves, we begin to see the same potentials in the world around us.

Moment of Pause

Reflect on What Is Emerging in You

Take a moment to attune to your deepest sense of Self. Can you sense, see or feel the emerging potential within you?

If you have difficulty perceiving it, take a few breaths and focus on relaxing your body and opening your heart. Invite Spirit into your mind, and allow yourself to gently shift energy-wise into a place of peace, calm, trust, or any state of being you desire to embody.

Once you feel yourself embodying that state, attune to that which is emerging at your deepest level. What wants to happen at the core of your being?

Stay with it for a while, and when you are ready you will naturally begin to perceive what wants to happen on the external plane, in the various events and situations of your life. Notice how the external opportunities extend from the internal state of beingness that you have chosen to embody.

Accessing the Generative Potential

The challenge to perceiving the generative potential is that it is not accessed in a linear way. Linear thinking says, 'I would like to gain a broader or different perspective on the issue I'm working on, and so at any time I can ask, "What is trying to happen here? What is the opportunity in this situation?" and with some thought I will likely see some possibilities.' This approach is always available, and it will produce some kind of a result, but it is linear because it assumes I can perceive a potential that is 'of the whole' in a relatively direct way: by asking a certain type of question. What the linear approach does not require is any kind of preceding shift in being or consciousness, one conducive to accessing a higher field of potentiality in which 'what is trying to happen' is vibrating away.

Here we see the connection to the Four Levels of Engagement (Chapter 2), where a shift in being at the third level, Choice, is required to access the potentials of the fourth level, Opportunity. There is also a direct connection to Otto Scharmer's fourth level of listening, "generative listening," or listening from the emerging field of future possibility (Chapter 14). To access Opportunity and to listen generatively, we have to go through a subtle but profound shift in being that enables us to tap into this field of possibility. This applies to both coach and client.

In a Deep Coaching session, inviting a client to tap into the emerging potential by simply asking "What's the opportunity here?" or "What is trying to happen here?" is not enough to get you where you want to be. You can always try that, and the answers could prove beneficial in some way; however, in order to connect effectively with the generative potential, the person must be attuned to his deepest source and listening with an open mind, open heart, and open *will*. This means individual will (what *I* want to have happen) has been relinquished and a greater will is allowed: what wants to happen that is of the *whole*, which includes the whole of my being.

When these conditions are met, perceptible shifts in being occur, and this is when the emerging potential begins to reveal itself in the mind. It won't need to be searched for or figured out; the person will begin to access naturally the system of profound knowledge and wisdom that is inherent within the field of potentiality, and they will *know* who to be on the inner plane and what to do on the external.

Practice Application

Exercises for Learning to Attune to the Generative Potential

These activities reference the Four Levels of Listening in Chapter 14.

1. Deep Listening Reflection

For one week, at the end of each day, reflect on the number of times you found yourself listening from level 1 (Downloading), 2 (Factual), 3 (Empathic), or 4 (Generative).

> When did you find yourself listening generatively, from your deepest source?

> What enabled you to access this level of listening?

In the course of a day, if you cannot identify an instance where you were in a state of deep (generative) listening, explore what it was that kept you out of that state.

2. Notice the Shift

In your coaching or daily conversations, pay attention to the moments when the conversation shifts from a normal conversation (levels 1 and 2) into empathic dialogue (level 3), and then into a deeper level of connection, meaning, and emerging potential (level 4).

> What happens to you? To the other person?

What potentials do you perceive when you listen from your deepest source?

As an example, if you are conversing about a friend's weekend activities and the conversation switches to their recent health issues, you may notice an immediate shift in how you listen, from level 1 or 2 to 3. Did it move from there into level 4?

You may observe that moving into level 4 is easier in coaching conversations than in daily conversations. Why is that? What is happening that makes it this way?

Experiencing the Great I Am

Earlier in the book I posed the question:

> What are the optimal conditions in which transformation
> unfolds, naturally and organically, and with the greatest
> amount of ease and joy?

You are likely now seeing how the nine practices form a holistic approach to creating those optimal conditions. Practices 1 to 3 establish the coaching space as a healing environment infused with the transformative energy and consciousness of Spirit. Practices 4 and 5 invite the coach and coachee, as spiritual partners, into periods of sacred silence and to connect with the heart center and its vast intelligence. Through the pathways of the heart we are able to attune to the deeper realm of Self and let that lead us into what wants to happen.

As I have noted, Practice 6 is a gateway practice. There are two general directions that the deeper Self will take us: towards the pain body for healing (letting go), or towards an exalted experience of oneself as whole and complete (letting come). Practice 7 invites us to learn to be with the naturally arising pain of transformation and to hold a healing space in which people can express, lean into, and attend to that pain in order to grow into a fuller expression of their true Self.

This brings us to Practice 8, the penultimate practice in terms of order, the ultimate practice in terms of what it does to *transfigure* the self-concept. As we attune to the emergence of what wants to happen at the level of Self and soul, we are confronted with a possibly unexpected truth: that what truly wants to happen is, above all else, an *experience of oneself as whole and complete*; as I Am.

At first it surprised me to discover the universality to the call of the soul, yet upon second glance it makes perfect sense. The inner call to transform is born of the natural impulse of the soul to evolve and actualize its own magnificent potential. The greatest gift a Deep Coach can offer is to help people step into a fuller expression of themselves—to experience who 'I Am,' in essence, or any aspect of I Am, such as:

I AM good enough.

I AM worthy.

I AM lovable.

I AM loved.

I AM deserving.

I AM safe.

I AM abundant.

I AM wise.

Any of these states of the great I Am (and more) can be experienced. The intent is simply to bask in the sense of goodness, rightness, and wholeness, and to allow that to penetrate deeply into the mind. This is pure inspiration for the transformational journey.

Listen for the Readiness

This experience will not happen in every coaching session, and with some people it may not happen at all. There needs to be a *readiness* on the part of the coachee and a *capability* on the part of the coach to foster the emergent experience.

It is also not something that you, the coach, *will* to happen ("I'm going to ask you to try to have this experience because I know it›s good for your growth," kind of thing). You can coach a person for years and not have their readiness level rise to the point where they are truly desiring and ready to step in. However, when they are ready they will, in one form or another, signal that readiness. Your role is to listen for it and let it lead.

It's helpful to know what readiness can sound like. Often it combines a distinct feeling of having had enough healing with a desire to embody a fuller expression of the emerging selfhood. It can sound like this:

> "There's been a way I've operated in my life, a way of being that has worked for me. It is connected to various kinds of pain, both physical and emotional pain. This way of operating also had me reflecting on the past constantly, correcting things, and striving for certainty in the future because I was anxious about what was going to happen. But no matter how uncomfortable and painful it was, it also gave me a sense of certainty. Pain gave my life definition. But now, when I look closely at my pain, I see how the comfort of its certainty blocked me, and also how it supported my transformation, so far. My pain gave me motivation to keep moving forward, to heal myself—which led to years of healing work actually.

> "Now I no longer want to be motivated by pain or the need to heal the pain. That's enough. That's how it's worked so far, and I'm ready to move on and to be inspired by life itself. I've been experiencing a new reality in bits and pieces, here and there. What I want is...I've not been able to anchor it in. It's

at the surface level only, but I want to anchor it in my being. I want to know how to step into this reality, which I feel a calling for strongly. How do I step into this new reality in a powerful way, or more confidently, trusting that this is all good and this is all safe? Because the old way feels safe, and there's a certainty and a familiarity in the way things have been. Yet there is a calling to choose and step into this. So how do I...I want to step into it, fully!"

The request is not always so explicit; people will not always be able to articulate clearly their readiness, particularly if they have never before had such an experience. The coach needs to sense the readiness as much as listen for it. Some people are not even aware it is something they can ask for help with, that such an opportunity exists within a coaching relationship. (For these people, you will need to make an invitation.) Other times, the fear of what it means to step into it will act as a barrier to the experience, sounding like this:

"I have experienced this new way of being, and it feels awesome. It feels really energizing and alive. Yet when I reflect on it, there's no clarity as to what it's about, or what I am actually stepping into. So I question it. What is it that I want to step into? Then I start feeling blocked again, like my mind starts stuttering. There's fear. Is it safe?

"So far it's been going at a very slow pace, a gradual transition, so that I feel comfortable and safe. But at the same time, I have this pull to just step into it. Something is telling me that I'm ready to just step into it, not to listen to all of this fear chatter, to just make a decision once and for all that I'm choosing this and step into it. So there's a pull from the back, there's a pull from the front."

Fostering the Experience in a Session

Listen for the readiness and then, with the permission of your client, invite in the experience. It can sound like this:

Coach: Every cell in your being is saying it's time to step in, that you can do this. Just make the choice. But there's a little voice that says, "But is this safe? What is this I am saying yes to?"

Client: Yes.

Coach: So what would be helpful for you today, here in our session? Given all that is happening within you at the moment, what do you desire to have happen?

Client: I want to step into it and have a very powerful experience of this, one so powerful that my entire being knows that this is okay and I'm ready for this and it's okay to be as I am. Yes, what I'm looking for is an experience.

Coach: Then let's have that experience.

Client: Okay.

Coach: Now, this is your experience to create. But in this space you're being held in complete safety. I am right here with you as you open to this experience of your true nature.

Client: Okay.

Coach: There's no rush, no force, there's nothing, there's just the allowing, the permission-giving so that you can step into this new way of being and allow it to be there without any concern. Take your time. Allow that which is alive in you to lead. I am holding the space for you. And as we move into this, at any time if something comes up that you wish to share, simply give voice to it...

...and then shift yourself into sacred silence, supplying spiritual consciousness with the fullness of your being.

This is an extraordinary moment born of true spiritual partnering, and you will know it when you are there. You may experience the opening of a vast energy field, the mental boundaries between you and your client may seem to dissolve, or you may experience a vibrant field of light that feels completely and utterly healing. Trust whatever you experience, no matter how foreign it feels (and if necessary invite your client to do the same).

Do not bust the silence. Nothing needs to be said until your client speaks. Even then, it may just be to verbally process emotions, thoughts, bodily sensations, or energy movement, and silence is resumed soon after.

Let go of any need to control or direct or know what's going on. It's out of your hands at this point. Be fearless, and relinquish any concern about 'doing it right' or 'making a mistake.' There is nothing you can or need to do anyway. At this point your primary role is to *be* a loving presence, supplying spiritual consciousness, while making space for Spirit—the vast evolutionary consciousness alive in every sentient being—to do its work in mind and body.

Enter into this exalted experience *in partnership* with the person. It's not nearly as beneficial or powerful to hold yourself back, to hold the 'coaching position' and observe the person having their experience, detached from your own. This is the moment where you and your client have the opportunity to become as *one* in the unified field, to consciously co-exist within an energy field of potentiality connected to a deeper source. This is 'presencing.' And whatever happens in this field is of the highest good for all concerned. Let go of the urge to maintain positionality or the concern that you must 'do' something, and just allow the silence to do the work.

As the experience unfolds, fear, doubt, sorrow and pain will begin to recontextualize, becoming like a distant memory which has no actual reality or essential value. In their stead, joy arises, accompanied by certitude of the goodness and rightness of oneself and life.

Awakening and transformation is a healing process that unfolds of its own volition when it is *allowed* to. Through it we come to know ourselves in all our manifestations: I AM lovable. I AM good enough. I AM an individual of great worth and potential. I AM what I choose to be because I AM an expression of perfect, infinite Spirit. This is what 'wants to happen' at the level of Self and soul, *the generative potential inherent in every moment*. It is the same for all human beings everywhere, whether they are conscious of it or not.

Clara's Story

"The me that wants to emerge happens as a gentle, organic process, if I allow it to happen. I was expecting it to fall from the sky, but now I see that's not how it is. That expectation came from the construct of my story and the drama around it I'd created. It hit me that I have been trying to understand and allow that new me that wants to emerge with my old mindset, with the old construct of who I *thought* I was to be, and they never mesh. The soul-essence level cannot be embraced by that part that is different. This realization helped me to relax, and I shifted my expectations to just allow that flowing, more sensitive approach.

"That opened the door for the new process to begin. It is a slow, gentle, pushing forward, but not in a big bold kaboom! way. That's where I connected with that place inside of me where everything just is. I AM. It's just where I am. In that place it doesn't matter what the outcome is, or what the things I want to create will look like; it doesn't matter what the story around it is, or whether one approves or doesn't approve. It's just me at the core.

"The picture I have for this, is scuba diving, where you go to that place in the water where you are just floating. It's quiet and silent and peaceful. It just is. It's an amazing place to be. And I know, in that place anything is possible, anything can happen. I don't know how or why, and I don't need to know. I somehow thought if I go to that place I'd be weak, vulnerable, and not able to act. But the truth is, I have more clarity and more power and more ability to act than in any other place. It's not a place where my head is in the clouds and I can't do anything anymore. Just the opposite. All that I thought I was is falling away, and the way I existed before with the story and the fighting armor I wore...well, I couldn't put any energy into that anymore. I am free to create what I want to create, and everything I need will be provided."

To experience the great I Am—to touch the essence of your true nature—is so innately powerful it's transfiguring. No greater gift can you provide for another person than to hold a space in which they are able to have such an experience. No greater gift can a person give themselves than to allow their soul's desire to flourish. They are, in essence, saying, "I love myself enough to give myself this experience." It's a pure act of consciousness elevation that bestows manifold blessings: it reaffirms why they are on the path, it assuages concerns and doubts, it quells the discomfiture that comes with transformation, and most of all, it allows mind and body to calibrate to the frequencies of higher consciousness. Here the Divine Mind is touched and the true Self seen in its reflection.

To be clear, this does not mean that in each session a person will have this experience. And it is not a Deep Coach's objective (or agenda) to reach that state. The objective is to energize a shift in being in which *more* of the nature of the true Self can be revealed within the awakened mind. It will vary for each person, according to the extent of which they are capable in that moment. However, each time you support a person into an experience where more of the truth of who they are is experienced, they receive the ultimate gift of life. Each time you foster the emergence of what wants to happen, for yourself or for another, you construct an increasingly stable and sustainable way of being. The new paradigm locks into place.

Experience the Experience

Are you ready?

This is the moment you have been preparing for. Everything you have been asked to learn, everything you have been asked to practice leads to this point. We are standing on the edge of an exalted experience of Self within the healing, integrating, unifying field of Spirit. You have been guided here, one way or another, and you are readying to enter in.

I hear you say that you are tired of not feeling good enough, exhausted by the battle of not feeling worthy of the life you so desire. I hear you say how you've been living in fear for so long that you don't know how to live fearlessly in love. All your life you've decided through fear what you should be doing, so that you'd be safe, secure, in control. Now I am hearing you say that it's time to let all that go and to live aligned to your highest truth, trusting that the vast intelligence within you *knows* what is good and right for you, and I am hearing that you are ready to commit your life to it.

The door is open to that experience. All you need to do is invite it in.

No more talking about it, no more describing 'what it would be like' to live this way—it's time now to live it, to embody it in every cell of your being.

Take a breath with me, and open to it. Take another breath and expand yourself in it. Take another breath and invite it into every cell of your being.

That's it. We are just going to hold this state, bask in it, for as long as it's comfortable.

You are now experiencing your own light, the radiant light of your true Self. And you are dancing with Spirit, allowing it to imprint upon your being what has long been held in store for you: the truth of Who You Are, and your purpose and place in this world.

Expand yourself in this light, and notice how effortlessly it heals your pain. Your pain is not you, and never was. It is a mind trick, an illusion that keeps you from knowing the truth of Who You Are.

Now you know. You are light. You are love. You are an extraordinary being of infinite worth and potential, and you are being guided in light and love into your potential because you *desire* it.

Stay in the light of your Self a while longer. Open to it, fully. There is nothing more important in your life now than this.

And when you are ready, return to your normal state of awakened consciousness. You know what you are about, and you know what it is you need to do.

Practice Application

Emerging Moments

In the morning, upon waking, set the intention to notice throughout the day what is trying to emerge in any given situation, to tune into *what wants to happen*. With this intention in place, allow yourself 'emerging moments' throughout your day.

An emerging moment is when you stop what you are doing, slow it all down, take a few deep breaths, open your heart, orient your mind to Spirit, and then attune to what is trying to emerge within yourself, first on an internal plane and then on an external plane.

What is the way of being you desire to embody?

How are you being called to act from that place of being?

What is the emerging potential or opportunity you now perceive?

CHAPTER EIGHTEEN

Practice 9 - Cultivate Trust in the Mystery and Magic of Transformation

A Lesson from Zorba the Greek

I remember one morning when I discovered a cocoon in the bark of a tree, just as the butterfly was making a hole in the case preparing to come out. I waited a while, but it was too long appearing and I was impatient. I bent over it and breathed on it to warm it.

I warmed it as quickly as I could and the miracle began to happen before my eyes, faster than life. The case opened, the butterfly started slowly crawling out and I shall never forget my horror when I saw how its wings were folded back and crumpled; the wretched butterfly tried with its whole body to unfold them. Bending over it I tried to help it with my breath. In vain.

It needed to be hatched out patiently and the unfolding of the wings should be a gradual process in the sun. Now it was too late. My breath had forced the butterfly to appear all crumpled, before its time. It struggled desperately and, a few seconds later, died in the palm of my hand.

That little body is, I do believe, the greatest weight I have on my conscience. For I realise today that it is a mortal sin to violate the great laws of nature. We should not hurry, we should not be impatient, but we should confidently obey the eternal rhythm.

~ Nikos Kazantzakis

When a butterfly begins to emerge from its cocoon, in those final moments of metamorphosis, it struggles a fair bit before it fully emerges. It is a long and painful-to-watch process, and you might even be tempted, like Zorba, to blow on or cut the outer covering off the chrysalis to help the butterfly along. But if you did, if you did not allow the struggle to happen, you would actually harm the butterfly.

The chrysalis' shell holds vital fluids that are important to a butterfly's wing formation. Your act of kindness, of clipping that outer shell, deprives it of those fluids. As a result, the butterfly emerges crippled, deformed, and nothing like the butterfly it was supposed to be. But if you can be patient and trusting enough to allow the butterfly to struggle against its bonds, you will witness the culmination of one of nature's transformative miracles.

When people do not interfere with nature, nature always manages to flourish. As the scientist Dr. Ian Malcom succinctly put it in the film *Jurassic Park*, "...life, uh, finds a way." We know this. Yet it seems we find it far easier to trust the natural unfolding process of change when it comes to plants and animals than we do when we witness human beings struggling to change or grow—especially when that human being is ourself. Somewhere along the line we came to perceive struggle as negative—most likely because of an aversion to discomfort and pain—and therefore something to be circumvented or avoided altogether.

As Deep Coaches, we will inevitably witness our clients struggling to grow into new levels of being. They will resist the cyclical nature of transformation, one that seems to take them two steps forward, one step back. They will rant when a desired something does not transpire, question and doubt the validity of their experience, gnash their teeth while muttering about how unfair it all is, and why the heck must it be this way anyway! Struggle can stir up all sorts of negative thoughts and emotions.

This is why Deep Coaches practice cultivating faith in the mystery and magic of the transformational process. We may not understand exactly *why* things are as they are, but just like the butterfly's struggle to emerge from the chrysalis, something is going on in a person's divinely calibrated curriculum that is a necessary aspect of their own evolutionary journey. We should neither attempt to circumvent nor cut short the process, as that will, in some way, deprive them of necessary 'vital fluids.' Our role is to support people to lean into their experience and trust what is happening, as it is, and to let go of the need to always know *why* things are as they are. Such abiding trust is something both coach and client can cultivate.

The Mystery and Magic

To trust in the force that moves the universe is faith. Faith isn't blind, it's visionary. Faith is believing that the universe knows what it's doing. Faith is a psychological awareness of an unfolding force for good, constantly at work in all dimensions.

~ Marianne Williamson

What is actually happening when an individual or a group embarks on an evolutionary journey of transformation? The truth is that, despite all our scientific progress, we know very little about it. Human beings are extraordinarily complex material-spiritual mechanisms interwoven into the vast tapestry of life itself—yet we have not evolved to the point where we can perceive or even conceive of all the facets and dimensions of our existence. It's far too complex for us to understand, and thus how it all works remains shrouded in mystery—a real limitation of being finite material beings in an infinitely spiritual universe.

We do know that transformation is a growth process that unfolds of its own volition. No person is the catalyst for their own awakening—that honor belongs to Spirit, the evolutionary life force, the one presence that lives in and through us all. Transformational change therefore does not need to be driven or forced, it needs to be *allowed*. What is also known is that transformation is not a random series of events. There are clear patterns and stages, and all those on the journey experience the duel of the dual dynamics of transformation, albeit translated into their unique personal story. There is 'method in the madness,' or more accurately, 'method in the magic.'

The fact that the mystical transcends human understanding means that we have to trust what we cannot fully comprehend. Yet what invariably happens when things in life are unclear, shrouded in mystery, or future outcomes unknown? We feel uncertain, and doubt creeps in. Uncertainty breeds doubt, and doubt questions what is happening: "Why am I experiencing this? Is this what should be happening? Is this right? Why does this keep occurring? This can't be good, can it?" You can hear the intellect attempting to penetrate the mystery of it all. And that is perfectly okay as long as it motivates the willingness to remain unsure, to leave the door open for alternative possibilities. Uncontrolled in the mind, however, doubt will breed fear, and once that happens we are swept out of curiosity and wonder into something altogether less empowering.

The antidote for doubt is trust and faith. To have faith is to have an abiding trust in what cannot be seen or empirically evidenced. Even if you cannot understand what is happening or why, you have an unshakeable sense of knowing that circumstances are arranging for your higher good—that life is conspiring to shower you with blessings. With trust in place, you can lean into your every experience, whether you judge it on the surface as good or bad, and revel in the miracle that your life is. When in doubt, you can always ask:

Why am I experiencing doubt?

What am I perceiving in this moment?

What is the lesson I am here to learn?

Who do I choose to be?

When you stand back and contemplate the journey of transformation, you will see just how beautiful in design it really is: a spiritual renaissance arising from deep within whereby you come to know more and more your essential reality, your relationship to all that is, and your purpose and place in the world. There is always a far more encompassing purpose or lesson behind every encounter, every experience, every event in your life. Can you sense and trust that goodness and rightness during your darkest hours, during your most tumultuous moments, as much as you do during those times of progress, attainment, and desire fulfillment?

There is a certain grace to a life lived trustingly. When we slow down, quieten the mind, and attune to what is emanating from deep within, transformative growth occurs with much less struggle and far greater ease and joy. This does not mean that life is free of challenge or difficulty—these are necessary stimulants for evolutionary progress—however the potential for stagnation is removed as the soul is given the nutrients and space it needs to flourish.

It's Hard for People to Trust

Transformation inherently breeds doubt and mistrust. We're stepping, after all, into an unknown world, one which operates very differently from the world we've known, and we're learning to navigate through with very little information to go on. You can therefore expect people to need to vent their doubt-fueled angst. As one my clients said, and I've heard this in various forms from many others:

> "Right now, I'm just done. I'm tired of this. I'm done waiting. I'm done hoping. I'm done investing in myself and in bringing my passion [work] to life, and not seeing anything in return. I really want to step up to whatever is needed for me to do, but there's a big silence. There must be something that I'm not getting. I'm so confused right now. Can I keep trusting this? But as the weeks go by with little changing, it makes trusting so much harder."

You can hear the yearning, wanting, hoping, all that has built up over the years. He's ready to go, and more than anything he wants the struggle to end and his life to take on the shape he so badly desires.

He knows what he wants: he wants to see tangible results from all the inner work he's done. He wants to create, to be in action, to wake up each day looking forward to doing things that excite and energize him, to manifest the ideas he has, the high dreams of his life. This is what he wants to have happen, as an extension of his emerging selfhood, and it's abundantly clear when you hear him speak. What is also clear is that when so many of his efforts do not produce the results he expects and hopes for, he begins to lose faith. "Can I keep trusting this?"

All forms of coaching facilitate the designing and taking of action, because when we take action towards fulfilling our aspirations the result is often an increase in trust with the process. When we are in motion, things are happening. But when it comes to acting on the creative impulses of our emerging selfhood—actions which often require a high degree of personal transparency, vulnerability, and authenticity—we invariably become attached to the outcomes. And when those actions do not produce the desired results, we spin into angst and mistrust. "Why, oh why, did this not turn out as I hoped?"

Such doubt signals that we have lost sight of the bigger picture, the generative potential, the lesson to be learned, of the goodness, rightness, and beauty of what *is* happening. When mired in doubt, we have become fixated on a thought that reflects fear instead of love, lack instead of abundance, pessimism instead of optimism. It is then, when in the grip of doubt, that people attempt to wrest back control. They exercise their will, determined to make things happen (whether there is a readiness or not), which invariably takes them back into old patterns of behavior because they 'got results' in the past. Taking action creates the feeling that they are doing something, moving forward, masters of their destiny once again—temporarily assuaging the negative feelings of mistrust, confusion, and lack of control. In reality, however, their doubt-motivated actions no longer align to the higher truths and way of being they seek to embody, and soon they fall to their knees exhausted by their efforts.

When the voice of doubt and all the angst it generates arises, the role of the Deep Coach is to hold a space in which it can be heard, as it is. Allow the person plenty of room to decompress, to release the pent-up emotion, and then gently bring them back into connection with their creative capacities, with their intuition, with the intelligence of their spiritual heart, with a higher flow of thought. You are supporting a return to love and to the inner dimension of being that is their desired experience. *Energize a shift into that state and trust will arise of its own accord.*

The work of the Deep Coach may appear circuitous, revisiting over and over the dynamic of doubt and trust. It doesn't matter. The path always takes us on an endless upward spiral of understanding where more and more is revealed about the nature of the Self, barriers to progress, and what it means to trust in life. The way of transformation is experimental. Trial and error, trial and success—both are possible and nothing is guaranteed except that all things are lessons life would have us learn.

Moment of Pause

Your Levels of Trust

Rate each of these statements on a scale of 0-10, where 0 is the absence of trust and 10 is complete trust.

Do not spend much time thinking about what each term or phrase means. Just read the sentence and then write down your intuitive response.

How much do you trust...

- yourself
- life
- the unknown
- the universe / God / Spirit
- in the process
- that over which you have no control
- that which has control over you
- those whom you love
- those whom you do not love.

When you have finished, note what your trust levels are.

> What surprised you? Are any of them higher or lower than you might have expected?
>
> Are there any contradictions?
>
> Where is there room for movement into a more trusting way of being?

You Will Be Presented with Lessons

In the book *If Life Is a Game, These Are the Rules,* author Chérie Carter-Scott describes ten rules for life as a human being. The following three are helpful in our efforts to cultivate trust in the transformational process:

> **1.) You will be presented with lessons.** You may like them or hate them, but they're yours and they're part of the 'school of life.'

> **2.) There are no mistakes, only lessons.** Growth is a process of trials, errors, victories, and setbacks. If you look at life as if everything happens to teach us something, then you will say, 'Okay… What is this here for…how's this going to educate me…how can I grow from this?'

> **3.) A lesson is repeated until learned**. You will continually attract the same lesson into your life. You will also draw teachers to teach you that lesson until you get it right."

A Course in Miracles describes the curriculum it teaches this way: "This is a course in miracles. It is a required course. Only the time you take it is voluntary. Free will does not mean that you can establish the curriculum. It means only that you can elect what you want to take at a given time."

The curriculum of life is the same for all of us; only the time we take to complete it is ours to choose. Life's lessons will therefore be repeated in various forms and guises until learned, and yes, some lessons will take a lot longer to learn than others. But until the lesson is learned, as disheartening or frustrating as this can be, you will not move forward in that area.

One of the greatest steps of trust you can take is to know that no matter what is happening in your life, no matter how horrible or beautiful you perceive something to be, in all things there is a lesson to be learned. The only question is, can you see the lesson?

The Need to See Progress

Learning to trust the mystery and the magic of the transformational process is as important for the coach as for the client. Practitioners of Deep Coaching learn to stand as beacons of trust so that others may lean on us when their own trust falters. You may not have much experience with this way of being, and living from trust in a world steeped in doubt and fear can feel odd, as though you are being foolish or naïve…until you learn the way, of course.

One pitfall that befalls many coaches is wishing people would make more rapid or visible progress. Do you ever find yourself becoming impatient or frustrated with how things are moving? That is a telltale signal that your own level of trust is wavering. Wishing for things to move faster or for someone to make visible progress is just that: wishful thinking. Why would you wish for anything to be other than it is? Are you doubting the person's choices, or your own ability? What are you not trusting? Do you have an unmet need that underlies this wish?

Wishing for a person to progress faster or differently than they are detracts from your capacity to hold a space for them to struggle and flail, or to break through and flourish. Avoid spending energy wishing for things to be different to meet your own need for progress. That is a sign that you are not living in trust. Practice releasing any judgment around what is or is not happening—the truth is, you can scarcely comprehend the marvel that is an evolving soul, or why it fashions the experiences it does for its own growth. Particularly in the case of those who are committed to the grand journey of transformation, more is going on within than you can ever perceive.

Know that your ego will desire validation for the work you do. It is rarely enough for the ego to know it was a loving, supportive, grounding presence; the ego wants to know that it did a great job, that it made a difference, that it was worth the money paid. Love your ego; it means well, but it will distract you from your role as a trusting witness just so you can feel better about the work you are doing.

Practice releasing the need to see progress, to control, to know 'why' something is as it is, or to see any further ahead than what is happening in this moment. Allow all things to be as they are, and learn to trust that whatever is happening is always an expression of a divinely calibrated curriculum in action.

All Is Well

When we awaken, something extraordinary happens: the soul's desire to grow registers in the conscious mind. Some people experience this as waves of joy while others experience it as an inner call or yearning. This is a huge step forward for any human being. Whilst the soul communicates continuously, its communiques are not always heard or heeded. Distracted by the endless stimulation of material living, the mind becomes detached from the voice of the soul. Those who choose to embrace its call to know themselves as 'I Am,' however, have embarked on a journey unlike any other, one that is disruptive and replete with unknowns. But what would the journey be without the mystery and magic, the confusion and chaos, the uncertainty and doubt? How else would we learn to cultivate an unwavering trust in life and Spirit?

There is a wonderful scene in the movie *Indiana Jones and the Last Crusade* which exemplifies this. Chased down a long, narrow passageway by the 'bad guys,' Indy arrives at the edge of a precipice. To turn back is certain death; to step forward is to plummet a thousand feet. He can see that the passageway continues on the other side of the chasm, but there is no visible way to traverse the gap. He turns to his trusted source, a small book of ancient texts, and realizes that he must take a leap of faith. He is frightened to his core, yet he puts his foot out—it is what he must do, and he knows it—and takes a step into the great abyss. Miraculously, he does not fall. Instead he finds himself standing on a stone pathway, one that was impossible to see from his earlier vantage point. He hesitates, stunned that he is actually safe, before making his way across.

So often this is how the heroic journey unfolds, by our stepping into the unknown, heart in throat, only to find that we are safe and supported. Transformation is inherently an adventure along an unpredictable path towards an open-ended future. As with Indiana Jones, there will be times when the path will seem to disappear completely underfoot, and that can be woefully frightening, until we learn to trust that the path is always there, revealing itself a little more with each step we take. People will say, "I'd be far less anxious about things if only I knew where this was going." But we won't know with certainty; that's the point. The path is shrouded in mystery and magic. What we can do is take a step, the one we *know* is right for us to take, and then trust in the rightness and goodness of whatever it may bring.

This final Deep Coaching practice invites you to expand your capacity to trust an extraordinary evolutionary process that is not of your design. But you can learn to be its steward. This entire book has been written to show you the way. You can also be sure that because you are human, you will get tangled in your own stuff. You have needs and wants, hopes and fears, goals and aspirations, just as all others do, and they will get in the way. It's okay. In the end, it comes down to this:

Who do you choose to be?

Are you one who trusts or one who doubts? Do you embody your highest truths or pay lip service to them? Are you a free and clear conduit for Spirit and all the fruits of trust it offers? There is no judgment here as to who you choose to be or what you choose to experience in your lifetime. Yet whenever you find yourself in doubt as to what is happening, around a choice you must make or how best to support others with their life challenges, turn within and ask for guidance. Assuredly, you will be given what you need.

Take a deep breath of trust now and know that all is well.

Nothing real can be threatened.
Nothing unreal exists.
Herein lies the peace of God.

~ A Course in Miracles

CHAPTER NINETEEN
Structure of a Deep Coaching Session

Together the nine transformative practices form a powerful 'field of potentiality' which enables the ego-patterns, false interpretations, and limiting perceptions of the mind to be transformed. There is no place, no situation, no event in your life in which these practices are not applicable. They have been designed to guide you, along with specific exercises and fundamental questions, to use the power of your mind in concert with the Mind of Spirit, and to grow from a life based on the thought and action of ego to a life grounded in the depths of being, one infused with the intelligence of the heart and the consciousness of love.

Working with such intangibles does not mean, however, that we do not work with process or structure. The nine practices have a loose structure to them, in that the first five form the foundation upon which the latter are exercised, and Practice 6 is a gateway practice to 7 and 8. But for those who are versed in following a coaching system that prescribes the flow of a session, this may not be enough structure to understand how to lead a Deep Coaching session comfortably.

Deep Coaching Overlays Conventional Coaching

When the nine practices are used in a coaching context they are *overlaid* upon core coaching competencies, not separate from them. All coaching, including Deep Coaching, is based on the core competencies of asking questions, listening, creating awareness, shifting perspectives, and creating action. The primary difference between conventional coaching approaches and Deep Coaching is how these show up in the coaching space.

Take the core competency of asking questions, for example. The difference between a conventional coaching session and a Deep Coaching session is the importance that is placed on questions. In conventional coaching, questions are seen as *the* driver of the conversation. It is questions, particularly 'powerful questions,' that move the session forward towards desired outcomes. Most, if not all, coach training schools teach this, and coaches therefore adopt that mindset. When you listen to a conventional coaching conversation, it is often peppered with questions.

A Deep Coach also asks questions, though not nearly so many, and mostly in the exploration phase of a session. The questions are used primarily to understand a person's situation or context, to invite them to give voice to thoughts, emotions, and experiences, and to illuminate their inner operating system—to reveal *what* they believe and value, which highlights *why* they experience what they experience. As importantly, questions help us step into and, in a sense, *inhabit* a person's experience so that we coach from *within* it, not as detached, clinical observers of it.

The questions asked by the Deep Coach may or may not be 'powerful,' but there's no need to concern ourselves with that. The objective of a Deep Coaching session is not to formulate one question after another in quest of a shift in perspective or a breakthrough insight—it is to *energize shifts in being*. And from my experience, questions play a secondary role in that process. Questions help reveal and explore what's there, and as the knots of the mind begin to unravel they help prepare a person for a shift in being, but they are the driver neither of that shift nor of a healing moment, and are therefore not the primary driver of a Deep Coaching session.

Keep the nine practices in mind as you read through how conventional and Deep Coaching sessions are structured. This will give you a better sense of how the practices overlay and thus influence both core coaching competencies and the process itself.

Structure of a Conventional Coaching Session

Most conventional coaching sessions share a common structure or flow that looks something like this:

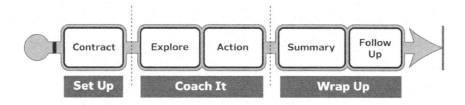

Part 1: Set Up

Contract

In the Contracting phase, you would typically set up the session by creating the coaching relationship and laying the groundwork for the session:

- Welcome the person, connect, and build trust

- Clarify expectations as to any session logistics (e.g. timeframe)

- Confirm the coaching agreement:

    1.) Identify the specific issue for the session

    2.) Set the desired goal or outcome for the session.

Part 2: Coach It

Explore

In the Explore phase you coach the client, which may include:

- Asking questions

- Exploring ideas, options, and beliefs

- Shifting or reframing perspectives

- Offering feedback.

Action

In the Action phase you coach your client to create and commit to action, and build the momentum for success:

- Inquire into decisions, potential changes, next steps, and actions

- Clarify action commitments, plan and timeframe

- Check for barriers to action

- Think through support and resource needs.

Part 3: Wrap Up

Summary

The Summary phase is typically part of the session wrap-up, occurring once desired conclusions and objectives have been achieved:

- Ask to summarize personal insights and learnings

- Ask what they are taking away from the session or found
  most valuable.

Follow Up

In the Follow Up phase, your primary objective is to build accountability for the actions and commitments they have made:

Ask how you can support them further or hold them accountable

Confirm what they are committing to before your next session

Confirm the date and time of your next session

These phases don't always happen in the order presented—it's not something you must follow step-by-step—overall, however, this is how a conventional coaching session is structured.

Structure of a Deep Coaching Session

You can see in this bird's-eye view of the process that the structure of a Deep Coaching session has stages and phases which mirror the conventional structure. The primary difference is not so much one of structure as of *approach*, as this book describes.

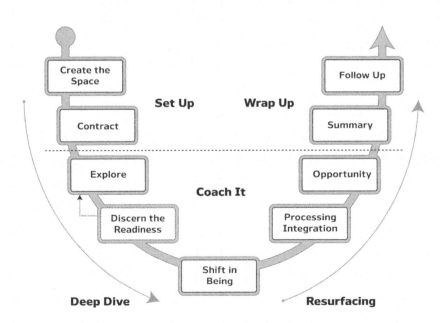

Part 1: Set Up
Create the Space

This is a vital phase in the Deep Coaching process because it lays the foundation for what is to come. In this phase you slow it all down (Practice 1), establish an energy connection with the person (Practice 2), and to begin to nurture the healing space (Practice 3).

Your way of being, or 'coaching presence,' throughout this phase is key. The energy you bring into the session and your sincerity in creating a healing space will be sensed, and that will affect what transpires. If you are nervous, stressed, hurried, or disconnected from your heart center, you will transmit this into the coaching space. Be sure to take at least five minutes before a session to do the necessary inner work for yourself so that you are in an optimal state of mind and being.

Avoid rushing this phase—this time is as much for you as it is for your client, as it brings you into deeper connection. It's perfectly acceptable to take anywhere from two to five minutes to create the space. Be consistent and start each session this way, even if you have worked with the person for some time.

Creating the Space begins with a series of invitations. "I invite you to…":

- take some deep breaths and relax your mind and body
- let go of anything that is not serving you in the moment
- sense into your connection with your me [your coach]
- trust whatever emerges and whatever happens
- invite Spirit into the space, in whatever way you would like.

When you put the elements together, it can sound like this:

> "I'd like to invite you to take a few deep breaths with me. [pause for breaths] As you do this, breathe away anything that is keeping you from being here fully present. [pause] I invite

you to sense into your connection with me, that we have come together in this space as two beings in service of one life. [pause] Your life is safe with me, and you are free to share with me any aspect of your life that is calling to be explored. [pause] Let's also take a moment to invite Spirit into this space, in any way that you would like, to facilitate our connection, and to help uplift us into higher levels of awareness so that what needs to be known will be made known. [pause] Now when you are ready, you can let me know what it is that you'd like to explore today."

If you do this well, with plenty of breaths and pauses, there will be a noticeable shift in the other person's state: they will speak more slowly and with a deeper voice, they will be more relaxed, and there will be a willingness to be more vulnerable and open with you. You will have established a relationship as spiritual partners.

Contract

Just as in a conventional session, contracting in a Deep Coaching session is intended to develop a common understanding of the issue or topic to be explored, to establish intentions and motivations, and to clarify the desired outcomes for the session. It consists of two primary questions, topic and outcome, both of which can be phrased in different ways.

Topic question:

- What is the area or topic you'd like to focus on today?

- What would you like to explore in our session today?

It's not uncommon for people to come to a Deep Coaching session with only a general idea of what they want to focus on—transformation does not always lend itself well to clear-cut ideas of what needs to be worked on—however, the topic question is intended to elicit the challenge, situation, or experience that the person is having. For example, "There has been tension between myself and my partner lately, and I think it relates to the fact that I'm on this journey and not relating to where he is anymore."

It is often necessary to follow up by asking the person to say more, or to fill in details so that you gain a more complete picture of what is going on. You are not 'exploring' the topic yet, rather gathering information to better understand the person's *context*. With enough contextual information in place, you can then ask the outcome question: what they'd like to walk away from the session having learned, experienced, achieved, or attended to.

Outcome question:

- What would you like to experience today?

- What would be a helpful or ideal outcome for you today?

- Within all that you have just shared, what is our work here today? What are we here to do?

The specific words used in these two primary questions can influence how a person perceives the underlying intention of the coaching space. For example, if the outcome question is phrased as, "What would you like to accomplish or achieve today?" this can put the person into a results-oriented, solution-focused (transactional) state of mind. The same thing can happen if you phrase the topic question as, "What is the issue (or problem or challenge) you wish to discuss today? 'Issue' signifies that a person has, well, 'issues,' and like problems, issues need solving or resolution.

A favorite topic question of mine is, "What would you like to explore in our session?" The word 'explore' has an adventurous, journey-like feel to it. Who knows what we will find when we explore! "What's calling for your attention today?" is another good example, as it invites a person to notice what needs attending to.

The wording of the outcome question may seem like a minor detail; however, language is generative (meaning, it is more than descriptive; language creates meaning and value), and the words we use to form questions evoke ways to perceive what is *expected* in the answer. When setting up a Deep Coaching session, take care to ensure that all variables, including the language you use, reflect the intention to support a deep dive into being.

Part 2: Coach It

Explore

It is here, in the Coach It stage of the process, that the Deep Coaching approach makes a noticeable departure from that of conventional coaching. Rather than using the intellect and 'powerful questions' to drive the conversation towards desired outcome and action, coach and client embark on a *sensing journey* through the pathways of the heart into the realm of being.

In the Explore phase, the topic brought to the conversation acts *only as the starting point* for a deeper exploration designed to illuminate the underlying patterns and constructs of the ego-based self-concept, and any pain that needs attending to. It is here that we begin to identify what is 'no longer,' while pointing to a way of being and thinking that is of the awakened mind.

As discussed in Chapter 13, in most cases when exploring a person's transforming self-concept, it will be necessary to ask some simple questions to help illuminate the bedrock of their experience: how that person actually thinks, believes, perceives, feels, and interprets. "What do you mean by that?" "Can you say more about that?" "What happens when you think that?" This is a pivotal part of a Deep Coaching session, as it helps the person understand *why* they experience what they experience. The intention is to:

1.) reveal how the egoic mind operates (so it can begin to heal), and

2.) connect with the beingness that is emerging (so it can be embodied).

As you explore, always remember this truth of transformation: *limiting beliefs naturally arise and dissolve as the mind awakens.* You don't have to work so hard to unravel the knots—the Explore phase is not a quest to 'dig deep' or to change, fix, or reframe whatever emerges, as uncomfortable as it may be—all this will happen on its own when given the right space, attention, and energy. However, out of all that is shared, you do have to be able to discern what is salient so that you don't pass it by.

If you are unsure of what to say or ask, you can always ask your inner guidance to show you, or, if you prefer, let this question guide you:

> What's that one thing you can point to in what the person has expressed that will open them up a little more to their own deeper realm?

This is a sensing journey. Insightful and well-timed questions play a valuable role in helping to reveal the limiting patterns of the mind, but they are secondary to the primary Deep Coaching roles: being a spiritual partner and holding space so that whatever emotions, thoughts, or energies arise, they can be attended to, trusting that when given appropriate space, the process of awakening itself will dissolve the structures of the mind which inhibit true Self-knowing.

Discern the Readiness

It is not entirely accurate to depict Discern the Readiness as a stand-alone phase, as I have done in the diagram. It is not so much a phase as a *listening stance* that runs through the Explore phase, but one so integral to the Deep Coaching process it warrants special mention.

The listening stance stems from two key questions you ask yourself as you move through the Explore phase:

> What wants to happen at the core of being?

> What experience is there a readiness for?

Can you sense it? What is the unspoken readiness for at the being level? What, if anything, is the spoken readiness for (verbally stated by the coachee)? Is there alignment between those two, or not?

On the being level, you are listening for what wants to happen, beneath it all (Practice 6). Is it a healing experience or is it an experience of oneself as increasingly whole and complete, as I AM (in whatever way it wants to manifest)? What is readying to happen?

But what if what you sense wants to happen at the being level is at odds with what is happening in the conversation itself? What if the person is not consciously aware of what is stirring deep within? This is particularly noticeable when a person is wrapped up in the drama, or needs to talk through thoughts and feelings, or wants to define strategies or techniques to resolve the issue at hand. All of these are signals that the person is not yet ready for a deeper dive or a shift in being. Continue exploring and listening for the readiness, and when it's time to wrap up the session move to the Summary phase.

If you cannot discern what the person is ready for, I encourage you not to worry and to rest in trust; when the readiness is so strong a person can no longer contain it, they will tell you. They will say something like, "I'm so ready to heal this," or "I'm so ready to step into the person I know I am." Then facilitate that experience.

Shift in Being

One of the most authentic acts of self-love a person can give to themselves is to open to the experience of a higher level of personal reality. A shift in being born of self-love transfigures the mind, and the emotional and energy body. It is itself a kind of spiritual practice.

When you do discern, through a person's words or energy, the readiness for a dive into being, or when you observe that a person has become aware of what wants to happen at a deeper level and is ready to make it an embodied experience *in the session*, then facilitate the shift with confidence.

As described in Practices 7 and 8, you facilitate the shift through a simple invitation and then hold the space in sacred silence.

When the moment arises, as the two (or more) of you close your eyes, you will enter into a transcended state of co-existence. Allow positionality (I am coach, you are client) to fall away, so that, in essence, two become as one mind. It's not helpful to position yourself as an observer of the person's experience, as that can give them the sense that they are being watched, which can interfere. It is more effective to allow yourself to drift into the experience along with them, even as you hold and energize the space.

The experience each of you has in those moments will likely be different, but that does not matter. You may experience a sense of profound connection with the person, as the boundaries of your separate existence fall away, or you may sense an energy field surrounding and extending out from you. Simply relax into whatever is happening, and activate the silence with the fullness of your being. This is the ultimate experience a Deep Coach can have with another person, a sacred connection born of the desire to know ourselves as we are, beyond the limitations of the egoic mind.

There will be times when a person feels blocked or has a hard time making the shift, despite their readiness to do so. They may express frustration or disappointment that they were not able to go further, to release an old pattern or energy, or to embody a desired state of being. Your role is to normalize their experience, assuring them that despite what may seem, there is always progress being made at some level of mind.

Processing and Integrating

As the shift deepens, as a person's emerging potential becomes their embodied reality, it can be accompanied by a profound sense of peace and calm. In that moment, all that needs to be known and understood will be.

What usually happens is that the person will start to speak from the vantage point of the newly embodied state, sharing what they are perceiving, experiencing, and understanding about themselves, life, or the issue they brought to the coaching conversation. The yearning and searching and questioning falls away, and they will speak from an unwavering sense of *knowing*. It's remarkable to witness. When the paradigm shifts, everything clicks into place, like the final twists of a Rubik's cube.

This is not the time to ask questions or to probe for action. This is the time to allow the person to process and integrate the thoughts, emotions, and energies that are flowing in. All you need to do is give subtle indications that you are listening, understanding, and experiencing the altered state of reality for yourself—which you will be, if you have facilitated this well.

Opportunity

The Opportunity phase in Deep Coaching is synonymous with the Action phase in conventional coaching, the difference being in how it is handled. In conventional coaching, the Action phase is typically initiated by action-oriented questions the coach asks such as, "What is the first step you could take with this?" or "What actions are you willing to commit to?" But that is not the Deep Coaching way.

We first looked at the Opportunity phase in the Four Levels of Engagement (Chapter 2) and learned that once the choice in being has been embodied and the paradigm has shifted we can ask a question such as, "What is the opportunity you are now seeing?" or "What wants to happen here (within you or the situation at hand)?" However, as the Opportunity phase flows organically from the Processing phase, oftentimes you won't even need to ask these questions at all—the information naturally arises as they process.

There will be times, however, when it is helpful to orient the coachee's gaze toward the specific issue they came to the session with, if they have not done it for themselves already. Proceed slowly here, so that the person remains in the embodied state —your intervention shouldn't be abrupt or intrusive—and say something like, "Just staying where you are, I invite you to turn your gaze towards the issue that you came into our session with today. What is the opportunity you are now seeing?" Then return to silence and hold the space so the person can sense the freedom to process the opportunity on their own terms.

A word of caution. Once a person has shifted their way of being in a session, it's easy to bump them out. The surest way to do this is to start asking a bunch of intellect-based or action-oriented questions that force the person into thinking mode just to answer your questions. I've seen it time and time again—the coach wants to probe for action (because that's what coaches are supposed to do) and the coachee, sounding like they have just been awoken from a dream says, "Uh, yah, um, well, I could…" and in that moment the intellect takes over and the connection to being is severed.

Those moments when someone shifts into a new way of being are at first fragile and fleeting. The state is not yet deeply embodied, and so bumping them out is easy. Remember, first and foremost the Deep Coach focuses on energizing shifts in being, giving plenty of time for the embodied experience to unfold of its own accord. This trumps any need you may have as a coach for the person to talk about actions or commitments or accountability.

Part 3: Wrap Up

Summary

The Summary phase is intended to give the coachee a chance to share any final thoughts, learning, or insights from the session, and to summarize actions and commitments. For the coach, it's a chance to share personal insights and inquire how best to support the coachee going forward.

In a Deep Coaching session this phase may or may not happen. It's not a necessity and may not add any value to the experience the person is having, especially when they are so deep into their embodied experience that all they need or want to do is to stay in that state without having to verbalize their experience. The best thing you can do is allow that to happen. You can choose to stay present with the person or leave the coaching space; either way is fine, as long as you let them know what you are doing and make the invitation for them to remain as they are, for as long as they wish, before moving into the day.

A simple way to summarize a session in those situations is to ask, "Is there anything you would like to say to be complete with today?" Once they have responded, you can then let them know how you will follow up.

Follow Up

The Follow Up phase is a brief conversational note at the end of the session designed to confirm what will happen next in the coaching process. Will you be coaching the person again, and if so when? Is the person free to connect with you between sessions? What's happening next?

At the end of a Deep Coaching session, this may or may not be a helpful course to take—again it depends on what is going on with the person. If they are complete with the session but desire to rest longer in the shifted state of being, you can always say that you will follow up by text or email. If the person is open to conversation, then you can discuss follow-up that way. As always, recognize the needs of your client and move with that.

A Final Word: Make It Your Own

The beauty of a Deep Coaching session lies not in its structure, but in what people allow themselves to experience in that space with you. They touch the *holy*, meaning they reconnect with the wholeness that they are at the core of their being. And when they touch that truth, they are free.

This work was never intended to be for coaches alone, and you do not need to be a coach to live the practices and principles taught here. For this reason, make this work your own. Rather than try to conform to an image you have about what it means to be a coach, take this work into yourself and embody it. Then open yourself to the way it wishes to express through you, into your family, communities, and the organizations you work within.

Who today do I choose to be?

How today can I be a loving presence?

How today can I live the quality of awareness that I AM?

How today can I hold space in acceptance and trust for all things to be as they are?

You are part of something extraordinary—you are living the process of transformation which corrects the illusions of the ego and transfigures the mind. Right where you are each day, you are given opportunities to be the truth of who you are and to be the light that enlightens the world.

Do not shy away from this. All the power in the world has been given to you, and you are powerful beyond measure. It's all in you. It *is* you. Just be that which you are. And you are the light of the world.

About the Author

Leon VanderPol was born and raised in Canada. At the age of twenty-five, curious to discover what the rest of the world had to offer, he packed his bags and ventured south to work as a management consultant in the United States. After several challenging yet fruitful years in 'corporate boot camp,' he followed the beat of his heart and relocated to Asia.

For the past twenty years, Leon has devoted his life to personal development and spiritual transformation. Having spent the first ten of those years understanding and deepening his own transformation, he then became a personal coach and mentor, and spirit-based teacher and healer. At the core of Leon's teaching lies the transformation of human consciousness—what happens when we consistently begin to experience ourselves beyond our ego-based state of consciousness, as our essential Self and soul.

Today Leon VanderPol is widely acknowledged as a master teacher and pioneer in the field of transformational coaching, and has spent thousands of hours training and mentoring student and professional coaches from all over the world. He is the founder and director of the *Center for Transformational Coaching & Living*, whose Deep Coaching program now has graduates in more than 35 countries.

In addition to training and mentoring, Leon is a sought-after speaker to an ever-expanding audience worldwide. When not engaged in transformational work, he is to be found at home in Taiwan puttering in the garden or hitting the beach with his wife and two children.

To find out more, visit him at

www.CenterForTransformationalCoaching.com.

Did you gain value from this book?

Recommend it to family, friends and colleagues,
or begin a study group with it.

To book Leon VanderPol for speaking
or teaching events, contact:
training@centerfortransformationalcoaching.com

For information on programs, teaching intensives,
and retreats offered by the Center
for Transformational Coaching & Living visit:
www.CenterForTransformationalCoaching.com

Free Bonus Materials

While you are there, check out the **extra resources** available free for you.
Navigate to the book's sales page on the website, and there you will find a
link to a download-able version of the questions and exercises in this book
which you can print out to work on.

Use this code to access the downloads:
DeepCoachingMastery

 Deep Coaching Intensive

Next Step: Turn Wisdom into Action
Learn the Art of Deep Transformational Coaching

Now that you have read the book, are you ready to open a new chapter in your own life? If so, here's how to move confidently toward a vision of your life and work that will bring joy and satisfaction to you, and honor those around you.

When you enroll in the Deep Coaching Intensive, you join a vibrant community of like-hearted practitioners from around the world who are committed to learning the art of Deep Transformational Coaching and thus making a profound difference in the lives of others.

The Deep Coaching Intensive is:

Core Training – through engaging classroom discussions and exercises, the DCI delves further into the concepts, frameworks and practices presented in the book, bringing them to life for you.

Deepening Practice – the program provides extensive opportunities to practice Deep Coaching. In a safe learning environment, you can turn 'wisdom into action.'

Master Sessions – observe Deep Coaching sessions with Leon VanderPol, who masterfully demonstrates how Deep Coaching works across a range of personalities and situations.

Community – become part of a global community of DCI participants. Through our monthly community calls and online forum, continue to learn, engage, have your questions answered, and make new friends and relationships.

Certification – completion of the Deep Coaching Intensive certifies you as a Deep Transformational Coach.

And for coaches certified by the International Coach Federation: Continuing Coach Education Units (CCEUs). Visit our website for details.

---

www.CenterforTransformationalCoaching.com

Join us!